D1258048

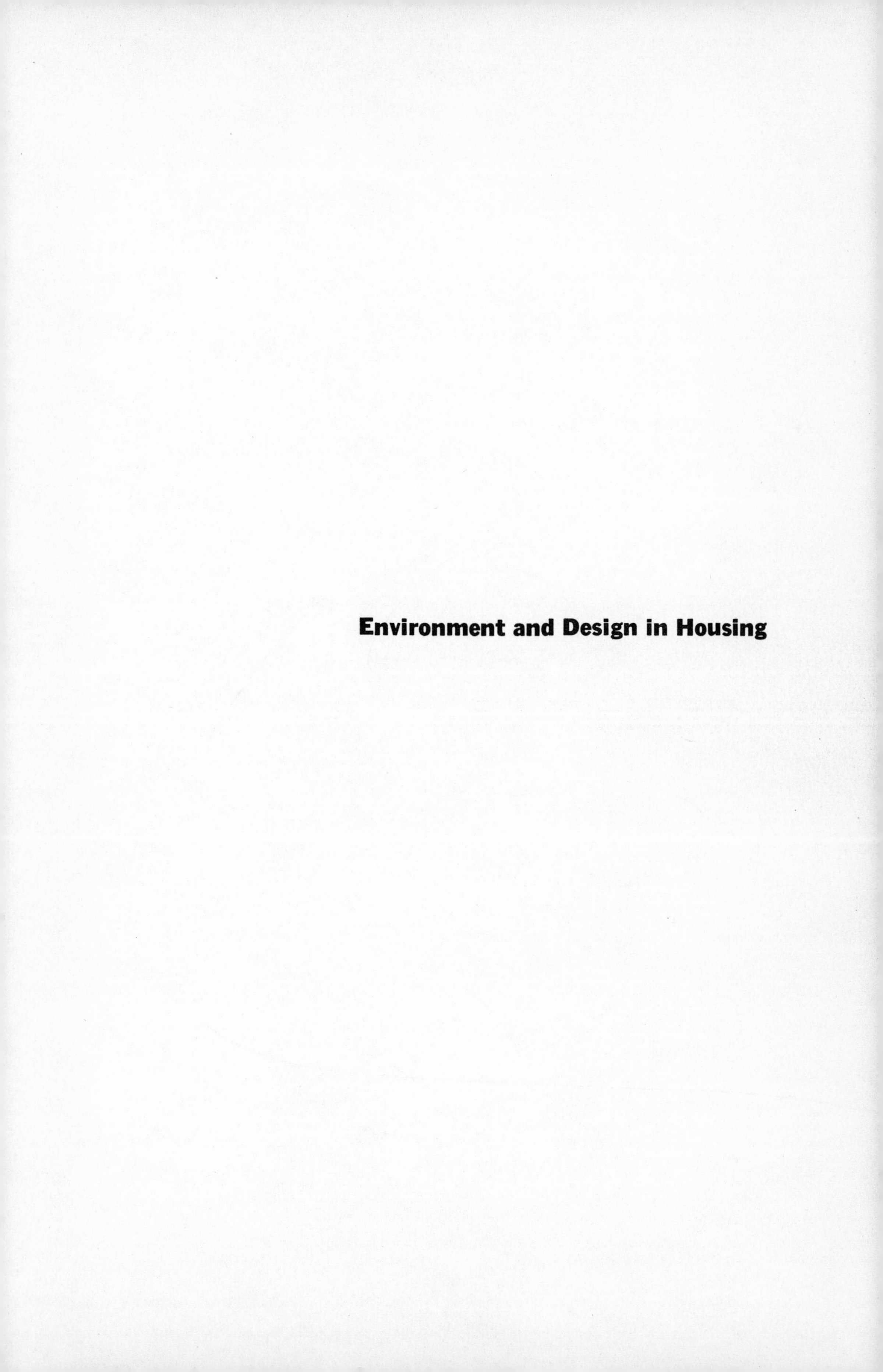

Environment and Design in Housing

From a jumble of broken glass

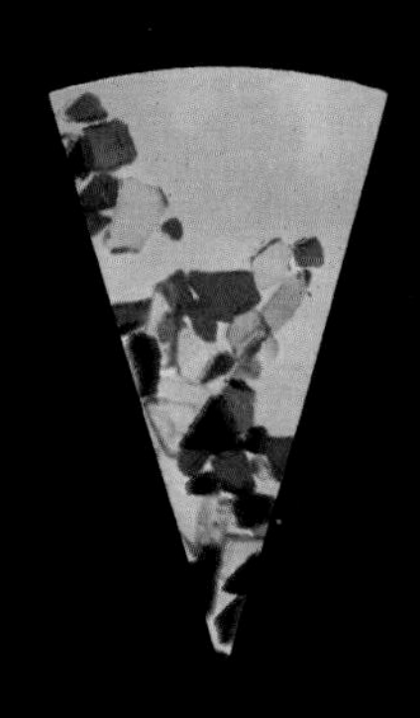

the mirrors of the kaleidoscope
create order and form.

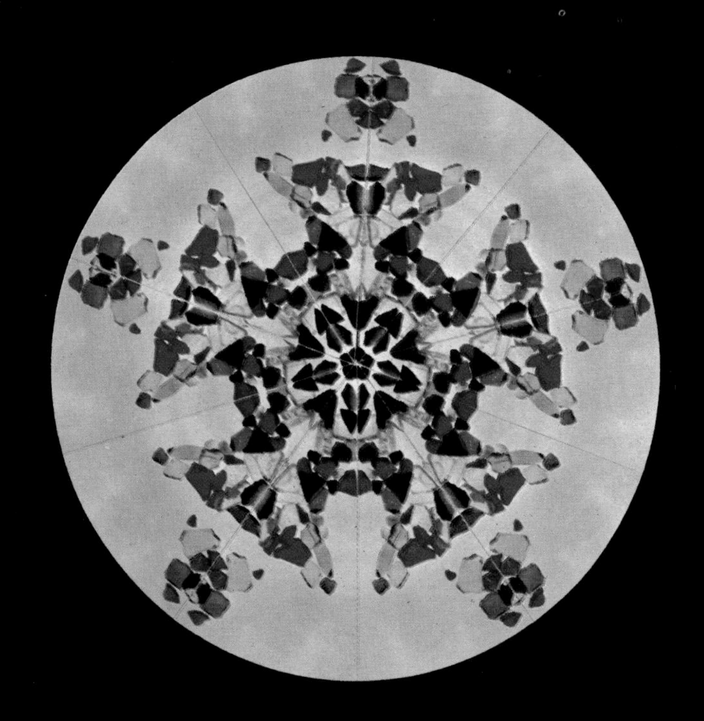

It is not the materials
but how they are organized
that is the essence of good design.

PHOTOGRAPH: ROBERT GOTTLIEB

Environment and Design in Housing

LOIS DAVIDSON GOTTLIEB
Lecturer, University of California, Riverside

JULIUS SHULMAN, *Photography Consultant*

The Macmillan Company, New York Collier-Macmillan Limited, London

First Printing

Library of Congress catalog card number: 65–16560

THE MACMILLAN COMPANY, NEW YORK
COLLIER-MACMILLAN CANADA, LTD.,
TORONTO, ONTARIO

Printed in the United States of America

Designed by SUSAN SIEN

PREFACE

When I first joined Frank Lloyd Wright's Taliesin Fellowship, it was winter and Mr. and Mrs. Wright and their group of apprentices were living at their desert camp in Arizona. I arrived, sleeping bag and baggage, and Mrs. Wright led me out into the desert to a tiny, pyramidal tent. She said, "This is your tent and it is up to you to make it beautiful."

My first need was a place to sleep—a platform for my sleeping bag. After acquiring a hammer, a saw, and a few other tools, I found some wood and built a "bed." Next I needed a place where I could put my possessions, so I made some shelves out of boards. Soon my clothes were so covered with desert dust that I realized that I had to have some coverings for the shelves. I put doors on them and made them into cabinets.

Later I wanted a chair. I had heard of the problem of making all the legs of a chair equal so that it would not wobble, and about cutting a tiny bit off one leg and then another until there were no legs left. Since I am not the world's best carpenter, I decided to solve this problem by putting only three legs on the chair so that it would be steady despite my amateur craftsmanship. The result was an unusual and satisfactory chair.

This experience was a turning point in my life, and ever since I have found it most rewarding to try to make various corners of the world a little more comfortable and beautiful. Today, because I have instilled in my husband this same desire, he is cutting another board into another shelf to hold our expanding possessions and make another wall of our home into something useful, interesting, and beautiful.

I mention these incidents with the hope that the reader will remember them if he or she is reading this book and wonders, "What has this got to do with me? I cannot produce a Taj Mahal or have Frank Lloyd Wright build me a fifty-thousand-dollar house." Well, neither can I. Nevertheless, I have found that by understanding the greatest architecture and by being able to better evaluate the physical world around me, I can improve my own environment and have some influence on the community as well.

The author suggests that you, the reader, do what you might be inclined to do anyway, and look at the "Conclusions" first. This will quickly give you a better idea of what to expect and what not to expect from this book.

This book was not written in an effort to make an amateur architect out of anyone. Planning and architectural design are complex arts and cannot be learned quickly or easily any more than one can learn to play the piano in ten easy lessons. For this reason such planning guides as bath and kitchen plans, minimum room sizes, and descriptions of L- or U-shaped house plans are not included. A plan is developed out of the requirements of the situation and the needs and desires of the people to live there. For this reason the understanding of how a plan develops is more important than trying to fit one's specific needs into generalized, ready-made plans and formulas.

Engineering data such as the insulating values of materials and other technical information sometimes found in housing texts are also kept to a minimum, since the home owner can obtain this information from local manufacturers or dealers, engineers or builders in a much more complete and practical form than this book could hope to include.

This is not a "how to do it" book. It is a "how to think about it" book as well as a "how to find out how to do it" book. It does not attempt to suggest what should be done in your home or try to solve your particular housing problems. However, the information here is offered to help you evaluate your real needs and thereby get the most out of whatever you have to deal with—be it a house, a fifty-dollar-a-month apartment, or a tent.

LOIS DAVIDSON GOTTLIEB

ACKNOWLEDGMENTS

I wish to acknowledge the help given by the many people who have taken an interest in this book. In particular:

Robert Gottlieb, my husband, who patiently lived through its writing, and also edited it for me.

Karen and Mark Gottlieb, my children, who also had to have great patience and understanding while I spent so much time on the manuscript.

Julius Shulman, who not only supplied most of the photographs, but gave so generously of his time to compile and edit them.

The Macmillan Company, which was helpful in bringing the book to completion.

The home economists Molly Larson, Velma Bradfield, and Dorothy Schnell, all of whom helped further this project.

Hilary Fry of Alameda State College, Hayward, California, and Sister Emelda Maria of the College of the Holy Names, Oakland, California, both of whom made it possible for me to give the courses on which the book is based.

John Kewell, architect, who gave assistance with information concerning his tract house which is used in the book as an example.

Dorothy Dunbar, landscape architect, who helped with the chapter on landscape architects.

Gay Ross, who read and gave advice and encouragement as the manuscript developed.

Sonia Brown, whose idea it was for me to give such a course and write such a book.

Frank Lloyd Wright, whose philosophy, great inspiration, and teaching made the book possible.

LOIS DAVIDSON GOTTLIEB

CONTENTS

ILLUSTRATIONS

V

VI

I

THE MEANING OF ENVIRONMENT AND DESIGN

ENVIRONMENT

The word "environment" is defined not only as one's surroundings, but as all conditions affecting life and human behavior. This book deals with our physical environment, and its purpose is to show that this environment we each create for ourselves and our families does affect every part of our lives.

Not only do our surroundings affect us, but we can affect and control them. Man is the only animal that can adapt his environment to his needs. While giraffes have developed longer necks with which to reach and be able to eat tree leaves, we have developed shorter fruit trees and ladders to simplify the problem. Whereas polar bears developed heavier fur coats, we developed clothing, shelter, and heating systems. In the days of Mohammed the mountain would not come to him—but today we can move mountains, we can create lakes where there were none, and we can literally change the shape of the earth's surface.

When man was busy with a pick and shovel changing his surroundings to fit his needs, mistakes were not too serious because they were not too large or destructive. Today, however, with the widespread use of bulldozers and other earth-moving equipment, and tomorrow with nuclear energy to make even bigger and possibly worse dents in our landscape, it is tremendously important that we know what we are doing and why we are doing it.

PHOTOGRAPHER: JULIUS SHULMAN

1. Man and his machines cut a flat site for a house.

The increase in population and the decrease in available land each year is forcing more and more dramatic changes in our surroundings. Human beings who have not grown fur like the polar bears are going to insist on being sheltered in one way or another. If they spread out as they have in the past, they won't all fit on the earth. If they crowd into prisonlike slum areas, they won't be happy. New solutions for shelter and community living are being developed and must be used. Unfortunately, too many of our present-day buildings are based on custom rather than actual need.

It is easy to give up thinking about the real needs and assume that traditional ways are "the way" to do things. For example, when man migrated to colder climates thousands of years ago, he developed form-fitting clothes designed particularly for cold climates. Today, even in the most tropical climates, Western man still wears those form-fitting clothes. To counteract this custom he has created "air conditioning." And now, in even moderate climates, a building is not considered truly modern without a totally artificial atmosphere inside. Then, to achieve maximum efficiency, the windows don't open even if you would like to let in a breath of fresh air.

There is nothing wrong with form-fitting clothes or air conditioning, but it is worth considering what these things were designed for, and whether it might not be just as pleasant to feel a gentle breeze or hear a passing bird from the window once in a while. But this lack, too, has been overcome by piped-in music—and, of course, there is nothing *really* wrong with piped-in music.

It seems that the wonders of science have now been able to cope with most of our physical needs very neatly, but the cost is great. In an age when everyone is concerned with costs and the complexities of everyday living, all efforts to adapt and readapt our surroundings to our needs are expensive. It is, therefore, good sense to examine one's needs and to consider what is, and what is not, worth spending money on.

You may wonder what this has to do with making a better home. You may not be planning to make any rash changes in your environment or move any mountains in the near future, but neither were the owners of the house in the picture (Illustration 1). They only wanted to have a flat spot for a house. But so did others above them. They were living at the bottom of a large hill happily enjoying their electric kitchen and other modern conveniences. As level land became scarce, more and more ledges were cut into the hills above for houses. Many of these were left uncovered by houses or plants temporarily, so when the rains came there was nothing to hold the soil. It formed a mud river, clogged up the drains and culverts, and finally poured down the hills to cause landslides.

This may seem like an extreme example, and it is. Yet it is becoming more and more common to read of floods, broken dams, and other great damage due to man's efforts to change the contours of the land. This is just one dramatic example of the many ways in which one's total environment can affect one's dwelling. The elaborateness of the kitchen equipment or the color scheme in the living room are but minor considerations. In choosing a place to live it is essential to be aware of the entire surroundings.

PHOTOGRAPHER: JULIUS SHULMAN

2. Nature takes over.

DESIGN

The next question is, how are we going to stop the kind of catastrophe just described? The answer—more planning and more design.

What is design? What do we mean by great design? What makes something beautiful? What constitutes a work of art? Why are only a few men able to create works of art that no one else can produce? The works of Leonardo da Vinci, Beethoven, and others have been studied, analyzed,

PHOTOGRAPHER: JULIUS SHULMAN

3. The result! The gadgets in the kitchen no longer matter.

and copied time and time again, yet their imitators never seem to produce quite the same results. When Frank Lloyd Wright was asked what made his houses *feel* different from all others, he said, "It's magic." This may seem vague, yet if it were more clear everyone would be able to produce the same results. Call it inspiration, call it genius, call it whatever you like. There are some things about a work of art that cannot be analyzed.

On the other hand, there are prerequisites to good design which are clear and can apply to all the arts. It does not matter whether one is designing a dress, composing a piece of music, writing a story, building a house, or arranging a room. The first prerequisite is to have an *idea* or a purpose. There are several facets to an idea. There is the intellectual part —the facts—that relate to how we think about a situation or thing. And then there is the emotional part that relates to how we feel about that situation or thing. Sometimes one part, sometimes the other, is more important and is emphasized. Newspaper writing is a good example of writing designed primarily to inform. It makes the facts as clear as possible, in contrast to a poem which is designed primarily to express a feeling. Often the facts of the situation are not as explicit as a poem, yet the feelings, atmosphere, or attitudes of the people involved become more vivid. Although detailed information may be left out, the impression of the scene may stick with the reader much longer.

For example, one could report that in Burma the sun rose in the East at 6:27 A.M., and the sky was very red. This statistical information is neither very earthshaking nor memorable, and yet Rudyard Kipling's expression of such a scene has stuck in the minds of millions of people for years.

On the Road to Mandalay,
Where the flyin'-fishes play
An' the dawn comes up like thunder
Outer China 'crost the Bay!

The difference between a dwelling that is merely a place to keep the rain off one's head and keep one's things, and one that is well designed is just as great as the difference between the above comment on a particular sunrise and Kipling's poem. In literature the artist has used words to express his idea, whereas in architecture, building materials and space are used.

In the design of buildings, large or small, the problem of achieving aesthetic results is greatly complicated, and for this reason it becomes fascinating. The artist, or architect in this case, is expressing his interpretation of the client's values and way of living. If the project to be built is an apartment, he must rely on his own insight and understanding of the situation to decide what would be best for the type of family that would rent such a dwelling.

The factual parts of the house or apartment are such things as the number of rooms, their size, a roof that doesn't leak, plumbing that works, etc. All are essential to good living, but they are not enough. A home is not something like a newspaper which is read and thrown out. A home is to be lived in and with for years, and it should be a delight and an inspiration each day. This means that certain feelings must be expressed—a certain atmosphere created.

An example of a home that has stirred the imagination of as many people as has Kipling's poem is "Falling Water" by Frank Lloyd Wright. One might say that it is beautiful because it is a large and expensive house. Naturally, this helped, as it probably helped Kipling to have had the in-

ARCHITECT: FRANK LLOYD WRIGHT; PHOTOGRAPHER: BILL HEDRICH

4. The "magic" of Falling Water. Here, on a difficult site, the equilibrium of the natural terrain is not destroyed, so that the owners can partake of the beauty around them while the man-made structure compliments rather than defaces the site.

spiration of a trip to Mandalay. It is also true that most people cannot afford such a site or house. Nevertheless, many thousands of expensive houses have large rooms, substantial roofs, and good plumbing. But at Falling Water it is the intangible atmosphere that is memorable. The perfection of design creates a feeling that it grows out of the hill as naturally and inevitably as the rock around it. It is the architect's expression of the owner's love of the site.

One aspect of any work of art such as this is that the ideas, both fact and feeling, be clearly stated. Unfortunately, this does not mean that it will always be clearly understood by everyone or by even most people at the time. It often takes a certain amount of previous knowledge to be able to grasp a new idea. The most exquisite Chinese poem cannot be enjoyed if one does not know Chinese. There is also the problem of adjusting our ears and eyes to new sounds or sights. For example, many people thought Debussy's music strange and ugly at the time it was composed, yet now it is considered beautiful. Often we are equally shocked by a new design in clothes, which after a year or two seems like the normal thing and we are all wearing it.

A direct way in which the artist may express himself most clearly is for him to develop *one idea at a time.* In a painting this is called the "center of interest" or theme, and since the viewer sees the whole painting at a glance, it is usually clear what the main theme is. If you are looking at a table, this is usually apparent too. For one thing, the whole table can be seen at a glance; and secondly, everyone is used to the idea of a table—a flat surface on which to put things so that they are more convenient than if placed on the floor.

Within the painting there may be several things going on. There may even be other pictures, as there may be a play within a play. But for the picture to be successful, the main thought or idea must be clear. In the case of the table, it may have a drawer in it or a bookshelf underneath, but if too many gadgets get attached to it so that the flat surface on top is no longer useful, it will not be successful as a table design.

In the case of a house or other building it is not so simple. Compare a newspaper article and a book. The article describes one incident and can usually be read and understood immediately. The book describes many incidents, people, and places, and it usually takes a matter of hours or days to read; so it requires some ingenuity on the part of the writer to organize his material so that the reader may grasp the whole thing. It is the same with a house. A table can be seen at a glance, but a house cannot. A house is not only too big, but has many sides, inside walls, and sometimes many levels. In addition, a house has many functions. Almost any building has many activities and usually a number of people are involved with it. Add to this the problems of the site and the various materials and appliances and it is no wonder that the whole form can get very complex.

It is the job of the designer to organize these complexities into a unified form. He is like a composer of a symphony who carefully organizes his melodies and rhythms, and balances all the different sounds of the orchestra. If the composer does not carefully make each note fit with all the others, the result will be only noise. Such chaos is exactly what happens to a house or apartment without this same kind of careful organization of building materials and decoration.

A symphony cannot be composed by simply adding random notes together. Neither can a house be designed by adding rooms and windows and gadgets together. A symphony is the elaboration, with repetition and variation, on a central theme. So must a house be, or it is a visual noise as horrible as an unplanned symphony.

The problem of furnishing a single room is not as severe as that of furnishing a whole house. It is like composing a song with accompaniment as compared to writing a composition for an orchestra. The noise cannot be as large, as chaotic, or as hideous because there is not as much of it. Nevertheless, just as the singer and accompanist must go well together, so must the objects in a room go well together. And in turn each room must be part of the whole dwelling.

It is imperative that all the following aspects of house design be considered and analyzed. There is (1) the purpose of the structure, (2) the needs of the owner and his family, (3) the site, (4) the materials available, (5) the equipment to be used, (6) the budget, etc. The designer who can see the problems and solve *most* of them within a unified concept will come closest to creating a "work of art." It is this solving of problems in combination with the expressing of an idea which produces what has been called "great architecture."

To relate all this once again to the landslide (Illustration 2), what went wrong there? The people who cut this ledge did the expedient thing. There were sewers and culverts to carry off any normal rainfall, so there seemed to be no danger. To terrace and retain and plant the hillside would have taken much more thought, time, and effort. But not anticipated was the fact that, due to excessive bulldozing, what came down the hill was mud, not water. This carried with it rocks, brush, and other debris, since much of the area was no longer in its state of natural equilibrium and it was this that clogged the sewers and culverts and finally created slides.

What was the *idea* behind bulldozing such level areas? It was a very simple, straightforward one—a good one from certain standpoints. It was based on the fact that most people want a one-story house if possible. Two good reasons for this are that it is easier to live in a house where one doesn't have to run up and down stairs, and it is usually considered cheaper to build on a flat site where elaborate foundations are not needed.

And why were other sites bulldozed and left bare? Suppose you want to build a house. A real estate man shows you a lovely hillside covered with oaks and underbrush. You stand on the road because you don't want to get the thorns in your stockings and you prefer not to step into the poison oak or poison ivy. You think it is all very charming, but where will you put the house, and where will the children play? To make a long story short (and looking for a place to live is always a long story), you find it all too discouraging and end up in a nice flat house on a nice flat lot somewhere where everything is obviously convenient. The people who are in the business of selling land have seen this happen time and time again, so in order to expose the vast possibilities of their hillsides, they cut a large flat area in them, bring in a road, and eliminate all thorns and poison oak. It becomes easy to walk around, and everyone is happy—that is, so long as there is no unusual weather.

This landslide problem is not universal. No problem is. But this example is shown as one possibility of what can happen, and how serious it is, as a result of a type of thinking typical of our civilization which honors speed as its essence and immediate efficiency as its goal. It is the same kind of simple problem-solving that went on in some orphanages years ago when the girls' heads were shaved in order to solve the problem of dirt and lice getting into their hair. The problem of the dirt and lice was solved directly, totally, and completely; but now there would be concern that other more serious problems might well develop from taking away such a basic adornment as a girl's hair. Of course there may have been some girls who were not bothered by this, as there are some hills that have been bulldozed without too much harm. But, in general, the indiscriminate cutting away of what nature intended or any other rash move without thinking through all the possibilities—without planning or design—is apt to end in disaster or at least ugliness. Immediate convenience is often *not* an economy. Wise planning with a long-range point of view for the entire area will benefit the most people, be the most economical in the long run, and create the greatest beauty which can be enjoyed for years. This is design.

HISTORICAL BACKGROUND

STYLES OF THE PAST

How have the problems of other civilizations been solved? How did these solutions express themselves in design, and how does this relate to what is being done today?

Man's first environmental problem was to shelter and protect himself physically against both the elements and other animals and men. Primitive man did this in two ways, either by finding ready-made shelter in the form of caves, or by constructing little shelters or huts out of available materials. In some areas the huts were made of trees or reeds. In other areas, where stones were available, these were piled up to form little dwellings of a different type. Other groups of people learned to make simple frames and cover them with thatch, animal skins, or bark, thus producing tents or teepees. In the Arctic, people made shelters called igloos out of the only available material, ice. These various forms of shelter could be called the first "architectural styles." They were all intended to solve the same need and to express the same idea—that of providing physical protection in the simplest possible way. However, the reason a stone hut, an Indian teepee, and an Eskimo igloo all look so different is that each is made of entirely different material. The irregularly shaped stone huts resulted from finding stones, piling them up, and fitting them together as well as possible; but even a primitive person with a few tools could cut blocks of ice

PHOTOGRAPHER: JULIUS SHULMAN

5. Wherever there is wood and grass, the first architectural styles are remarkably similar throughout the world.

to exactly the shape he wanted and thus an igloo could be a very regular dome-shaped dwelling. On the other hand, a tent or reed hut depended on using flexible materials such as small trees or reeds and tying them together with grasses or some other flexible fiber, which produced characteristic shapes.

6. The portable shelters of Nomadic people create different forms.

PHOTOGRAPHERS: STUDIOS CINEMATOGRAPHIQUES, RABAT, MOROCCO (COURTESY SERVICE GENERAL DE L'INFORMATION, MOROCCO)

PHOTOGRAPHER: J. BELIN (COURTESY SERVICE GENERAL DE L'INFORMATION, MOROCCO)

7. A whole community piled up out of mud blocks. People grouped together for companionship and protection.

These methods—one of piling up rigid blocks and the other of tying together flexible materials and covering this framework with a skin—are essentially the way most homes are built today. Now stones can be cut to any size or shape, synthetic stones called concrete blocks can be made, wood can be cut into regular sizes, and flexible "reeds" can be made of steel. These can all be put together with mortar, nails, and bolts, and covered with synthetic skins such as paper, plywood, metal sheeting, or plastics. Water and electricity can be run in and out of this dwelling. But it is essentially the same idea that was used ten thousand years ago.

What, then, are the differences? Several facets of life have changed greatly since people began building those little huts and were satisfied with them. When one has no physical shelter it becomes one's primary concern. But after shelter has been achieved and its comfort has been enjoyed for a while, man begins to turn his mind to other things. Groups of people or communities form. By acquiring more security and greater strength in numbers, they are then able to furnish themselves and their leaders with more comforts. They then become concerned with spiritual values and religious ideas. It is the thoughts and achievements of these groups that have created the cultures of the past.

DRAWING: KARL WERNER (FROM: EGYPT, BY G. EBBERS. CASSELL, PETTER, & GALPIN, 1878)

8. An entire mountain is used to create eternal architecture.

Although the individual dwelling formed the immediate shelter for each family, this soon became a part of the larger shelter of the community. It was both physical shelter from the elements and intruders, and psychological shelter for a feeling of protection, security, and privacy.

Even man's first shelter, the cave, has been made into whole communities. At Petra, Jordan, gigantic temples were cut out of the cliffs and elaborate façades imitating Roman buildings were carved on the front of the cliffs.

At Abu Simbel, which overlooks the Nile river in Egypt, the main room of the rock temple inside the mountain is four stories high, and the ornamental carving on the front of it is as high as a ten-story building. Obviously when this temple was built—about 1300 B.C.—the purpose was more than physical protection or comfort. It was one of the most colossal expressions of religion built by man. Although it physically does not resemble Egypt's pyramids at Giza, it has the same purpose. It is a monument that attempted to preserve the soul of a God-king. The first requirement of both this cave temple and the pyramids was that they should last for eternity. There could be conceived no more stable form than the pyramid unless it would be the use of an entire mountain as one's structure, as was done at Abu Simbel. What a difference in time concept this is from our civilization which tears down a fifty- or one-hundred-year-old building if it is considered too old to be efficient.

And where were the dwellings of the people of this civilization which was dedicated to preserving its God-kings? They were there, but they were so insignificant in comparison to the structures for the Pharaohs that there is hardly a trace of them left. The difference in importance between the king and his subjects is clearly stated in the facade of Abu Simbel. Here there are four statues of Ramses II, each 65 feet high, and the figures of other people are hardly noticeable at his feet.

Now, as the importance of life today for all men supersedes the perpetuating of the body and spirit of one man, one of the most important projects of the Egyptian government is the building of a dam to control the Nile river and provide water and power for everyone living there. It is ironic that the lake to be formed by this dam will cover Abu Simbel and Ramses II, if he and his mountain are not jacked up above the new water level.

One could suggest that the dam is being built now and not before because we now have the materials and equipment to build it. And, to be sure, it is a bigger project than even the pyramids of Giza. But not that much bigger. The pyramids and other tombs of Egypt built as long as five thousand years ago were accomplished with such fantastic efforts and sacrifices, it appears that if anyone had had the idea of controlling the Nile for the betterment of the nation as a whole that they would have at least tried it. The structures they did conceive and build clearly express the prime interest of that civilization.

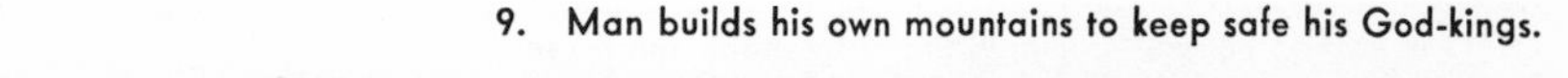

9. Man builds his own mountains to keep safe his God-kings.

DRAWING: F. C. WELSCH (FROM: EGYPT, BY G. EBBERS. CASSELL, PETTER, & GALPIN, 1878)

FROM: A HISTORY OF ART, BY W. H. GOODYEAR. A. S. BARNES, 1896

10. The Acropolis, Athens, built to glorify man and his virtues.

11. The Roman Forum—a tribute to the splendor and power of the Roman state.

FROM: A HISTORY OF ART, BY W. H. GOODYEAR. A. S. BARNES, 1896

Compare all this with other great landmarks in architectural history, the Acropolis and the Agora in Athens. Although the Acropolis is primarily a place of worship, it is a different type of worship. The buildings are magnificent with the idea of being magnificent when they were built rather than eternal in character. Marble was used throughout because it was readily available and it was also the best, most beautiful building material. The roof structures the Greeks knew how to build could span only a short distance, so many rows of columns were needed to support them. All the ornament depicted their gods in the form of idealized man. Not just one man—a God-king—but the idealized Greek man.

These men, who felt that human life was important, also built the Agora. It was a market place, or business district, for everyone; and it was built with as much concern as was the Acropolis. Man and his life at the time were of primary importance and the buildings of Greece were built to facilitate that life.

By the time Rome was at its zenith the temples and religious architecture there were overshadowed by the civic buildings. The Romans' great interest in ruling themselves and others demanded many buildings for this activity. Another indication of their interest in power and the things that go with it were the many triumphal arches, pillars of victory, and amphitheaters or arenas. However, these arenas were not primarily intended for plays, as in Greece, but for gladiatorial combats and races. Here they trained and displayed their warriors and made spectacles of their conquered slaves.

Although many of the Roman buildings were essentially copies of Greek architecture, the ornament became more elaborate. The columns became mere decoration as the interior space was surrounded by walls that could support the roof without the columns. But the appearance of Rome was changed, not only by a different type of thinking, but by new structural methods using the arch, the dome, and concrete. The arch was not invented in Rome. There are arches at Giza which were built five thousand years ago, but while in both Egypt and Greece there were adequate supplies of large stones, in Rome the stones were small and had to be fitted together in some way to span large areas. The result of this need produced a mass use of the keystone arch and its three-dimensional counterparts, the vault and the dome. Baked clay, or bricks, were used in the same way. Accordingly, with these new materials and techniques and the interest of the Roman rulers in a display of wealth that would assure everyone that they were the rulers of the world, architecture became more vast and more grand, and its scale dwarfed the individual.

After the disintegration of the Roman Empire and the decay of its culture, the primary need of the European people was once again protection. This time not only from the elements but from the barbarian hordes which ravaged Europe. Out of this need grew the feudal system and the castles of the Middle Ages. Ravaging had become a familiar incident in life and peace was only an interlude between assaults. The few who could afford to build castles surrounded them with high walls and moats, and then traded the protection therein and the use of the land around for the work and

PHOTOGRAPHER: ROBERT GOTTLIEB

12. A medieval castle. The greatest virtue of this home was that it was impenetrable to intruders.

loyalty of the many who could not afford such things. So the typical European community developed into a castle-fort with its cluster of dwellings and farmlands around it.

The castle walls were of stone because it was the most impenetrable material known. At the top of many, "crenelated parapets" were constructed. These protecting walls which extended above a flat roof had a lower section every few feet resembling a window without a top. This motif is still seen today in the more expensive residential sections of the United States where people have wanted to preserve the "elegance" and "charm" of medieval life in their own homes. Actually the idea behind these picturesque parapets was not so elegant or charming. They were designed so that one could stand behind the high part of the wall and throw rocks or boiling water onto any attackers below.

Lower down on the walls there were windows, but they were not there to let in the sun or to be able to look out at the view. These were enjoyments which the noble people of the Middle Ages could not afford. The castle windows were built tall and narrow to let in a little light and air and to allow just enough space for someone to shoot arrows out. These castle windows are often copied today to give the home owner a feeling of being the "lord of the manor." What is often the result of grim necessity in one era becomes a sign of distinction and is copied by later generations.

Later in the Gothic era, life again changed with the growth of towns and cities, and the development of Christianity. The towns varied with climate and terrain, but almost all had one thing in common; the largest and most central edifice in each town was the church. Instead of clustering around a castle for protection, the people now grouped themselves around these churches which were the centers of spiritual and social life. This type of community can be seen today in small New England towns, in most Mexican villages, and in a few remaining California Mission communities. The church is the core of life and it produces a different picture than the typical American city where the "downtown" area is the business section.

In the Renaissance, Europe developed economically and politically to a point that men could turn more of their attention to the pursuits of the intellect. They rediscovered the cultures of Greece and Rome and wanted to surround themselves with these. All buildings were covered with Greek or Roman motifs. The columns that used to support Greek roofs were now plastered on the front of buildings like embroidery on a dress. The pediments which used to indicate the shape of Greek roofs now became masks which hid a new type of roof structure or were appliquéd over windows and door openings like frosting on a cake. The plans and structure of these buildings gradually changed to meet the needs of the time, but façades continued to be a tribute to the past.

These examples from man's early attempts to make an environment to fit his needs are not intended to comprise an architectural history. They are, however, included to give some idea of how the problems of creating homes and communities have been dealt with in the past.

Architecture can be read as easily as a book. The edifices that man creates show clearly which are his greatest interests and needs. When the

PHOTOGRAPHER: ROBERT GOTTLIEB

13. The most significant building in this town is the church.

FROM: A HISTORY OF ART, BY W. H. GOODYEAR. A. S. BARNES, 1896

14. St. Peter's church, 16th century, Rome. All architectural ornament is appliqued like icing on a cake, and is a tribute to the past glories of Rome.

focal point of a town is its church, it is quite a different type of place than a town centered around a business district, a university, or a resort. It is the same in a dwelling. Is the focal point of the living room a table for the family to gather around, a wall of books, or a TV set? Just as archaeologists and historians have deduced most of the facts about early civilization without seeing the people, but from buildings and artifacts left by them, so today one can tell a great deal about another person from his home without ever meeting him.

The distinguishing characteristics of the environment one creates for himself—that is, the way he solves the problems of making a home for himself—is his style. When whole communities or countries solve their problems in a similar fashion this style takes on the name of that area, such as the Greek, Roman, or Cape Cod style. When the communities or countries do the same thing for a long period of time, the style is often labeled by the name of that time period in history—the Medieval, the Renaissance, or Colonial style. Essentially all these styles that developed during the last five thousand years represent solutions to the design problems of the particular places and times in which they originated.

If we can realize that all the styles of the past were direct solutions to the problems and needs of the past, we will realize that the styles of today must come from solving our own problems and fulfilling our own needs rather than by mimicking the past.

THE BACKGROUND OF CONTEMPORARY ARCHITECTURE

The coming of the Industrial Revolution brought drastic changes which affected the way most people lived and how they arranged their environment. With the sudden development of machine power around 1800, a population which was primarily rural in northern Europe and England developed into an urban one. Factories were built and people clustered around these to live and work.

Since everyone had to be within walking distance of the factory, people crowded together more and more. Land values increased as the need to be near the factories grew. People were gradually squashed into a strange two-dimensional world. Stranger yet, we now accept this two-dimensional living as quite normal. In the country, the simplest dwelling had been a three-dimensional structure (that is, it had four or more sides with windows or openings on all sides and some semblance of light and air). In the industrial towns and cities, land became so valuable that the houses were packed in next to each other with a common wall between each. Thus

15. Row housing—it is the front that counts.

PHOTOGRAPHER: JULIUS SHULMAN

PHOTOGRAPHER: JULIUS SHULMAN

16. The front is from Hansel and Gretel; the garage from medieval England, and the side apparently does not matter, although one window has shutters.

there were only two outside walls, a front and back, where there were windows, and the front façade was all that was seen or important. It was a good method to get the most people into the least space and get the most profit out of each foot of land, but it was hardly made for comfortable living. These dwellings were dark inside and the sanitation was practically nonexistent. This profiteering from land was the idea behind "row housing," and it continues to be built even today.

These houses have been gradually made more sanitary and planned with good light and air, and there is great variation now that it is possible to use the land better by piling people up in apartments rather than just squeezing them together. But these first row houses were the beginning of a change in thinking about architecture from a three-dimensional to a two-dimensional form.

There had been two-dimensional buildings built in early cities, but most people lived in the country where buildings were detached from one another. They were made of the same material all around. This may not seem significant, but one would be very surprised to see a woman in an elegant satin party dress turn around and reveal a back made of gingham. There is one type of suit made in which only the front is important. Some mortuaries sell such a front half of a suit—a sort of "dickey suit" to be buried in if one doesn't have a good suit of his own. This idea is most likely based on the assumption that once a person is lying in the coffin he will no longer turn around. And with the same idea that only the front is important, city row houses were built with fancy fronts and plain backs. They have been referred to as wearing a "Queen Anne front and a Mary Ann back." It is the same type of thinking and economy that produces some "well-dressed women" with the fashionable dress and the dirty or torn underwear.

This is often seen today in the concrete or brick buildings with the marble or stone fronts that are on every downtown street. Even many suburban houses that are detached, with all sides exposed, have only the

PHOTOGRAPHER: JULIUS SHULMAN

17. The front. It is obviously designed to make an impression.

18. View of the house in Illustration 17 from the back. This design apparently "grew like Topsy," and yet here is where the family would spend most of their time.

PHOTOGRAPHER: JULIUS SHULMAN

false front decorated with brick or something to look like a "California ranch" or a "Cape Cod" or some other "style." They are like little stage sets which lose all illusions the moment one peeks around the side. This idea of the fancy front is apparently based on the concept that it is first impressions that count.

Although the increase in land values and overcrowding of people continued, faster transportation has solved the problem somewhat by making it possible for many people to spread out again and come to work by trains, cars, or buses. But although there could now be space between houses, the old idea of the decoration on only the front of the dwelling persists.

These developments in transportation have produced other physical changes in our surroundings as well. Formerly, signs used to be designed to attract the passing pedestrian. Now the signs have to be large enough to be seen while driving at at least twenty-five miles per hour. On some highways the signs are designed to be seen at sixty miles per hour. Such signs were unnecessary fifty years ago and now create a different look in our cities.

More changes due to the automobile and machines are that multitudes of families have become mobile. Migrations have happened before and still happen each year in such places as Afghanistan where whole communities of fifty thousand people and a hundred thousand animals walk

19. This street sign, the lights, and the flowers were made for those who had time to look and enjoy them.

PHOTOGRAPHER: ROBERT GOTTLIEB

PHOTOGRAPHER: JULIUS SHULMAN

20. These "shrieks for attention" make one want to flee, but there are few places left in the world where they can be escaped.

21. The store façade draws you in rather than merely shouting about its wares. The architectural design has become the symbol and trademark of this elegant shop.

ARCHITECT: FRANK LLOYD WRIGHT; PHOTOGRAPHER: JULIUS SHULMAN

over mountains and through rivers and snow each year in search of grass for forage. And these and other nomadic peoples in the Middle East and other areas of the world usually have dwellings designed to carry with them. (See Illustration 6.) But there has never been such a migration in the history of man as that which has gone on, and is still going on, in the United States from the East to the West. Before, nomadic people depended on staying in groups to defend and support themselves. The basis of these groups was the large family or tribe. But now, with the advent of the machine, one man is able to support his wife and children without the help of the greater family unit. As a result, each individual family is able to separate itself from the larger family and become a self-sufficient unit. This again changed the look of dwellings. Where once it was common for a house to be large enough for a family of three or four generations, now each generation and each man in that generation expects to have his own house or apartment—smaller, indeed, but nevertheless his own. Not only are some homes smaller because there are fewer people living together, but because the building costs as well as the wages of servants required to take care of these houses have gone up. For all these reasons fewer very large homes are built today as compared to fifty or one hundred years ago.

On the other hand, the number of medium-sized homes for the middle-income group has increased enormously, and most of these are in urban areas.

Another socioeconomic change that produced a new environment was the increase of leisure time. In the days when most people were involved with farming, they worked from dawn till dark. Later, in the nineteenth century, factory workers labored even longer. Children worked twelve and fourteen hours a day, and it was considered revolutionary when laws were passed limiting their working day to ten hours. For these people there was no problem of what to do with their spare time—there wasn't any. But now a good deal of our effort goes into construction of civic buildings, parks, and recreational areas within our own dwellings purely for the enjoyment of leisure hours. It would seem that with this leisure time people would have more time to plan and build and dream of the future. But the opposite has happened. Most people dash so fast from one activity to another and one place to another that the criterion of excellence has become speed rather than quality.

The whole pace of life has increased, and with it the pace of building. Not only are buildings built in less time now, but they are not expected to last as long. Because homes as well as public buildings used to be built to last many generations, more time and thought were put into them. Today almost no one builds his home with the idea that it will be used by the family for generations. In fact, most homes are no longer thought of as a root for even a lifetime. Some tract builders even construct new models of houses every year and trade them for last year's models much like cars are traded. When a home becomes a temporary dwelling it is treated quite differently from the beloved "family home" of yesteryear.

Because this vast mobile population has neither the time, interest, nor money to build their own homes, the apartment, the builder's house, and the tract have come into being. This situation has brought about a new motive for building, which is not to make something the most beautiful, but to make it the most salable and profitable. Many of the builders are conscientious, do a good job, and in many ways give a family more for their money than they could get by building for themselves. But, however numerous the advantages of these dwellings, when a house or apartment is built to sell to someone else at a profit many of the decisions of design and construction are approached differently from the way they would be approached if one were building for oneself.

With today's frequent turnover of housing, most people are interested in having everything new and different. While before the industrial revolution changes of environment were hardly noticeable within a lifetime, now, due to the efficiency of industry, changes can be constantly made and spread rapidly throughout the world. New materials, new appliances, new gadgets, are all remarkable. They are familiar to everyone, and are desired by almost everyone. The cheapest tract house or apartment is equipped with dozens of these modern conveniences and the value of the dwelling is often based on the number included.

22. Architects communicate in schools and publications. This hotel and that shown in Illustration 23 are half a world apart and of two entirely different cultures but have the same concrete structures, balconies, fins, pools, metal railings, furniture—and almost the same tourists.

ARCHITECTS: WELTON BECKET & ASSOCIATES; PHOTOGRAPHER: JULIUS SHULMAN

PHOTOGRAPHER: BERNARD ROUGET, CASABLANCA (COURTESY SERVICE GENERAL DE L'INFORMATION, MOROCCO)

23. Hotel in Morocco.

These conveniences are wonderful but must be well incorporated into the total design of the home. The problem in design is to relate them to the structure in a simple, unified manner. This is not easy. It was much easier to design a thatched hut or an adobe house of one hundred years ago and come up with something beautiful. It is relatively easy to make order out of a few simple materials; it is very difficult to take one hundred different items and materials and combine them into a unified form.

The startling paradox of our modern world is that although most people are anxious to have something "different," never has the man-made world looked so much the same. Whereas it used to be easy to see differences between the various towns and buildings throughout the world, it is now almost impossible to tell a modern building in Cairo from one in Athens, Rome, or Chicago. Whereas the ideas and ways of living used to be very different in each area, now, through constant communication and travel, the building materials and ideas of Western civilization are relatively the same, so their results in building today are also similar. Furthermore, the ease of communication has made it possible for architects to be informed of what is being done in all sections of the world. It used to take years and sometimes centuries for these ideas to travel from one region to another. Now the ideas and the architects can travel by air in a few hours.

Formerly, buildings used to be designed to fit the particular terrain, climate, and materials at hand; now all these can be manufactured synthetically by bulldozers, air conditioners, and factories.

Most people are aware of what bulldozers and earth-moving equipment can do and have experienced the comforts of heating and air conditioning. However, it is also the production of new materials and methods in the past one hundred and fifty years that has significantly changed our lives. It is the use of these new materials as well as the new needs and values which have arisen that have made "modern architecture."

CONTEMPORARY MATERIALS AND METHODS

Iron

To go back again to about 1800, one of the first and most important new materials of the machine age was iron. It had been used previously, but now the significant difference was that it could be mass-produced. Iron was first used as a framework and covered with masonry. The early iron buildings looked much the same as those that preceded them, except that they were strengthened inside with iron. It is typical in the history of design for designers to have new materials take an old form. One may see the merits of a new material (greater strength, for example), but the mind, rather than let the new material suggest its own new forms, easily retains the images and ideas of past structures.

One of the first men to realize the esthetic possibilities of iron as well as its structural strength was the engineer Alexandre Gustave Eiffel. He built many buildings in Paris, but is known chiefly for the famous Eiffel Tower. But steel beams alone were not enough to make possible such a structure as this giant tower. The beams had to be connected, and the mass production of bolts, rivets, and other connectors was just as important as the main parts of the structure. Also, the invention of the elevator to provide easy access to the top of the tower was essential to the whole idea of these tall structures.

Glass

Glass was another material that could be mass-produced and it fitted in well with the light and open feeling of iron. Previously, glass had been made only in tiny pieces so that windowpanes were either small or had to be fitted together out of many pieces, as in the leaded glass window. By 1850 factories could turn out pieces of glass 4 feet long, and this material made possible such buildings as the Crystal Palace in England and the various International Exhibition halls of Paris done in the second half of the nineteenth century. In contrast to the heavy masonry buildings of the previous eras, these new buildings were transparent lacework structures.

ARCHITECT: GEORGE H. WYMAN; PHOTOGRAPHER: JULIUS SHULMAN

24. A new "tall" building of 1892 made possible with iron, glass, and elevators for ascent.

ARCHITECTS: TROST & TROST; PHOTOGRAPHER: JULIUS SHULMAN

25. An early concrete "skyscraper."

Reinforced Concrete

Another important new material that has made modern architecture possible is reinforced concrete. Concrete is a synthetic stone. In contrast to the natural process whereby sand lies under the ocean or some other enormous weight for a few million years, consolidates, and becomes rock, man has now developed a process for accomplishing this in a few hours.

Concrete is produced by mixing sand and gravel with an adhesive agent called cement. Water is then added to this mixture, which becomes as hard as rock when it dries. By making a form out of wood or metal the wet mixture will take the shape of the form just as a cake takes the shape of the pan in which it is baked. The problem with concrete, however, is that it is as brittle as a cracker or a piece of glass. It can stand a good deal of weight if it is well supported from below, but if suspended from its edges and pressed down at the middle, it will break under relatively little pressure.

So, concrete was fine for piling up in blocks, but if one tried to hang it between two objects, as a roof hangs between two walls, it sagged and broke. On the other hand, a rod of metal, such as iron, can easily hang between two objects, and even if it bends, it will not break. So the idea was conceived to combine the strong qualities of both these materials by putting the iron rods inside the concrete and thus producing "reinforced concrete." This was first done about 1800, but it was not until 1900 that it became widely used. With its tremendous strength and spanning capacity larger rooms could be built. Roofs were stronger and needed less frequent use of supports, and buildings became not only bigger but taller.

Prefabrication

Not only were there new materials introduced in the machine age, but new methods for handling old materials were developed. It was the standard practice to bring all building materials to the site and then prepare them for use. Now, most materials are either partially or totally prepared in factories and require less handling at the site. The inevitable result of this method is that more of the building components of houses will be assembled in the factories, and eventually whole houses will probably be delivered to the site in one complete unit. There may come a day when handmade houses will be as rare as handmade cars are today.

This development toward the prefabrication of buildings is the result of high labor costs. Building materials used to be, and still are, expensive in most countries outside the United States. However, this expense is offset by the fact that the labor costs are relatively small. Today in the United States, the cost of labor amounts to at least two-thirds of the total cost of the building. This means that if it costs $20 to put together $10 worth of the cheapest wood, $30 has been spent, and a poor quality product is produced. If an additional $5 is spent on a better grade of wood, a much finer product can be produced for $35. In other words, the high cost of labor makes it pay to buy the best materials. Unfortunately, this situation also encourages a great deal of waste in our present building methods. For instance, if one needs a door and has an old door in good condition, it may cost less money to buy a new door rather than pay for several hours of a man's time to cut down the old door, plane it, sand it, reset the hinges, and rehang it.

Concrete Shells

It is this cost ratio in the United States that makes it expensive to build the delicately curved concrete shell structures seen in Europe and Latin America. Reinforced-concrete shells use very little material but require a vast amount of labor to make the wood forms. So for this reason they are little used in the United States.

The Balloon Frame

Another significant labor-saving building method today is the "balloon-frame" system of construction. In the field of individual housing, there has probably never been a more significant development. Surely at least 90 percent of the houses built in the last fifty years have been constructed on this

26. The "balloon frame" before being covered with its skin of wood or plaster.

PHOTOGRAPHER: ROBERT GOTTLIEB

DRAWING ROOM FROM THE POWEL HOUSE, PHILADELPHIA, 1768. PHILADELPHIA MUSEUM OF ART

27. Patterns and ornament everywhere.

system. Even the few masonry houses built now usually have their interior partitions made of hollow "stud walls" which are essentially the balloon-frame system.

This system may be considered as the modern version of the reed hut or teepee. The walls are not solid but are a framework of wood covered with one of many varieties of skin such as thin wood strips, plaster, shingles, etc. Most parts of the skeleton construction are made of "2 × 4s." These are long mill cuttings of wood 2 inches thick and 4 inches across, and in balloon frame constructions the vertical 2 × 4s are called "studs." They are usually put every 16 inches along the wall and nailed to a horizontal piece both at the top and the bottom. This most-used building system is only about a hundred years old and depends totally on the machine for its existence. Before the age of machine saws it was easier and cheaper to pile up solid round or squared-off logs into a solid wall. This was the wall system of the log cabin and the logs were overlapped at the corners like "Lincoln logs." This method used a good deal of wood and required expert craftsmen to put it together. Today, with machined wood of uniform dimensions and machine-made nails, a structure can be built in a fraction of the time with less wood as well as less skilled craftsmanship.

Machine-Made Ornament

Mass-produced ornament was another product of the machine age particularly noticeable in the Victorian era. Before this time all carvings and paintings were handmade and a luxury. Now, suddenly, machine lathes could make a piece of wood into a corkscrew or just about anything else in a few minutes. The presses and power looms could quickly turn out the most complicated patterns on paper and fabrics. Ornament was everywhere, on the floors, the walls, the ceilings, the banisters, inside and outside and everywhere. There was hardly a place left that did not bombard the eyes with patterns, impressions, and activity of line.

Style and Purpose

Today there is a similar enthusiasm over plastics, chrome, and "streamlining." "If it is new it must be good," is the motto. Maybe it is good, but there is also the possibility that it isn't good. Or, more to the point, what is good for one purpose may not be good for all purposes. Just because it is good for an airplane to be streamlined it does not follow that everything in one's household need also be streamlined, unless these objects are going somewhere fast. It is also a matter of degree. If a car is going to the moon it should definitely be designed like a rocket. If it is intended for driving around in downtown traffic, the rocket shape with fins and multiple taillights to simulate exhausts no longer applies. And, if a car runs on gasoline, there is no use feeding it bales of hay.

28. Hay for the car and "built-in birds" add the really authentic touch to this "California ranch."

PHOTOGRAPHER: JULIUS SHULMAN

Review

Briefly, here is what has happened to our man-made environment from five thousand years ago until now. Between the dawn of man and the machine age, architectural ideas and styles developed and changed slowly. Each region had its own style which developed out of its own terrain, climate, materials, and way of living. In areas where there was travel some ideas were borrowed from other places and cultures, but, in general, each culture had its own unique way of building to fit its environment. Thus each area had unity of design, but there was diversity of design throughout the world.

Now, with the exchange of ideas, the manufacture and transportation of synthetic materials, and the possibility of creating artificial terrain and climate, buildings are becoming more and more similar throughout the world. But there is much diversity within each area. Today, any town can have both ideas and materials from anywhere in the world. The result has been that, in general, everyone is better housed, but the fascinations of each country's differences are diminishing. The conglomeration of ideas often seen on a single street is chaotic and almost frightening. This chaos results in part from the number of meaningless imitations of past styles used without an understanding of how their original forms developed. If contemporary architecture is to be as successful today as past styles were in their days, both the original ideas behind these traditional styles as well as the basic ideas of modern architecture must be understood.

CONTEMPORARY ARCHITECTURE

The term "contemporary architecture" is often used to define a particular style of building. However, in this chapter the term is used in its more correct and original connotation to mean anything that has been built recently or within about the last fifty years.

Although the buildings we see around us are new because they were built recently, very few of them are new ideas most suitable to the current ways of living. For several reasons this is particularly true in the field of housing.

Most people feel most comfortable in the surroundings they are accustomed to. It may be exciting to meet new people or see new places, but for "feeling at home" most people are more at ease with old friends in surroundings with which they are familiar. At times people will cling to what is familiar or what they are used to, no matter how uncomfortable or impractical the situation. An extreme case in point can be seen when prisoners who have been offered their freedom after many years prefer to stay in jail. Generations of farmers have kept their gardens on the slopes of the volcano Agua in Guatemala, even though boiling water erupts periodically from it and pours down the slope.

Such examples of the innate tenacity of man to cling to the known, no matter what the consequences, indicate that, for many people, a change from their familiar surroundings is difficult, if not almost impossible. Now, even though architects may feel that there are better methods of building than most people make use of, this need to change is certainly not a life-and-death matter, so a change in architectural environment is even less likely than for people who actually live in dangerous situations.

It is also true that most people are influenced by what they hear and see around them. This, in turn, produces contemporary dwellings that are influenced by the past. An idea which is seen or heard may not register consciously at the time, and yet it comes forth later as something remembered or even as something one may think his own. One may see a beautiful house, for example, and later, when that person needs a house, the first thought is of that beautiful house already seen rather than of the actual housing requirements which would produce their own unique architectural solution. Not only are past impressions strong influences, but by common usage they become symbols; status symbols and other kinds of symbols. Some government buildings are still being built in a "classic" style because this style is a symbol of the Greek or Roman eras which supposedly were eras of good government. So, by inference, if the Greeks had good government in such a building, we, too, will have good government in this style of building. The probable reason the Greeks had good government was that they were able to solve their governmental problems with the same straightforward, creative thinking that produced the architecture we all admire. Today, however, there is often less concern with how they solved the problems of governing themselves and more concern with the outward symbols —their buildings.

Styles in clothing are also influenced by impressions heard and seen. Until about 1950 most American men wore undershirts. Then, a famous movie star who was regarded as masculine, courageous, and strong, had a scene in a movie which disclosed that he was not wearing an undershirt. The conclusion was that if this strong and courageous man on the screen did not wear an undershirt, then all strong and courageous men did not wear undershirts, and by not wearing an undershirt one would be certain to appear strong and courageous. For a period following the release of this movie the men's undershirt business practically died out.

Hair styles, entertainment, toothpaste, dwellings, or what have you, are also influenced by what is seen and heard. The successful results achieved by advertising products with the endorsements of famous people are based on this fact. Because a man is an outstanding ball player does not mean he knows anything about toothpaste or hair lotion. His teeth and hair may even be falling out, but unfortunately it is easy to associate achievements in one field with knowledge in all fields. If the movies show successful, rich people in certain types of houses, these houses then become symbols of what successful people should have. Whether we realize it or not, the material things around us, particularly our dwellings, are to a great extent outward symbols of our aspirations, and a reflection of our values insofar as we are able to make them so.

Perhaps the most important reason for our reliance on the ideas of the past is that new ideas are hard to come by. Even most education is based on studying the past, admiring it, and imitating it rather than teaching the student to find the principles on which the solutions of the past were based and to search for new ideas. Today there is too much stress placed on conformity in order to succeed. We tend to teach "the way" rather than trying to encourage various possible ways of doing things that would lead the student to discover his own method as a result of his own thinking. With such single-minded concepts goes an inference that different ways of doing things are strange, abnormal, wrong, or at least peculiar. But our ways may actually be peculiar to others and should be constantly reexamined.

Several years ago an Arabic magazine carried an article on "a quaint American custom called dating." It described dating with as much disbelief and amazement as an American magazine would describe some African bloodletting ceremony. The author could not understand why a boy would save up his money and then spend it all taking a girl to dinner or a movie. Although this custom is very new in world history it is no longer questioned in the United States. It is "the way." And neither is the fact that most houses are far from beautiful or truly comfortable. They are also accepted as "the way."

If our minds are so firmly fixed on "the way" of doing things as if there were no other, and we tend to look with such caution on new or different ways, it is therefore not surprising that new ideas often receive little encouragement. It usually takes a good deal of time to form a new idea as well as to work it out, and since our civilization is in such haste, it is no wonder that many intelligent people are discouraged from pursuing new thoughts.

Despite all these difficulties new ideas do emerge and our surroundings do change. There have been a few architects in the past seventy-five years who have been able to think almost independently of the past and solve architectural problems in a manner suitable for contemporary living. However, there are also many houses built today which imitate older styles; therefore a brief analysis of the most common traditional styles of American housing will be presented first, in order that the total scene we find on the streets today will be more comprehensible.

"TRADITIONAL" STYLES

The variety of traditional styles in American architecture is vast and often confusing. Actually, the variations on the many traditions are almost as endless as the people who live in the houses. However, for the sake of having some basis of understanding of the most common styles, they can be divided into a few main groups corresponding roughly to the main periods in our history and the different locations in which the buildings were built.

The Colonial period during the sixteenth and seventeenth centuries pro-

ARCHITECT: BERNARD MAYBECK; PHOTOGRAPHER: JULIUS SHULMAN

29. Forms and ideas of the past need not be either forgotten or slavishly copied, but can be used where they apply.

duced styles called Early Colonial, Northern Colonial, Cape Cod, the Salt Box, and Dutch Colonial. During the eighteenth century the Spanish Colonial or Mediterranean style and the French Provincial style were introduced in the Southern and Western regions where the Spanish and French colonized. In the North the "New England Colonial" was replaced by the "Georgian" or "Regency" style.

After the American revolution the people of the East Coast became interested in the classic and Greek styles, and from these Thomas Jefferson and other architects of the South developed the neoclassic and Southern Colonial style. During the late nineteenth century copies of all European styles were built. These included Greek, Venetian, French Renaissance, English Romanesque or Norman, Medieval English and English Half-Timber, and combinations of these styles. And during the twentieth century copies of these copies (see Illustration 16) were built side by side with the new "modern architecture."

The Early Colonial Style

The earliest American houses were completely simple. As in the beginning of other civilizations, the first need was for shelter. The difference between the early American civilization and others was that it did not grow from a primitive state. Ours started with a group of people who came

30. This 200-year-old Early Colonial house is still in use. It is a simple, compact, honest shelter with the charm of these qualities.

PHOTOGRAPHER: JULIUS SHULMAN

from various European cultures, so many of these people brought with them the ideas and styles of their European homeland. Since New England was primarily populated with people from England and its climate was similar, the English style of architecture introduced there fitted well.

Early Colonial houses were compact because this form is easiest to build and heat. The materials used were stone, clay made into bricks, and timber. Since these were abundant in this area, the materials were put together crudely in the early houses because there were few skilled workmen, but the textures produced were beautiful because they were put together in a simple, straightforward manner. Windows were few and small since glass could be made in only small pieces at that time. Also it was imported and taxed by the English government. The shutters were not ornaments, but were there to protect the windows in the winter. Roofs were generously sloped to shed the snow, and the massive chimneys extending from them stemmed from centrally located fireplaces. All household activities went on as close to these great fireplaces as possible since these furnished the only heat available, and so were essential to life. (See Illustration 98.)

Most of the houses were built of wood and the hand-hewn beams were left exposed in many rooms. It is easy to comprehend the structure and design in these early houses since the beams are visible. It is like seeing a simple piece of machinery work and being able to understand how it functions—it is worth watching. However, if what is happening cannot be comprehended, interest is often lost.

The Early Colonial houses took on various modifications in their shapes to suit the materials at hand and the backgrounds of the people building them. Various names were given to these modifications. The style which developed around Massachusettes and Cape Cod was called the Cape Cod style. This was an unadorned rectangular shape with a sloping roof. It had one or one-and-a-half stories. In Connecticut some of them had an additional one-story wing behind a two-story structure with the upper roof running down over the lower story in back. Since this shape resembled that of the salt boxes used at the time, this type of house became known as the "Salt Box."

The Dutch Colonial style did not conform to the symmetrical concepts of other New England architecture. The Dutch settlers brought with them a type of roof that was flatter at the top and then dropped sharply near the edge. The advantage of this type of roof structure was that it produced more room upstairs under the gable.

The Georgian Style

As life in the Colonies became easier, there was more time to think of things other than pure shelter. Shelter from the New England climate was still important, but there was now time, materials, and craftsmen to produce more sophisticated structures and ornament which reflected the great interest in the past and European styles.

PHOTOGRAPHER: JULIUS SHULMAN

31. The more refined elegance of the Georgian style. There are more fireplaces, windows, and rooms, and the doorway indicates that the family has "good taste" and knowledge of the classics—important qualities in this era.

By the eighteenth century all respectable houses were larger, more refined, and painted. Many houses of this Georgian period were delicately ornamented with classic details. A third floor was added to many of them by inserting dormer windows in the sloping room, thus making the space under the gable more usable. More comfort was derived from the addition of fireplaces at each end of the house. Interiors were finished with plaster, paint, and wallpaper. To keep up this sort of house took many servants and slaves, but these, too, were plentiful. Structural elements in Georgian houses were no longer visible. Each room was a box totally sealed off from the rest of the house with the exception of a door for entry and a window or two to admit light and provide some view. The whole house became more

COURTESY OF METROPOLITAN MUSEUM OF ART, NEW YORK

32. This interior expresses the same interest in elegance and European culture as does the exterior.

complex with the addition of more wings; kitchens, servants' quarters, and offices extended out from the main structure. Over each door was some form of Greek pediment. It was pure ornament since it supported or protected nothing but was a symbol of elegance.

Neoclassic Style

By the end of the American Revolution, England was no longer revered and its architecture was not used as a model. Although the English architecture of the Georgian era was based on classic motives, by the end of the eighteenth century the American people preferred to go directly to the classics and produced the neoclassic style. Many, including Thomas Jefferson, traveled to Italy and Greece and brought back firsthand knowledge. The tiny pediments of the Georgian period now grew to resemble the proportions of small Greek temples. These classic façades were stuck onto the front of the house, and had no relation to the planning or structure within. Sometimes the temple façade was built to be used as a front porch or the columns extended up one story to support a balcony for the second story.

In Southern regions the columns became larger and were built around the sides of the house so as to give shade for coolness. These mansions typify the Southern Colonial style. The building materials for them were so elaborate that there are instances when whole ships were chartered to bring the materials and fittings from Europe.

33. A neoclassic house made elegant with a façade of Greek columns.

PHOTOGRAPHER: JULIUS SHULMAN

COURTESY OF NEW ORLEANS CHAMBER OF COMMERCE

34. The French Provincial style of New Orleans. Heavy, classic columns are replaced by lacelike ironwork.

French Provincial Style

Farther south the country was settled by the French and Spanish. In New Orleans the architecture was primarily influenced by that of France and the style which developed there is called French Provincial. Here the massive Greek columns were replaced by a delicate grillwork of iron. It was as gay and lacy as possible—as were the clothes and furnishings of the period. In the cities the houses were built around open courtyards. This is a typical house plan of the southern Mediterranean regions also, since the climate there makes it possible to enjoy the out-of-doors most of the year and such an interior garden affords privacy. Another distinctive feature of French Provincial architecture was the Mansard roof. (It was originally designed in France by the architect Nicolas François Mansard.) This type of roof was practically flat on top and dropped down steeply near the edges on all four sides. Dormer windows protruded from these sides.

Mediterranean and Monterey Styles

All southwestern Latin American Colonial architecture was influenced by the architecture of Spain and North Africa. In California and the Southwest this style is generally referred to as the Mediterranean style and can be seen at the California Missions. These were built out of the most available material, adobe. This clay was formed into blocks and set out into the sunlight to dry. Other blocks were baked into semicircular tiles for the roof. Adobe, being a heavy material, was a good insulator, and was well suited

35. Heavy, rough materials and planning for shade and outdoor living are characteristic of the Southwest and the Mediterranean style.

PHOTOGRAPHER: JULIUS SHULMAN

COURTESY OF MONTEREY CHAMBER OF COMMERCE

36. The Monterey style with heavy adobe walls, wood balconies and low-pitched tile roofs.

to the warm dry climate. The large scale of the adobe walls gives these "Mediterranean style" buildings a feeling of massive repose and simple elegance.

In Monterey, California, the heavy masonry walls of the Mediterranean style were combined with the woodwork of the New England carpenters, and became known as the Monterey style. The rooms were placed around courtyards and the surrounding balconies were built of wood. The roofs were pitched low since there was no snow, and the materials were used with the same simplicity and beauty of texture that characterized the early Eastern Colonial houses.

Eclectic Styles of the Late Nineteenth and Twentieth Centuries

During the last half of the nineteenth century there was a surge of eclecticism. Most of the American architects were trained in Europe and were primarily concerned with bringing the grandeur of the European styles to America. During the period many ornamental features of Greek architecture were appliquéd onto houses. Venetian, Renaissance, Romanesque, and Medieval English and English Half-Timber façades and details were also applied to the basic balloon-frame house. The earlier Colonial and Georgian styles were imitated as well. Many of the late nineteenth-century homes were beautifully designed and well built, but others combined so many styles that the aesthetic result could only be described as chaotic. As mentioned previously, the mass production of machine-made ornaments contributed its share to the maze of patterns. The technique of "appliqué" is basic to almost all architectural design at this time. This is where the ornament or the parts of the house that are there to be "beautiful," are put on or appliquéd on to the building after it is constructed. The ornament is not part of the basic structure.

Contemporary copies of English Half-Timber illustrate one example of how the appliqué technique has become totally unrelated to the structure itself. During medieval times in England the houses were built of heavy timbers that formed the supporting structure of the building. The spaces between the timbers were then filled in with bricks or some other material. When the beauty of these structural patterns formed by the exposed timbers was recognized, a conscious effort was made to make the timbers into more ornate patterns, but they still retained their structural function. The exposed timber patterns in the authentic English style can be compared to the branches of a tree. Even if a tree is gnarled and weatherbeaten, it reveals a structural beauty because the lines of growth can be comprehended.

37. A Victorian home. Obviously built for comfort and delight rather than efficiency alone.

COURTESY OF LOS ANGELES CHAMBER OF COMMERCE

Anne Hathaway's Cottage
OPEN

PHOTOGRAPHER: JULIUS SHULMAN

39. This house is slicker and obviously expensive, but the wood trim supports nothing and becomes meaningless.

This sense of growth and line continuity would be entirely lost if those same tree branches were lying on the ground in a heap. When the structural elements of the Half-Timber house become nothing more than a trim on the outside of a totally unrelated balloon-frame structure, this is no more comprehensible than the heap of branches. In these eclectic houses only the superficial look of the original form is there. The essential idea has been omitted, and even though one cannot perceive directly whether or not the exposed timber pieces are solid or trim, one is nevertheless able to "sense" it. It is similar to the difference between a girl with healthy and beautiful bone structure as opposed to a badly proportioned girl who attempts to cover this by painting perfect features on her face with make-up. What is inside can be sensed even though we can see only the outer surface.

Such distortion of an original idea by applying the form of it onto something else without substituting a new idea has left many homes without character. Though many of these may be referred to as charming, quaint, homey, or even cute, they are no longer an architectural structure of integrity. They are planned not with the thought of solving important problems of today's living, but merely to fit behind a façade of the past.

38. These timbers form a bold framework to support this house.
PHOTOGRAPHER: ROBERT GOTTLIEB

The Fluted Column

The past can be of help with both its ideas and inspiration, but it must be understood or the true idea and its value are lost. There are many past architectural ideas which have been permitted to dwindle into insignificance and irrelevance. One example of this which can be easily traced to its source five thousand years ago is the fluted column. There is nothing wrong with fluted columns—it is what has happened to them that is unfortunate.

There are imitation "Georgian" or "Colonial" houses built today which have fluted columns or pilasters (flattened-out columns) on either side of the front door, but inside have twentieth-century bathrooms and kitchens with every electrical gadget. The façades of these houses are copies of nineteenth-century replicas of eighteenth-century Georgian houses. Many of these are five-room houses copied from fifteen-room houses copied from the White House in Washington, D.C., or some other home which was large enough to carry the columns. Although these columns were built of wood in most cases, they were copied from the stone columns of the immense English Renaissance palaces built during the seventeenth century. Their scale of construction and their columns were almost as impressive as the scale achieved in the civic buildings of sixteenth-century Rome from which they were copied.

The models for these Italian Renaissance buildings were the original buildings of Rome built around the first century. The fluted columns on these early buildings were built of stone and measured as much as 50 feet high and 5 feet across. These columns were nevertheless as much an ornament as are the contemporary columns that measure only 10 feet high and 5 inches across. These Roman columns were copied from the less ornate fluted columns of Greece which were functional and held up the roofs of the temples. Since they were supporting something, the diameter had to be greater in proportion to the height than in the Roman columns, and they were more like their predecessors in Egypt.

This first fluted column in Egypt was designed almost five thousand years ago by the architect Imhotep. He was regarded so highly by his contemporaries that he was later deified. He used this column at Sakkara (near present-day Cairo). It was part of the first monumental stone structure built by man. The *concave* "flutes" of these columns were a variation of an earlier theme by Imhotep. In its first form the columns were carved with semicircular, *convex* ridges all around to imitate and stylize bundles of reeds in stone. Such reed bundles were tied together and used to form the first columns of the Nile valley.

40. The first fluted columns, built by Imhotep five thousand years ago in Egypt.
PHOTOGRAPHER: LOIS GOTTLIEB

What has happened is that a simple Egyptian structure, the reed column was elegantly used as a motif by a great designer, but it then was modified and gradually diminished in scale until the grandeur of the idea was gone. There has never been a more magnificent column designed than the original, but the watered-down replicas seen today which try by inference to depict the magnificence of Egypt or the beauty of Greece or the power of Rome are shorn of significance in comparison to the original form.

These pathetic imitations are particularly meaningless today because there are many more alternatives to build with than at any other time in history. We now have more materials, more control of these materials through machine power, and more knowledge than ever before. With these assets a new and better kind of environment can be made for everyone. The possibilities of this modern world have much more to offer everyone than the accomplishments of the past.

41. These imitation bamboo columns fail to give this room the true flavor and enchantment of Oriental architecture.

PHOTOGRAPHER: JULIUS SHULMAN

ARCHITECT: FRANK LLOYD WRIGHT; PHOTOGRAPHER: JULIUS SHULMAN

42. Crude materials made into an imaginative and dynamic new form.

MODERN ARCHITECTURE

Here the term "modern" architecture is used to describe those contemporary buildings which do not rely on past traditions to give them beauty or elegance. Such modern houses or other buildings are more difficult to describe than the traditional ones because they cannot be classified by outward effects. Although there exist endless variations of each traditional style, there are certain architectural forms such as sloping roofs, dormer windows, "classic" doorways or iron grillwork that have come to characterize each style. However, in good modern architecture, the style depends not so much on particular forms, but rather on ways of thinking, ways of solving the problems of environment, ways of using materials to their best advantage, and various ways of creating usable and beautiful space. Therefore the form of a modern building becomes different for each problem, and the results satisfy the particular requirements of the site and the needs of the people living there. Good modern style is not stuck on like make-up; it must grow out of the entire structure as the beauty that is the manifestation of total character.

The Misuse of Contemporary Ideas

One difficulty encountered in studying and understanding the values of modern architecture is that there is relatively little good modern architecture around, compared to the vast numbers of buildings that are poor imitations of the outward effects of these buildings. Good modern buildings have been copied just as were the ancient classic buildings and many of the results have been equally unfortunate.

For example, one commonly misused feature of modern architecture is the "picture window." In the early twentieth century architects began to design larger windows as large sheets of glass became available. The house was no longer a fortress, and it was better to have plenty of light and have the possibility of looking out at a beautiful view. Today many of the houses trying to be modern have picture windows which look out at telephone wires, streetcars, or the neighbor's laundry. In these houses the essential idea of the picture window, that of framing something worthy of being pictured, has been lost.

The Effort to Be Different

Other misuses of the principles of modern architecture manifest themselves in a sort of wild "Buck Rogers" structures. In such cases someone has tried to be "different," not different because there was a reason for it, but different just for the sake of being different. Suddenly a wall will veer off at some strange angle incongruent with the rest of the structure. If one asks why the wall is that way, one is apt to be told that it is "modern." Instead of solving basic problems of structure and design, such flights of fancy without purpose create only confusion and needless complexities. Since good modern architecture is designed to cope with the problems of the site and take into consideration the basic requirements of the owners, the design will therefore vary to adjust to different circumstances. The resulting house or building should, however, give one the feeling of "Well, naturally, what else would one do?" rather than "How different!" Sometimes this effort to be unique results in something outlandish. However, to be unique does not necessarily imply that the results be shocking or peculiar in form. The pyramids of Giza are certainly unique, but their form is a completely simple one even though it was far from simple to build them. The Egyptians of that time were not trying to be unique; they were simply trying to preserve the body and spirit of their leader in the simplest, most straightforward fashion they could devise.

Good Design Seems Obvious

The design of the pyramids now seems obvious, but it probably was not so obvious five thousand years ago.

Today the shapes of the airplane and rocket seem equally obvious. It would now seem that practically anyone could design one, but the fact is that it has taken over half a century and millions of hours of designing to arrive at these simple forms wherein every square inch of surface curvature is planned with mathematical precision. And yet contrast these with most modern automobiles. The only thing obvious about their design is its pretentiousness. Does it really take a 200-horsepower engine and more than a ton of machinery and metal to transport one person, or even six people? Is it necessary to take up 20 feet of road space or parking area for each car? If a fender is supposed to be something to protect a wheel, why should it extend halfway or all the way through the door? On the modern car chrome strips run here and there to give the effect of streamlining but never seem to be really placed where they are needed, such as where they might prevent the paint from getting scratched. Tail fins are attached vertically one year, horizontally the next year. All these things are not only costly to change, but were of no use to begin with. The same situation exists in many houses. False shapes and ornaments made to suggest grandeur only help to reveal a pretentious attitude toward living, when for the same money one could buy more space or something truly useful.

Simplicity in Contrast to Starkness

A common misconception about modern architecture is that it forsakes all use of ornament. Such impressions are understandable, since many people now live, work, or study in structures that would have been considered fit only for prisoners fifty years ago. These buildings have absolutely bare walls, hard surfaces, back-breaking furniture, and a grim determination to have it "honest" and cut to the bone. And they are supposed to be modern. It is more to the point to think of this type of contemporary building as being representative of our civilization's concern for cleanliness, efficiency, and laboratory sterility. These are all worthy attributes, but they do not solve man's emotional needs. There is no reason to assume that man's senses need to be delighted or uplifted only in the theater or the cathedral. If beautiful surroundings are to be reserved for only special occasions, it is not surprising that one's best behavior is too often reserved for only these special occasions. The places that matter the most in our lives are the places where we spend most of our time, at home, at work, and at school.

Although modern architecture has eliminated the ornament of the past, it is a mistake to assume that it need not be replaced with some other form of ornament to lift the spirit. The idea of simplicity should not be confused with plainness, dullness, or drabness. A most simple and elegant dress, for example, can be beautiful, but a simple gunny sack, which can serve the same function, will produce an opposite impression. A house can be designed simply, but it need not be the architectural equivalent of a gunny sack.

Form and Function

This unornamented starkness is often referred to as "functionalism," and it usually functions pretty well for one's physical needs; the roofs don't leak, there are the minimum number of steps between the kitchen and dining areas, and all the utilities work perfectly. But, since man is a feeling creature, it is just as necessary to take into account these feelings. A building must function in this realm, too.

The concept of functionalism stems from an idea expressed some seventy-five years ago by Louis Sullivan, the Chicago architect who designed some of the world's first skyscrapers. He said, "form follows function." He meant that the form or shape of a thing, anything, must be made so that it is best suited to the use to which it is being put. This process is seen in nature where animals or plants develop forms and characteristics to fit the needs of their environment. As previously mentioned, the giraffe's long neck is for a specific reason, to reach the leaves on trees since there is not enough grass in Africa. Such a neck would be useless in the Arctic where there are no trees. In the Arctic the main need is for protection from the severe cold. Here the fat and fur on the polar bear are for this function. As different environments have produced different forms in nature, so have the new forms of modern architecture developed out of their functions.

Criteria for a Good Architecture

To try to describe the modern house or building with a single description is like trying to use a single description for all animals. However, as all vertebrate animals have some sort of structure or skeleton to hold them up, so does a house. There must be some sort of central core with ducts to distribute fluids and gases, just as the animal has a heart and arteries. And there must be some sort of walls or skin to hold everything together and protect it. Further descriptions of the modern house must refer to a particular house, since few other generalities can apply to all. The size, types of structure, materials, textures, colors, and details can be limitless.

The following questions consider some of the most basic criteria of good modern architecture:

1. Does the building fit the site and the needs, interests, and values of the people who use it?

2. Is the building a three-dimensional object, or is it simply four flat planes designed individually and hooked together at the corners?

3. Are the spaces the structure creates usable and integrated so that there is a flow of space from one area to another without sacrificing privacy, or is the building a series of little boxes stuck together?

4. Is the structure itself beautiful or does it rely on being "decorated" or covered up in order to be beautiful?

5. Does the structure have a unified idea and form in relation to its total environment? Are all parts and proportions related to the whole structure?

The International Style and Organic Architecture

Although most architects would generally agree with the aforementioned concepts, there are within the realm of modern architecture many diverse schools of thought. Just as different writers or composers do things somewhat differently, so do architects. The ideas of modern architecture are constantly developing in wider directions, but almost all their sources can be traced back to the two important schools of architectural thought which prevailed during the first half of the century.

The "International school" developed from the ideas and buildings of such men as Alexander Gustave Eiffel who were vitally interested in the new materials of the machine age. With the realization that the material benefits of the Industrial Revolution had to be accompanied by a revolution in building techniques and forms, there was an increasing awareness that the tremendous potential of mass production could produce a better living standard for everyone. Modern concepts of design developed not only as a reaction against the excessively ornamental styles of the Victorian era, but also from the awareness that simplicity could be beautiful and just as satisfying as the great ornateness so valued at the time. This was not to be the simplicity of dullness or drabness, but the simplicity created by the highest order of organization of thought and materials. The crystalline forms produced in the 1920s became known as the "International style." As the name implies, this is an architecture of the machine age which is not regional in character as the styles of Europe had been previously. The International style is probably best known for the steel-and-glass skyscrapers and gigantic monolithic concrete buildings. Although there are today many excellent architects building in this idiom, the three men who were the most influential in developing the International style were Le Corbusier, Walter Gropius, and Mies Van der Rohe. Le Corbusier worked in France, whereas Gropius and Mies Van der Rohe began their careers in Germany and are now in the United States.

ARCHITECT: MIES VAN DER ROHE; PHOTOGRAPHER: JULIUS SHULMAN

43. Example of the crystalline forms of the "International style." The steel and glass "skyscraper" is probably the most representative type of building of the 20th century.

44. This house is representative of the type of thinking of the "International school."

ARCHITECT: PHILIP JOHNSON; PHOTOGRAPHER: JULIUS SHULMAN

ARCHITECT: FRANK LLOYD WRIGHT; PHOTOGRAPHER: JULIUS SHULMAN

45. Concrete block house.

The other most significant trend in modern architecture was developed by Frank Lloyd Wright. He started his career in the 1880s with Louis Sullivan who was then designing the first ten-story "skyscrapers" in Chicago. Frank Lloyd Wright's architectural career continued for the next seventy years until his death in 1961. During this time he initiated more innovations in building techniques and new concepts of design than any one person in the history of architecture. Mr. Wright referred to his architecture as "organic." By this he meant that his structural forms were developed from the same principles he found in the structures of nature. His new organic style of structures were designed to fit the nature of the site, the nature of the materials, and the nature of the people for whom he was building. The three houses shown in Illustrations 45 to 47 give some indication of the scope and diversity of his work. Each is tremendously complex, yet totally unified in idea and form.

ARCHITECT: FRANK LLOYD WRIGHT; PHOTOGRAPHER: JULIUS SHULMAN

46. Hillside house.

47. Desert house.

ARCHITECT: FRANK LLOYD WRIGHT; PHOTOGRAPHER: JULIUS SHULMAN

The remainder of this book is a study of the various factors that produce good "modern" architecture or good design of any kind. Good design is not primarily the result of "taste" but the result of knowledge, just as good nutrition is not a matter of what tastes good but what will produce good health. Although most children would prefer to eat ice cream sundaes rather than meat and vegetables, few parents would go along with this kind of basic diet. Most mothers insist that their children acquire a taste for nourishing foods since only a well-balanced diet will produce physical health. It should be the same in one's dwelling. The choice of style and furnishings should not be the result of what one "likes," but rather the result of a carefully thought-through plan of what would best fulfill the physical and mental needs of the family.

Although the principles of architectural design cannot all be expressed in such definite terms as the vitamin content of foods, nevertheless some of the basic principles of design can be analyzed. The starting point is to know what you are looking for. This has nothing to do with the amount of money to be spent. Although it is easier to build a beautiful fifty-thousand-dollar house than make the fifty-dollar-a-month apartment beautiful, it can be done—just as one can eat inexpensive, nutritious foods such as soya bean in place of steaks and cheese. In design, however, the difference is that one must work within many limitations. Nevertheless, these financial limitations, structural limitations, or limitations of area can often be a springboard for the imagination to produce something even more creative in the long run.

One common limiting factor of good design which is too often ignored today has to do with the total community. When most people think of making a place for their family to live, they think of fixing up or decorating a home or apartment. Although this is, of course, necessary, it will become a losing battle if the larger area of the community is not taken into consideration. It is like trying to keep one's own child healthy while the rest of the community is infected with epidemics. The most beautiful home or apartment will not be fully enjoyed if it is surrounded by community problems and ugliness. Even if the community in which you live is not crowded with other people as yet, statistics indicate that sooner or later it will be. The problems of the whole community are becoming more and more crucial to us all, and it has become imperative that these problems be considered and planned for when building today.

THE CITY

THE TOTAL ENVIRONMENT

A discussion of the community and city may seem beyond the scope of a book dealing with the home. But just as everything inside a well-designed dwelling must be discussed in relation to the whole, so must the dwelling be thought of in relation to its total environment. This becomes clear when we think of objects we use. For example, a particular piece of furniture may be perfectly suitable for one family's room, whereas the same furniture may be unusable or out of place in another family's room. The same is true with clothing. A dress may look charming on one girl and unbecoming on another. Applying this to houses, a particular house may be suitable to one location, because of a certain climate and environment, but to place this house in a totally different situation may make it lose its function and meaning. For instance, a weekend house designed for the mountains had a roof steeply sloped to frame a particular mountain in front of the house. At the same time this roof design gave protection on a windy site. (See Illustrations 129–134.) After it was built, pictures of this house appeared in a widely read magazine, and a few months later a drive-in restaurant in the middle of a large city was built with the same roof design. In this location the large roof framed a sign advertising hot dogs, masses of telephone wires, and the traffic rushing by. Although the form was there, the idea was gone.

The City

The total environment of any building is crucial to the design. A building out of place is like a plant out of place. It becomes a weed and a blot on the community.

The same sort of thing can happen to a well-designed house when the surroundings change. A house can have a picture window looking out on a lovely view. Gradually the city expands and now it is looking out at a freeway 50 feet in front of it and 20 feet above it. Although this house still provides the necessary shelter, it no longer provides the other benefits for which it was designed; the view, the quiet, and the clean air, are gone. A dwelling depends on more than interior decorating for comfort.

Population Growth

When one drives or flies across the country it is impossible to imagine that there could be a problem of living space. The wilderness and empty land may seem endless, but there is a limit to it. The following statistics show the increasing rate of population growth:

Since the time of Christ, two thousand years ago, the world population has increased ten times. In California the population will double in the next twenty years, and, at the present rate of increase, the world population will double in forty years.

In 1790 the United States had twenty-four urban communities of 2,500 people or more. At the time only 5 percent of the American people lived in these cities. Now there are 4,700 urban communities in which more than two-thirds of the American people live.

In 1900, half of the working people in the United States worked on farms. Now, due to the increased efficiency of the machine, all of the agricultural work is being done by only 10 percent of the workers in the country, while the remaining 90 percent work and live in towns and cities.

As these statistics indicate, there will be more people living everywhere; most of them will live in cities, which will also increase in number, and the cities will be larger. But how much larger?

Again the statistics are astonishing. For example, ten years ago a remote town in California had a population of 365 people. Now the city planners of that town are expecting it to reach a population of 50,000 people in another ten years. This town is situated far from a city and without industry. What will happen to the towns that are suburbs or industrial centers?

The city as such is no longer primarily a business and cultural center surrounded by residential areas and suburbs, and agricultural areas. In the areas of highest population, such as the East Coast and Southern California, the city has become an overextended strip of commerce and tracts. There is no city center or form, just buildings for hundreds of miles. Although certain large cities are losing population within their city limits, they are adding suburbs, thereby actually extending the limits. In the near future it is expected that there will be one big city or "megalopolis" from Virginia to Maine, with all communities adjacent to one another. The only visible indications that will distinguish one section from another will probably be the signs showing where former villages used to be. But as far as going into the city or going into the country, it will all be an indistinguishable and endless sameness. This uncontrolled city growth today is referred to as "urban sprawl."

There are, however, alternate solutions to this problem which can be accomplished only by planning ahead. Tearing down and rebuilding the mistakes of the past can only be a good deal more costly than taking the time and effort to plan on paper.

Urban Problems

People have been clustering together in cities for thousands of years, either for protection, as in the medieval cities, or because of a common interest such as religion, learning, or work opportunities. The same thing is happening today, but on a larger scale; it is this scale of growth, however, that is creating the major problems. As was mentioned before, it is not too serious if one moves too much or too little earth with a pick and shovel, but to bulldoze hills and mountains away without planning or allowing for natural consequences can be disastrous. The problems of city planning are related. If one building or road is in the wrong place, it doesn't matter much. But building single houses or small sections of road are no longer typical of today's city development. Houses are being built by the hundreds, road construction is increasing at the rate of hundreds of miles per year, and the increase in the number of cars is even greater. Without serious planning, what will all this lead to?

Perhaps the most startling example of what can happen is already becoming evident in Los Angeles, not because Los Angeles is essentially different from other cities, but because it is already the largest city in the world (in area). But some day most large cities will face these same problems. The most publicized problem of Los Angeles is its smog. It happens to be worse there, but all big cities have smog under certain atmospheric conditions, and will get more smog as the pollution of the air continues. There is simply too much matter being poured into the air to be absorbed and carried away.

Pollution of the water is another problem which is becoming more acute in Los Angeles. Sewage cannot be constantly poured into the ocean and go unnoticed. The ocean is very large, but the amount of sewage is getting to be more than even the ocean can absorb.

Still another problem is the water supply. Water may seem as unlimited as the air we breathe, but the fact is it isn't. Certain areas of the country are bound to run out if they continue to depend on only the present sources of supply. Food, too, must have space to be raised, and plans must be made to transport it since less and less open land is available close to the cities.

Transportation and mobility within a city constitutes another major problem today. What difference does it make how nice a home or apartment is if one can't get to or from it? Again, in Los Angeles it is nearly impossible to live without a car because of the great distances involved. Statistics for

PHOTOGRAPHER: JULIUS SHULMAN

48. Los Angeles already extends farther than the eye can see. This formless, unplanned maze of dwellings is what is now being referred to as "urban sprawl."

this city show that there is more than one car for every two inhabitants (this includes children). If everyone drove their cars out into the streets at the same time all of the roads would be completely covered with cars, and there are many roads. Thirty-five percent of the land of Los Angeles is devoted to roads and another 30 percent devoted to the garages, gas stations, and parking areas. In other words, about two-thirds of this large city is already devoted to the automobile, with more cars arriving each day. What is the solution?

You may feel that this is not your problem, but unless your city has a plan to cope with the inevitable expansion that is taking place, it may well be your problem before too long. Land must be used for the benefit and profit of the whole community, not for the profit of a few individuals. Just as one's living room can become cluttered with furniture until everyone is stumbling over it, so can the entire community become a chaotic scene in which there is neither mobility nor adequately planned living space.

While this expansion takes place on the outskirts of the city, the center areas usually have problems of deterioration which often result in slum areas. With this deterioration rents and land values decrease. Properties are then divided and redivided in order to maintain the same income from them. As more people are packed into these areas, the general decay makes even cleanliness difficult and many aspects of life deteriorate with the environment. The cheaper land then becomes more useful for commercial or industrial use, and the houses and apartments which now become mingled with industrial buildings lose more of their value, and so the spiral downward continues.

To help counteract these conditions of city deterioration, the Federal government has formed numerous redevelopment or urban renewal agencies throughout the country. In collaboration with the city governments these agencies select specific areas for redevelopment and replanning. Planners and architects study the entire situation and decide how the land can best be used to the advantage of most people. As a result of these governmental endeavors certain areas become zoned for industrial use, others for commercial use, and the remainder for residential and recreational use.

In residential areas traffic is controlled so that the fewest possible streets become main arteries of the city. Schools, parks, recreation areas, and public utilities are planned. The redevelopment agencies have the authority to condemn any building they see fit. When this is done, although some people will be unhappy to lose their homes, most people will benefit by the decision in the long run. It is also part of the agency's responsibility to find suitable housing for those whose houses have been condemned.

The work of renovating privately owned buildings is paid for by individual owners, and all the work on streets, recreation areas, schools, etc., is paid for by the government. Under the redevelopment agency's management the Federal government contributes two-thirds of the total cost, the remaining third being paid for by the local city government. The money loaned by the Federal government is repaid by increased tax revenues made possible by land and property improvements.

In spite of its many problems, the modern city offers great advantages as well. Job opportunities are more plentiful, and for many the city is the only place where they can practice their professions. Whatever kind of dwelling you like is probably there. Whatever kind of people you like are there, too. Whatever one's interests, be it collecting stamps or judo, one is likely to find others with the same interests in the city.

A large city can afford specialized educational opportunities as well. Because of the vast number of students to choose from and an excellent public transportation system, New York City can offer specialized high

Equal areas to house 24 families in equal-sized dwellings

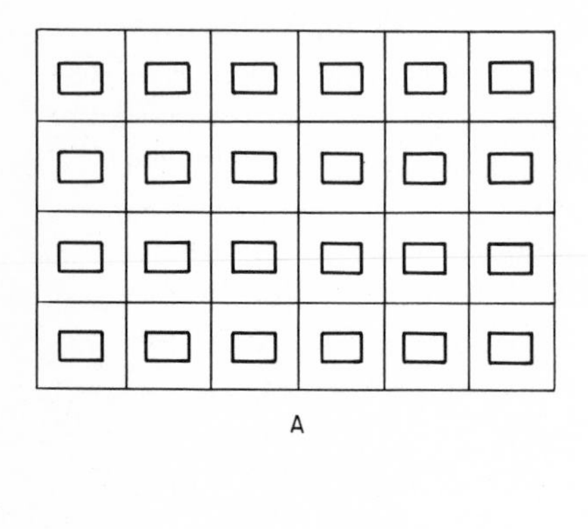

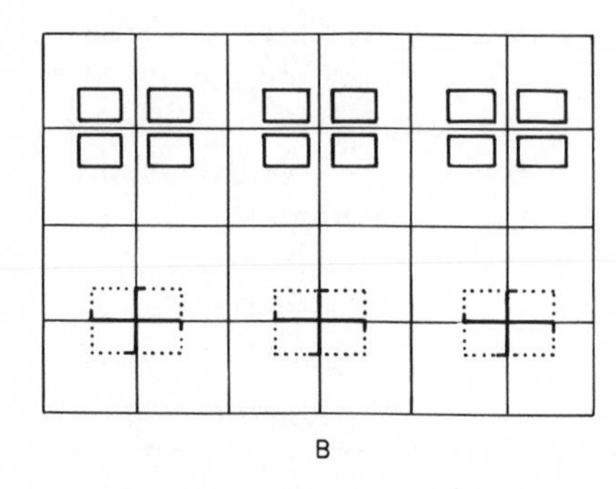

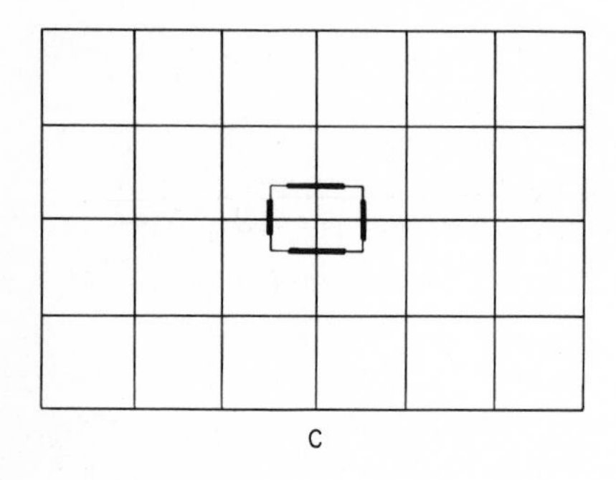

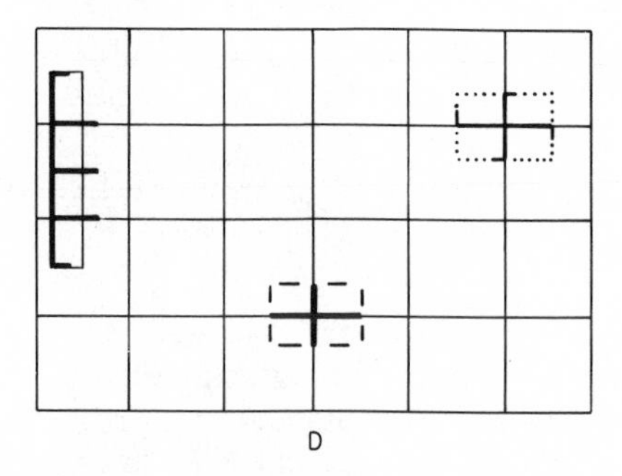

A. Tract type lots and housing. Each house is surrounded by a fringe of planting on all sides. At least one road as well as many driveways would be necessary for access to all houses.

B. Same lots with houses grouped to consolidate garden areas so as to be more useful and attractive. Privacy could be assured by arranging the utility areas of the houses where they would be adjacent to the other houses.

C. One six-story apartment surrounded by a park-like garden and playground which could be maintained by a single gardener.

D. The same area with various types of dwellings for different tastes. A group of four dwellings, a group of four row houses, and a four-story apartment. Again, surrounded by a park and play area.

Although this diagram shows an area for 24 families, the same type of planning could be done for 2,400 families.

49. There are many ways to house a number of families in a given area.
DIAGRAM: LOIS GOTTLIEB

PHOTOGRAPHER: JULIUS SHULMAN

50. Houses evenly distributed as in Diagram A. The focal point of the circle which has been left open culminates in an intersection rather than in something to benefit those living around it.

schools for talented children in the fields of science, music, and art. A smaller community could never hope to provide these educational advantages, nor could any large city that does not have such a well-planned transportation system.

Many people prefer the social anonymity of the city; others feel lonely in this crowd that is too big to be very concerned with the individual. Others feel that the main advantage of the city is its cultural activities. However, when one makes a decision as to whether or not to live in the city, one is basically choosing between these advantages and one's ability to buy or rent space. Space is the one commodity that the city loses as it grows, but it is an asset that can be provided for and even to some extent regained through proper planning. With proper city planning it is not so much a question of how many people there are per square mile, but how these people are distributed. City inhabitants can be evenly distributed in one flat plane so that there is a little space between each dwelling. They can be grouped together so that there is more space between each group, or they can be grouped together vertically as well as horizontally and have much more open space between them available for recreation. It is up to each person to decide in which arrangement he or she prefers to live.

51. Houses grouped around a common park and play area (Diagram B).

SITE PLANNER: CLARENCE STEIN; PHOTOGRAPHER: JULIUS SHULMAN

ARCHITECT: I. M. PEI; PHOTOGRAPHER: JULIUS SHULMAN

52. A combination of large apartments and single dwellings creates a high density of people but leaves ample free space for a park (Diagram D).

ARCHITECT: R. M. SCHINDLER; PHOTOGRAPHER: JULIUS SHULMAN

53. Garden apartments—another way to make it possible for many people to live close together comfortably.

IV

YOUR STYLE — THE DWELLING AS A PERSONAL EXPRESSION

CREATING ONE'S OWN STYLE

The examples of traditional architectural style referred to in the historical section of this book were included to show that styles vary with the character of the environment, and are an outgrowth of the thinking and ideas of particular eras. The chapter on modern architecture has further indicated that good modern style is concerned not so much with "a way" or "the way" of designing buildings, but rather with a more flexible kind of architecture catering more specifically to the individual requirements of environment. In other words, good modern architecture caters in a more meaningful way to the living and working requirements of the people who occupy it. Therefore, at its best the modern house will be an expression of one's individual style.

Webster's definition of *style* is: "The distinctive or characteristic mode of presentation, construction, or execution in any art, employment, or product. . . ."

Louis Sullivan summed it up in a more explicit way in relation to architecture when he said

What we so glibly call the styles are, and were, in their times and places, organizations or crystallizations of the thought and feeling of certain peoples. Hereafter, when you look on one of your contemporary "good

copies" of historical remains ask yourself the question: not in what style, but in what civilization is this building? *

It therefore becomes evident that when we think of creating our own architecture, dwelling, table setting, dress, or anything else, we have two alternatives to choose from. One is to copy a style of a past era, and the other is to create our own style, not for the sake of being modern or different, but rather to best utilize this knowledge and the material advantages of modern technology in a most meaningful way.

If you decide you would prefer to live surrounded by the styles of other civilizations, first make a thorough study of that era and its style of architecture to try to understand why the style developed as it did. If you want what this style offers, at least try to go back to the original buildings as models. These are always better than copying a copy of a copy. If your house style is to be meaningful, you should have some understanding of what the things you like about that style are expressing and why they are there. Don't copy the effect but see to it that the style you choose retains the idea or purpose for which it was originally designed. For example, if you want protection, don't defend yourself with a crenelated parapet but be equipped with the best means of defense possible today, just as the parapet was in its day. A telephone to call the police if you are attacked is cheaper, handier, and probably more efficient than pouring boiling oil from the roof.

If you decide to create your own style so that your dwelling is a portrait of you rather than of someone else, the first thing to do is to take a good look at yourself and your family, as if you were going to paint a self-portrait, or take a picture of your family. There is no use pointing the camera in any other direction; it has to be looking at you. To collect pictures of other people's rooms is fun, just as it is fun to make an album of pictures of your friends. But no matter how you arrange these pictures, you will never be able to make a picture of yourself out of them. You have to be looking at you.

An important question comes up at this point. How can this apply to people who are unable to build their own house? Starting with an old house is a limitation, to be sure, but it can be made into a dwelling that expresses your life. There are limitations in every building project, such as the site, an existing building, and the amount of money available, but these are stumbling blocks, not insurmountable hurdles. (These will be discussed on pages 94–101.) Another question is whether to paint this portrait yourself or hire an artist to do it. This will also be discussed. Whether you do it yourself or have professional help, it is first necessary to know what it is you are trying to do. This portrait is not only a physical portrait, but should be a reflection of one's total being: physical, mental, spiritual, etc. Nothing can be clearly reflected if it is not exposed and then organized.

Important questions which must be answered are:

* From *Kindergarten Charts* by Louis Henry Sullivan. Wittenborn, Schultz, Inc., 1947.

How do you want to live?
Where do you want to live and what do you want to live for?
What are your physical needs?
What are your interests, hobbies, work, recreation?
What people, things, and activities are most meaningful?

The answers to all these questions will determine the ideas you want to express in your house, and they will be as clearly stated as in an autobiography—clearer in some cases, because it is often easy to say what you think people want to hear with words, but the effort and cost of creating a dwelling are so great that one's real values must emerge. For example, few people would say that their first concern is with impressing other people, but there are a great many people with false fronts on their houses or apartments. Since they can't possibly be fooling themselves, it must be the visitors whom they want to convince that this place is really pretty elegant. They have made a very clear architectural statement to this effect.

Although style is the *way* something is said or expressed, the thing to be said, or the idea, must not be overlooked in the effort to gain style. The modern composer, Arnold Schoenberg, stated in his book, *Style and Idea,* "It is very regrettable that so many contemporary composers care so much about style and so little about idea."

This, unfortunately, is often true in other arts as well. In the field of design there are two comments that architects hear innumerable times. One is, "I can't visualize." The other is, "Will it look good?" Too often people feel that they can't attempt to create their own style if they don't know how it is going to look. They are concerned with the form rather than the idea, and because they are not trained to visualize the result, they lose faith in the idea. Certainly it is an asset to be able to visualize a plan, just as it is an asset for a musician to hear the sound of music from reading a score. However, many do not, and still produce music. It is equally possible to design your own environment without being able to visualize the physical results.

As to whether it will "look good," this is a difficult question. It is partly in the eyes and the mind of the viewer anyway. What may look good to one person may not look good to another, and what may look good this year may not look good five years from now. Styles in clothing illustrate our changing ideas of what looks good. For example, the dresses of five years ago were about six inches longer than they are now. It is hard to believe how unattractive these dresses now look to us. One is tempted to conclude that the dresses must have stretched or that girls must have shrunk. Since one's aesthetic evaluation of what looks good can change, there are few absolutes when it comes to "looking good." To be able to visualize beforehand will not necessarily guarantee that it will look good in architecture either.

A more important consideration than an arbitrary aesthetic judgment is whether or not the idea is good. Does the idea make sense? Is it related to the things around it? And is it in proportion to them? Satisfying these considerations will guarantee a much better chance of having it look good.

Even if a designer is capable of knowing what the result is going to look like first, the idea must come first and serve as a basis for any aesthetic decisions. The ability to visualize, although an admirable trait, is not a necessity for creating your own style.

Architectural style is created with ideas, and a very knowledgeable use of materials and techniques. As in writing an autobiography words are used, so in creating architecture, building materials, three-dimensional forms, structures, textures, and colors become the ingredients. The way you use and relate the ingredients will become your style.

SELECTING LOCATION AND TYPE OF DWELLING

The first considerations in choosing a dwelling are concerned with general location and the type of structure needed, such as the choice between a house, apartment, or trailer. Often the geographic location chosen will limit the choice of the type of structure. If you want to be in a large city, chances are that you may have fewer possibilities available other than an apartment; whereas in the country, even if one were looking for one, there might not be any. A sensible approach in making a decision is to narrow the available choices by starting with circumstances that cannot be altered. For example, many types of work can be done only in certain locations. Many people choose to sacrifice preferable aspects of living in order to be able to engage in a certain type of work or have a particular job that interests them.

Almost everyone must make compromises with their living conditions. Very few situations exist which would satisfy all one's needs and desires. The crucial point in choosing a dwelling that would best satisfy most needs is to be able to compromise with the less important rather than the more important needs. The problem is compounded because there are usually at least several people in the family to consider. It is easy to be tempted by a dwelling with some delightful aspects about it and then forget about other more important needs.

In choosing a dwelling the requirements of space and privacy must be thoroughly considered. To not provide these necessities can lead to minor irritations which may go unnoticed at first, but gradually these irritations become more noticeable and are reflected in the feelings of one or more members of the family. Insufficient space and lack of privacy may be very irritating to some; too much space and the effort to take care of it may overtire another; lack of safe outdoor play space or companionship for children can be very wearing on the most patient mother; a father too tired to be pleasant due to a long drive home from work may make the most beautiful home an unhappy one. All possible consequences must be considered. They are much more important than the color of the walls or the ruffles on the curtains, which can be thought of at a later time.

The following checklist gives some idea of the variety of considerations necessary for choosing a dwelling. This list is intended as a general guide and should be added to as individual needs become apparent. After checking those which relate to your situation, relist them in the order of their importance to you. This will help to clarify your thoughts on the subject of choosing a dwelling.

Geographic Considerations

1. *Convenience to Activities*

   a. Do you have to be near a particular job?
   b. Do you need public transportation?
   c. Do you need schools?
   d. Are there convenient shopping areas?
   e. Is there a special activity, some sport or cultural activity that it is important to be near?

2. *Climate*

   a. Are outdoor living and sports important?
   b. Does anyone in the family need a warm or dry climate for health reasons?
   c. In certain cities there are vast differences in climate even within a few blocks. Is this possible difference important to you?
   d. It is more difficult to live where small children must be kept indoors a good deal due to the climate. Is this important?

3. *Terrain*

   a. Hills often afford beautiful views.
   b. A hilly terrain can afford privacy.
   c. In a hot climate hills may be cooler.
   d. Hills can be more expensive to build on.
   e. Flat land and one-story houses are easier to take care of and provide play space more easily.

Social Considerations

1. *The City*

   a. One is close to large business and commercial opportunities.
   b. There are cultural advantages—music, theater, museums.
   c. There are more diverse and specialized people and groups.
   d. There are advantages for certain professions.
   e. There are possible educational advantages.
   f. High land values and rents produce crowded conditions.
   g. There is the possibility of too many activities and stimuli around one. (It is tempting to try to take advantage of all the activities a city offers and end up bewildered and exhausted.)

2. *The Suburb*

   a. It is close to the city with its advantages and has lower land-property values and less crowding.
   b. There is space and facilities for children.
   c. If the working members of the family commute, it can be time-consuming and exhausting.
   d. Transporting children to activities can also consume more time than planned or imagined.
   e. The possible need for a second car can be costly.
   f. Community activities can create less privacy, or there can be too much privacy in a neighborhood with no companionship, particularly for small children.

3. *The Tract*

   a. These houses offer the most new space for the money.
   b. The houses are designed for the convenience of families.
   c. Some tracts are designed to solve or minimize shopping problems for the homemaker and transportation and recreation problems for children. There are few tracts which cannot provide companionship for everyone.
   d. Most tract houses are designed for profit rather than excellence. The money is spent where it will show immediately and it is often later that it is noticeable where money has been saved.
   e. There is little feeling of architectural individuality in most tracts, and many of the groups of people are as similar as the designs; all on about the same income level, about the same age, and sometimes all work in the same industry. This sameness has certain advantages of togetherness, but it can also lack interest, and make privacy difficult to achieve.

4. *The Country or Rural Living*

   a. There is the most space for the money.
   b. It is impossible to practice certain professions here; however, other professions and specialized interests that cannot be done in the city must be done in the country.
   c. Sports and outdoor activities can best be done in the country.
   d. With few distractions, there may be more time to think. On the other hand, there may be less cultural stimulus than in the city to promote thinking.
   e. There are fewer services. One must be more self-sustaining, but there is more privacy.
   f. One may have to go further to educate children.

5. *Special Interests*

   a. Special interests or hobbies may make it worthwhile for a family to live in a special place. Boating, skiing, or fishing need special locations. Playing in an orchestra or theatergoing usually must be done where there is a greater population.

b. Most adults make their friends through common interests and can see each other if within driving distance. Children are usually limited to friends within walking distance, so this must be considered and worked out one way or another.

Aesthetic Considerations

1. Is the terrain, vegetation, and view attractive?
2. Are neighboring houses or structures attractive, or at least of equal value?
3. Is there noise or smog from freeways or industry?

Economic Considerations

1. *What Can You Afford?*

   a. Various economic tables give slightly different figures as to what percentage of one's income should be spent on shelter. Two rules of thumb are that the house should not cost more than approximately two years of one's income, and that the rent or monthly cost of a dwelling should not exceed one week's pay. Obviously these cannot be fixed rules, since some people may be more interested in their home than others and prefer to spend a greater amount of their income on it. But if a good deal more than this amount is spent on the dwelling, one will probably be sacrificing other things. The question is, then, is it worth it?

   b. After calculating the approximate number of dollars per month or year that you can afford to spend on housing, the next problem is to calculate the *actual* cost of a particular dwelling. Large signs along the highways frequently advertise tract houses for sale for as little as $67 per month. This may look like a great bargain, but is it? Before one can move in, there is usually a down payment. Then there are the "closing costs." These appear to be mere technicalities such as a loan fee, pro rata taxes, a title policy, and the recording of all these things, but these technicalities mount up to several hundred dollars. There is also the insurance to be paid for, the cost of moving, equipment, and furnishings necessary to the upkeep of the dwelling. Such things as light bulbs, garden hoses, and screwdrivers are needed almost immediately, not to mention other furnishings that make for comfort. Some repairs may have to be made before one is eligible for a loan. If one is not prepared to keep up a dwelling, its value will depreciate and the investment in it will be lost. There are also taxes and utilities to be paid, and these most likely will continue to go up gradually, so they should be thought about and provided for. To sum up the costs of owning a house, there are:

1. Mortgage or rent payments
2. Down payment and closing costs
3. Maintenance, repairs, and tools
4. Utilities (gas, electricity, water)
5. Insurance
6. Taxes
7. Furnishings and landscaping
8. Moving costs

Therefore, what may look like a $67-a-month cost at first glance can actually amount to something more like $167 a month by the time one is comfortably living in it.

c. There are also certain inevitable costs connected with living in some dwellings. For example, with larger and more spread-out cities and their suburbs all "conveniently" linked by freeways, more and more people are commuting in order to live in the suburbs where property and houses are more reasonably priced. But if the gasoline bills equal the difference in price between the suburban home and a city house of equal comfort that is close to one's work, nothing has been gained. For example, if you can rent or buy a suitable house near your work for $150 a month, it may be more economical than the $75 suburban house that necessitates $75 for gas to get to work. Both houses then cost $150 and one involves two hours of driving time per day. There may be other advantages, but there is rarely an economic advantage to long-distance commuting. These so-called "hidden costs" must be calculated to get a true financial picture of any dwelling.

2. *To Rent or Buy?*

The question of whether to rent or buy a house is as much a personal consideration as are all these other questions. In some cases it is cheaper to rent, whereas in other cases it is cheaper to buy your own house or apartment. The choice depends not only on what is available, but also on what you are able to do with it, and what your needs and values are. After you have some idea of how much you can afford to spend and approximately what the actual costs are going to be, you can look around with a practical basis for decision.

a. Can you afford to invest your capital or savings in your dwelling by buying one, or is it more advantageous for you to invest your money elsewhere and rent your dwelling?
b. Do you have enough money for a down payment? The more money you have for a down payment, the more bargaining power you have to make a more advantageous purchase. Then mortgage payments also decrease.
c. How much rent would you have to pay to get an apartment or house comparable to the one you could afford to buy, considering all the hidden costs? In calculating such comparative costs, realize that the

owner of the rented property is going to know all his costs, add his profits, and figure accordingly. Either way, one is paying for hidden costs. Banks usually consider that you should spend not more than 10 percent of your salary on monthly mortgage payments and another 10 percent on taxes and maintenance.

d. Do you feel permanently enough situated so that you would want to buy a dwelling?

e. Do you have sufficient interest in a home to want to take the responsibility for its upkeep and garden?

f. Could you consider your purchase an investment because you are able to improve it enough through your own abilities to later sell it at a profit?

g. The interest you pay which is included in the mortgage or loan payments can be deducted from your income tax. This figure should be taken into consideration when figuring actual costs.

h. To "lease" a piece of property is to sign a contract which entitles you to rent that property for a specified cost and length of time. The terms of such an agreement cannot be waived except upon mutual consent of both parties concerned. You cannot be evicted, but you are also liable for the continued payment of the rent for the duration of the lease whether or not you stay. If you have to move, it is possible to "sublease" it. That is, you continue to pay the owner and in turn get someone to lease it from you.

i. Another set of figures which must be analyzed if you consider buying is what the payments on the mortgage actually mount up to. There are various types of mortgages. Different banks and other companies will offer different terms and interest rates. A difference of 1 or even ½ percent in interest rates, or a different type of loan, does not seem like cause for concern, but over a period of ten or twenty years it can amount to a great deal. For example: If one needs to borrow $10,000 to buy a home, let us say that a bank is willing to lend the money at 5¾ percent interest over a period of twenty years. If it can be paid off at the rate of $70 per month, an amortized loan can be arranged. This means that both the interest and the $10,000 principal are paid off simultaneously. But if one can afford to spend only $47 per month, this will be enough to pay only the interest, so that at the end of the twenty years the original $10,000 will still be owed.

With $70 a month payment the total interest paid for the loan of the money amounts to $6,850, so the $10,000 house will ultimately cost $16,850.

If $47 is spent, only the interest is being paid. One borrows the $10,000 for the whole twenty years so the interest is $11,500. This plus the original $10,000 which must still be paid back brings the total cost to $21,500 which is the actual cost of this "$10,000 house."

When next you see one of those happy signs saying that you can have one of these houses for $67 a month, refigure the actual costs before you buy.

3. *Something Old or Something New?*

a. Since the cost of building has gone up a great deal in the last few years, one should consider the advantages of buying an older house. All the little refinements that a house needs will already be there, the garden will be established, and it will be pretty clear what kind of a neighborhood is around it. But, although one can usually get many more square feet per dollar in an old house, the question is not only how many square feet are there, but how the spaces are arranged. With better planning it is possible to have more convenience in a smaller house than a large one. And if it is more efficiently planned, it is easier to take care of. This can become an important consideration, especially with older, multiple-story houses.
b. Whether an old house is a good buy or not often depends on how much repair or remodeling it needs. (Remodeling will be discussed more in Parts V and VI.) For the moment let us say only that remodeling is not cheap. Its cost must be estimated and added to the purchase or rental price of the dwelling.
c. It is difficult not to be dazzled by a few stainless-steel gadgets. Often the same money spent on these will buy a great deal more comfort in the way of space, more beautiful materials and better craftsmanship. The stainless-steel gadgets can be added later.
d. Another economic advantage of older buildings is that in most cases the taxes are less.
e. If you are going to buy, the dwelling must be considered in relation to the whole neighborhood. A well-kept neighborhood will probably increase in value, whereas a neighborhood that is being permitted to get run-down will decrease in value. What may look like a good buy now may be worth even less in several years. The relative values of the surrounding dwellings are important to the extent that the same house or apartment can vary in value by thousands of dollars, depending on the neighborhood. If it is on a street with more valuable houses it is worth a great deal more than if it were on a street of houses or buildings worth less than it is.

4. *Building a House*

a. One needs more cash to begin with.
b. Usually the building cost is greater for a single dwelling than for one partially mass-produced, such as a tract house.
c. The over-all costs include not only the house itself but the land, landscaping, furnishings, and professional fees.
d. If a house is beautifully designed it may become worth a great deal more than the amount spent for it. Good architecture can increase in value just as any work of art does.

5. *Resale Value*

All the above considerations have to do with resale values. If you are absolutely sure you will want to be in a dwelling for life, you need worry only about your own needs; otherwise you must keep in the back of your mind the following possibility: "Will someone else want this too?"

Single- or Multiple-Family Dwellings

1. *The House*

   a. When you live in a single-family dwelling you usually have space all around you. Light and sun can come into the dwelling from all directions. There is usually a garden in the surrounding space which you may or may not consider an advantage.
   b. The exception to this is the row house or town house which is a single-dwelling house but built adjacent to a house on each side. Thus there are only two sides instead of four. This means less windows or openings and also less outdoor area to maintain. (See Illustrations 51 and 52.)
   c. The single detached house is unquestionably the most expensive to build. Some money is saved by the repetition and organization of the work by building many houses at once in a tract or housing development. The difference between the tract and housing development is that the tract is simply a group of houses built at one time in a larger community. The housing development is a totally planned community or town consisting of houses, shops, schools, etc. There are various degrees of completeness in these communities. Levittown, Pennsylvania, is such a planned community.

2. *The Multiple Dwelling or Apartment*

Apartment living used to imply being in a specific type of building. It was in a tall city building which was usually adjacent to other buildings, with little space or light between them. Each apartment opened out from a central hallway, and each one was rented or leased to the occupant. If one wanted to be outside, one got dressed up and walked to a public park. If there were children, they were taken to the park or, as was more often the case, they played in the streets. Although millions of people have learned to adjust to this kind of apartment-house living, even the animals in our zoos are not expected to survive under such overcrowded and unhealthy conditions as many poor urban apartment-house dwellers are subjected to. One cannot help but compare this existence to primitive countries where people may be living in a thatched hut without plumbing, but at least there is light and air and a place for children to run and play.

Fortunately this type of multiple dwelling is becoming a thing of the past, and today one can find instead all types or varieties of apartments to suit one's particular needs. (See Illustrations 52 and 53.)

The new ideas of apartment buildings are based on an attempt to make a better life for people, thus they form an extreme contrast to the older apartment buildings where the most people were fitted into the least space for the greatest profit for one person or a company. The modern apartment is based on the idea that if so many people per square mile are distributed over an area, it is possible for all of them to get more light, air, recreation, space, and open country around them if they all live in one or a few tall buildings. This "new" idea is not really new. Frank Lloyd Wright conceived St. Mark's Tower which was to be built in New York in 1929. It was not built then, but the idea was there; a tall building standing alone, surrounded by open space. As he described it, "The tree that escaped the crowded forest." Twenty-five years later he did build such a building in Oklahoma. This combined apartments for living and office space.

In the meantime Le Corbusier built the Unité d'Habitation in Marseilles, France. Here one entire city "block" houses a whole community. Most of the space is devoted to apartments, but also in the building are shops, communal services, a swimming pool, and a play area on the roof. The entire building is surrounded by a park.

a. ECONOMIC CONSIDERATIONS

1. In an urban area where land values are high, one can get the most living space for the money in a multiple dwelling of some sort.
2. If one is not interested in gardening or the responsibility and expense that go with owning a house, an apartment may be the ideal solution since it takes the least care.
3. Since one structure can serve many families, building and utility costs decrease.

b. TYPES OF APARTMENT BUILDINGS

1. Where large housing projects are being built, the apartment buildings are often surrounded by lower structures and parks so that every apartment gets light and sun, and can look out at the view as well. (See Illustration 52.)
2. The so-called "garden apartments" give the occupants a garden or terrace to step out on, thus combining some advantages of a house and apartment. (See Illustration 53.)
3. Some apartment buildings offer special advantages and conveniences for older people. Other multiple dwellings are made for families with young children. There is a play area either adjacent to the buildings or on the roof. Some even have nursery schools.
4. Another quite different type of multiple dwelling is the apartment which has been remodeled from an old house that was too large for one family. Many of these still have the same spaciousness that they originally had and a type of informality and charm that is often lacking in the newer, mass-produced apartment buildings.
5. The duplex is the structure with only two dwellings in it.
6. The Federal government has built and subsidized low-cost apartments which are available to people whose income is below a

certain level. These people are required to take care of the property adequately. These low-cost apartments can be rented from the Public Housing Administration and may provide an excellent answer for a student's housing needs while he is earning little or no money. These apartments are offered only as temporary aids to families in need until they can once again increase their income.

7. There is another type of apartment building in which one can own his own dwelling. This is usually purchased in either of the following ways:
   The Cooperative Apartment—the building is owned by a corporation and each apartment owner owns a percentage of the stock in the company. If one wants a larger apartment, he must buy a greater number of shares of stock. A smaller apartment requires less investment in stock. The costs of the lobbies, grounds, etc., are divided among all shareholders.
   The Condominium (which means "joint ownership") is different in that each person owns only his own unit and does not own a share of the common areas. He does, however, agree to pay so much per month for the upkeep of the public parts of the building and the grounds.
   In both of these cases your own apartment is totally yours, and you can change it, rent it, or sell it just as you would an individual home.

3. *The Trailer or Mobile Home*

The trailer or mobile home cannot really fall into either of the classifications of single or multiple dwellings. They have some features of each, plus their own advantages as well as the disadvantages of minimum space.

1. The travel trailer is essentially a one-room dwelling with kitchen and bath, and is small enough to be pulled by the average car. It costs little more than a good car, depending on its size and the number of accessories, and this vehicle is taxed with a license based on the same rate as a car.
2. The mobile home is larger and therefore becomes more stationary than a travel trailer; but it can be moved by truck for a reasonable cost. Many of these are larger than a small apartment and some are larger than some tract houses and have three bedrooms and two baths. They cost about the same as a tract house, but due to the use of metal in place of wood there is less upkeep and repair. Taxes are less and many people prefer to live in such homes even without intentions of moving them.

Both the trailer or mobile home can be parked in a Trailer Court or trailer park. The facilities depend on the price. The parks may be as simple as an ordinary parking lot with utilities to hook up to, or they may be as elaborate as a housing development with everything necessary for community living such as shops, swimming pools, and clubhouses. These seem to make for a special comradeship among the occupants. One can also be surrounded by landscaped areas without having to take care of them.

These dwellings may certainly be the answer for people whose work demands that they be constantly on the move, or for people who don't work and would like to travel and live in different parts of the country.

After checking through this list of ideas and possible dwellings, select the items that seem most important for your family. Rearrange them in their order of importance and add any other considerations that are important to you.

If some of your needs are still unclear to you, it is best to get advice from a professional person working in the field *before* making an expensive mistake. The advice will cost little or sometimes nothing and may save thousands of dollars or years of discomfort. (This is discussed at length in Part VII.)

When looking for a dwelling be sure of where you want to live and in what type of building you want to live. Carry the check list with you as your guide. It is easy to be enchanted with some minor detail of a dwelling and then forget everything else. Gadgets can be added; landscaping can be added; superficial improvements such as color can be easily changed; but space, sound structure, and craftsmanship are expensive and difficult to add.

Compromises are inevitable. To be able to find the dwelling best suited to your needs, it is necessary that one be able to make the right compromises. It is these important decisions and compromises that form the basis of one's architectural self-portrait.

PLANNING THE DWELLING FOR ACTIVITIES AND INTERESTS

To continue with this self-portrait, once you have decided where and in what type of structure you are going to live you can begin to think about planning the dwelling itself. If you are going to build it yourself you will have all your needs clearly in mind. If you are going to buy or rent a dwelling that is already built, a good selection can be based on the same thorough analysis that is used for building a home. Undoubtedly your needs will have to be adapted to what is available, but you will have the best chance of realizing these needs if you know what you are looking for.

The first considerations of planning are for the physical needs. There are also the more intangible needs such as the type of atmosphere one is trying to create. Then there are also the limitations such as the amount of money, the site, or an existing structure which must be worked with. These limitations should be clearly recognized and listed. They are there and will not go away by not looking at them.

The following outlines of family activities will show how the planning can be organized.

Physical Needs

1. List the activities of each member of the family individually. Indicate next to each activity or interest the space, furniture, or equipment needed for that activity. Here is an example of Family A.

HUSBAND

Studying	Desk, bookshelves, file, desk supplies
Music	Piano, string instruments, stands, music storage, space for chamber music
Woodwork	Workshop, counter, tool and wood storage
Photography	Darkroom, sink, counters, camera storage

WIFE

Housekeeping	Desk, telephone, bulletin board, cookbooks, fully equipped kitchen, laundry, mending equipment, wrapping materials and counter, garden supplies, cleaning supplies and space to store them
Studying	Desk, telephone, bookshelf, desk supplies and storage space for them, file, typewriter
Sewing	Table, sewing machine, storage for small equipment and for materials, iron, etc.

FOR EACH MEMBER OF FAMILY

Sleeping	Beds
Bathing	Baths, linen closets, etc.
Dressing	Clothes storage, mirrors

2. List the activities which the family does as a group, at home and away from home, which take transportation or equipment which must be provided for.

Example: Family A

Eating	Kitchen, food and dish storage Dining table indoors and outside Entertaining—space for 12 guests
Recreation	Living area Fireplace Seating for from 4 to 16 people Comfortable chairs, light, etc. for two to read Coffee table, bookshelves, etc. Musical instruments, piano, phonograph Slide projection equipment, games, etc. Outside area for sitting and playing

Travel	Cars (2) Storage for suitcases, camping equipment Outdoor clothes Space for maps, pamphlets, collections, etc. General storage of large and miscellaneous things

CHILDREN (each)

Indoor play	Large floor, large table, storage for toys
Outdoor play	Play yard and equipment, bikes, wagons, etc.

3. Group the activities or necessary spaces that would go together and thus should be adjacent.

Example: Family A

A. Living area
   Dining area
   Entry
   Outdoor area
B. Dining area
   Outdoor dining area
   Kitchen
C. Kitchen
   Dining
   Entry
   Utility area—laundry, ironing, sewing, packaging
D. Carport
   Workshop
   Entry
E. Sleeping areas
   Dressing and clothes storage
   Baths

4. List the activities that will probably not occur simultaneously and so could be done in the same space.

Example: Family A

Parents	[Sleeping Studying]	Bedroom, study
	[Sewing Visiting guest]	Guest and sewing room
	[Bathing (2nd bathroom) Photography (dark room)]	Bathroom
Children	[Sleeping Play]	Bedroom, playrooms

Furniture [Guest dining chairs / Desk chairs] Same style chair

Make a diagram from the previous lists. Group together the activities that go together in one room. Arrange these so that they connect with the activities that should be adjacent, i.e. dining-kitchen.

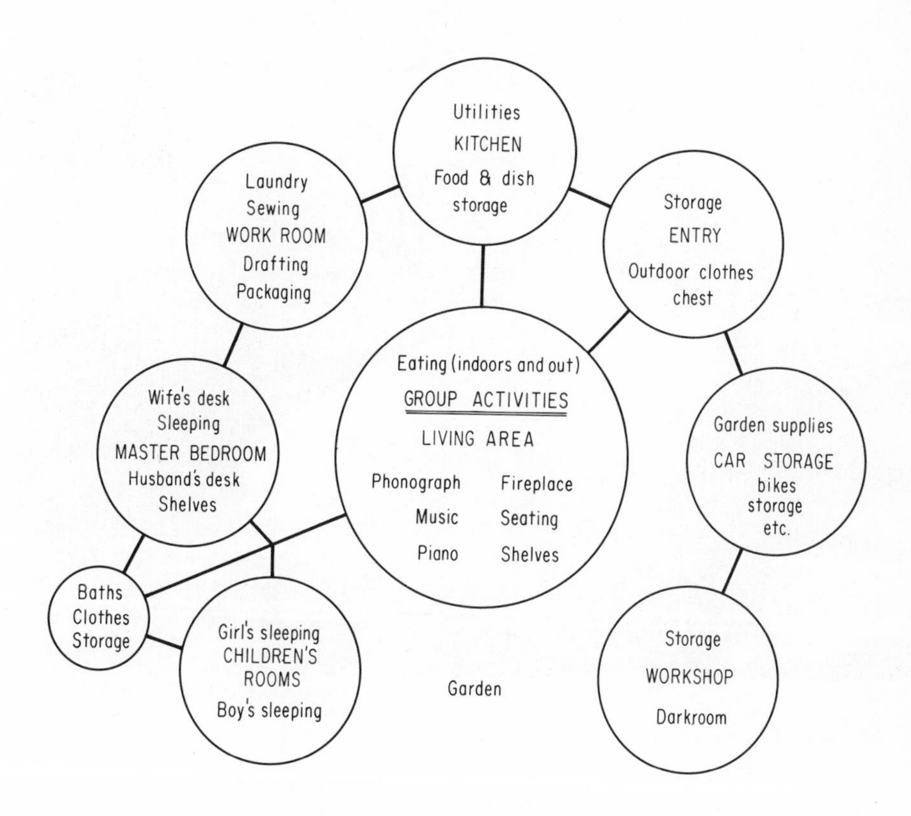

Diagram of Related Space Needed by Family A

This is not a plan, it is a diagram. The areas of the circles do not relate to the amount of space necessary, but the lines connecting the circle areas represent desired access from one area to another.

From such a diagram one can figure out the approximate number of square feet needed for each area. This, plus some extra for halls and such, will indicate the number of square feet of space needed for the entire house. Since building costs can be determined approximately on a square-foot basis (the cost per square foot can be obtained from a local contractor), this will furnish some clue as to how much the entire house will cost and how much is being spent on each activity.

This analysis of one's needs will often point out some startling facts. For example, more space, and thus more money, may be devoted to the car or cars than to any member of the family. This may be the way it has to

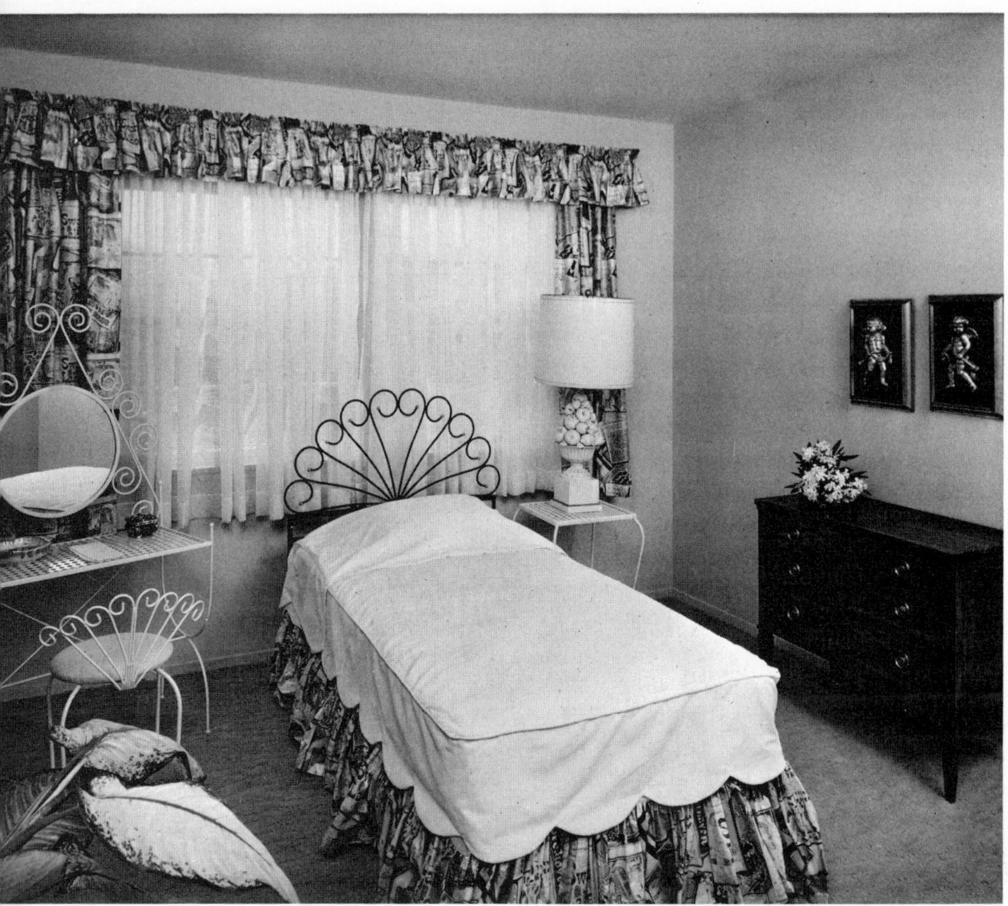

PHOTOGRAPHER: JULIUS SHULMAN

54. A small bedroom.

be; however, it is worthwhile knowing such facts while planning instead of regretting insufficient space for certain activities later on.

This clarification of family activities is the first step in planning a house. Whether you are going to design the house yourself or have the help of an architect, this apportionment of the space must be your own decision. However, it is not what space you have, but what is done with the space that makes for either real architecture and pleasant surroundings or an uninteresting box. What is to be done with this space depends on what sort of an atmosphere you are trying to create. The same space can be made into something formal or informal. The furnishings and equipment you already own must be considered. The sort of clothes you like to wear will indicate something about the way you want to live. How you want to entertain will influence the way in which things will be arranged. The ages of your children and the way you raise them will certainly be a decisive factor in planning the house.

ARCHITECTS: WILLIAMS & ASSOCIATES; PHOTOGRAPHER: JULIUS SHULMAN

55. Room of same size as that in illustration 54 which can be used for study during the day and for sleeping at night.

You may love chairs upholstered in pale blue satin, but it may be worth sacrificing them for a darker, sturdier material if you have small children and get tired of saying "No, no!" Or, if you don't mind the clutter of toys around, you don't have to plan space for children's possessions. But if this does disturb you, the only solution is to provide adequate storage space that is convenient for a child to use for himself, thereby keeping his room neat.

Many families solve the problem of informal living and more formal entertaining by having what may be called a "rumpus," "TV," or "family" room in addition to a living room. This may be the best solution, although it may also be an extravagant one, since it doubles the space devoted to group activities. Or, looked at another way, it divides the allotted space for family activity in two and produces two rooms half the size of one larger one. The choice here is determined by whether or not both of the areas are used sufficiently to merit such a separation of space. Will one of the rooms be used like a party dress, put on only once a month or twice a year?

The choice of materials also influences the atmosphere. Just as two dresses of same size and similar pattern can be totally different because one is satin and the other tweed, so two rooms of the same size and shape can be made to produce two totally different atmospheres by using a slick, smooth surface such as paint in one, and a rough variegated texture such as stone in the other.

The saying "It is not what you do, but how you do it" is all too true in all design.

CHOICES AND LIMITATIONS

Now, with some idea in mind of what one is going to do or what space one needs, the question is: How is it going to be done, or how is the space going to be developed? The crux of the matter is in knowing how to choose what to do with this space, and in not being discouraged by the limitations of each situation. Fortunately, one does not choose a result unless one moves into a furnished place and accepts it as it is. A result is developed; it emerges out of a myriad of limitations and small choices. Many people feel bad because they are limited by a shortage of money, a difficult site, or an unattractive house to begin with. However, the success of any design depends essentially on how well one can work within the limitations, rather than fight them or be discouraged by them. Actually, these limitations can be a spur to the imagination and become advantages rather than liabilities. If one has no limitations it is hard to know where to start or where one is going. As long as one is willing to stay within the limitations, they can serve as guideposts for decisions. Many of the most admired examples of architecture are the result of great limitations turned into assets. Falling Water (see Illustration 4) is the exciting house it is because it is built over a waterfall. This may have seemed like an impossible site, but actually it was the limitation of the site that created the idea for the house.

In the world of nature the limitations imposed by environment are seen everywhere in the forms of animals and plants. The heavy fur of the polar bear is an adaptation to the extreme limitations imposed by a cold climate. In the world of plants, the desert succulent has developed short, fleshy forms in order to better absorb and retain the small amounts of moisture available. Succulents are wonderful examples of plants which have adapted to the overwhelming limitations of poor soil, little water, and a hot climate, whereas the many varieties of animals and plants that have not adapted to the limitations around them are now extinct.

One can conclude from nature that almost any limitation can be adjusted to and worked with, but the situation must be faced, analyzed, and used to influence choice rather than be permitted to discourage or overwhelm.

The following pages list some of the more common limitations for most people. Again, consider your own situation and add anything that has not been included.

ARCHITECTS: WILLIAMS & ASSOCIATES; PHOTOGRAPHER: JULIUS SHULMAN

56. The desert cactus and other succulents develop fantastic forms in order to survive in their arid environment. This house, with its rough and massive qualities, also fits the desert.

Cost

The cost of building can be figured approximately on a square-foot basis. If you add up all the space you need and multiply it by the cost per square foot of building in your vicinity, you will be able to get some idea of what the house will cost. A very rough estimate is that in 1965 a simple house can be built for $10 to $15 per square foot, plus the cost of land, architecture, etc., and a more elaborate house can cost $20 to $30 per square foot. The only way to determine the approximate cost in a particular area of the country is to shop around and ask several contractors.

Most people want a little more house than they can afford. If they have $10,000 to spend, it seems as though they could be perfectly happy with what could be bought for $15,000. If $25,000 is available, their needs seem to increase slowly but surely up to what could be built for $35,000. For those who have $100,000, it seems that they cannot be truly comfortable in anything built for less than $150,000. When people do not face up to the costs involved, they usually end up by spending more than they had anticipated. A dwelling which has become too much of a financial burden becomes less enjoyable.

How do these costs increase? Most people who have shopped for clothes understand the buying of an outfit. The buying of a dwelling is comparable. For example: suppose a girl goes into a store with $15 to buy a dress and a sweater. She plans to spend about $10 on the dress and about $5 on the sweater. Suddenly she sees the perfect dress, it costs $15. At this point there are several possible decisions; one is for her to look further until she finds a $10 dress that will be satisfactory and be as happy as possible with it, and the second possibility is for her to find an extra $5 so she can buy this dress and a sweater too. A third way would be to buy the dress now and let the sweater go until later, when she could afford it. In any case, she will have to either increase her money or be satisfied with a $10 dress. Although this situation is a common one, no one would think of blaming the store for such a predicament. Yet, both architects and contractors are usually spoken of as necessary but expensive evils because a project has cost more than planned. Rarely does one of these dissatisfied owners say, "We just wanted more things in this house than we could afford."

Part of the problem is due to the fact that architects prefer quality materials and construction, so their advice applied to the girl who wants to buy the dress would be equivalent to saying: "The $10 dress may fall apart—better get the $15 one and manage without the sweater until you can afford it." However, even if architects tend to think this way, it is still the buyer who must make the final choice. The architect is not necessarily at fault if too many things or too costly things have been selected for the house.

A second aspect of the problem is that we are dealing with something much more complex than any other commodity anyone ever buys. If you shop to buy a dress and sweater, no matter what conclusions you come to or what you purchase, the compromises you have had to make or didn't make are not so crucial. In the case of a home, even a small remodeling project can involve thousands of pieces of material as well as many craftsmen to put them together. Since each individual part is not very expensive, it is easy to want to add a little here and a little there. A $10 item in one room, a $25 item in another, and so on, since none of these little decisions seem very significant or prohibitive. Then, to make a long story short, the bill from the builder is hundreds, perhaps thousands of dollars more than planned. Although these things have been authorized one by one, the sum total of their cost can be a complete surprise or shock. The process is comparable to buying a whole wardrobe for the next twenty years all at once. Anyone would probably be amazed at the total amount of money spent. Yet for a home it becomes immediately necessary to buy most of the things one will need for the next twenty years all at once. Another problem of costs is that in our culture we tend to regard things which are not expensive as not being worthy of much consideration. It is the amount of thought that has gone into something rather than the cost or value of the material that usually makes it worthwhile. For example, it is hard to find the everyday necessities of life in well-designed forms. If you hunt long enough you can usually find good-looking and good-feeling kitchen utensils and other equipment. These most-used items are the ones that should be given the most thought. Museums have exhibited inexpensive articles from the ten-cent stores that were well designed. These are hard to find but they do exist.

The same situation holds true for houses today. In general, the less money people have to spend on their dwelling, the less likely they are to give it the time and attention needed for it to be well designed. A common fallacy here is that only the person who has $50,000 to spend can afford an architect and good design. Actually, it is the person who can afford only a $15,000 house that is in most need of the very best design. With $50,000 to spend it would be hard for a competent builder to go totally wrong. There would be enough space, enough equipment, and enough good materials to please most people. But if you have a limited budget, every penny and every stick of wood has to be in the right place. Every inch of space has to be used to its greatest advantage, cheaper materials must be well used, and simple methods of putting them together must be devised. The less money there is to be spent, the more time and effort must be given to working out the most economical solutions on paper. Pencils and erasers are cheap as compared to wood and carpenters. Even a whole roll of paper costs nothing as compared to the remodeling which may become necessary if things are poorly planned at the start. As for the money spent on the designer, even if he is only moderately clever he can offer enough money-saving ideas from his past experience to pay for his fee and produce a better house as a bonus. No one has ever saved money in the long run by throwing something together quickly without planning. The less money one has, the more necessary it is to plan for spending it to its greatest advantage. (The cost and advantages of designers and architects are discussed in Part VII.)

The other aspect of costs that must not be overlooked is what might be called the "accessories." Let us again relate this to buying an outfit: Sometimes one has all the accessories that would go with a new dress, and need not buy more. But, if one is starting with nothing, an entire outfit will include the dress, underwear, shoes, a wrap, and maybe a hat, gloves, and purse. If you add up the probable costs of these items, you will find that the accessories will cost more than the dress. To clarify this point, let us assume that here is $50 to be spent. If $40 of it is spent on the dress, there won't be enough left to buy the other things. Some money must be allotted for the other parts of the outfit. The same costs must be provided for in a dwelling. Let us say that there is $20,000 to be spent on a dwelling. If this figure is quoted to an architect or builder, the result may be some bare walls, a roof, plumbing, an electric kitchen, and that is all. At this point more money for landscaping and furnishing is required, or things will have to be left in this uncomfortable state until money is obtained. It is more realistic to allot part of the money for these things initially.

The Site

The nature of the site may impose additional limitations. The size of the site and slope of the terrain may limit the size and shape of the building.

57. This entry was planned around the existing trees.

ARCHITECTS: JONES AND EMMONS; PHOTOGRAPHER: JULIUS SHULMAN

A hillside lot may make a one-story house almost impossible or at least financially impractical. The exposure and view will probably prescribe the way the rooms will face. Trees already on the site can be preserved if the house is planned around them. The surrounding buildings and general neighborhood will in many ways influence the design of a house. To simply superimpose plans made for one site onto another will, nine times out of ten, not fit, or at least not make the best use of the land. Mistakes can be avoided and money saved by consulting both an architect and landscape architect before the site is purchased or bulldozed. (See Part VII.)

Remodeling

Planning for the remodeling of a house is done in exactly the same manner as building one, the only difference being that one starts out with the limitations of the existing structure. The existing space, the style, the scale, and its value must all be considered, just as the terrain or trees on a site influence the design of a new structure.

If the changes in an existing building are to be very great, it must first be determined whether or not it is worth remodeling or whether it would be better to start with another building. Will values in the neighborhood warrant paying the cost of the original building plus the remodeling costs? Will you be able to realize your total investment if you have to sell it?

Many well-designed buildings or houses have been ruined by modernization or the addition of new parts which are totally unrelated to the old in style. Why appliqué a 1960 cliché over a 1920 façade? Does it improve the building? Or is it simply trying to look new, or up-to-date? Always ask yourself, in what way does this genuinely improve the building? When thinking of making an addition, ask yourself "Does it look and feel like part of the whole or is it stuck on like a sore thumb?"

The Apartment

When remodeling an apartment, one may encounter severe limitations in the space available. Usually there is no possibility of going beyond the outside walls, and rarely can any of the structure be changed. Also, because the apartment is usually rented the amount of money most people would want to spend on remodeling is limited. But the same principles of design continue to apply within the confines of what does exist.

Materials

The great variety of synthetic materials available to everyone today may seem wonderful. This variety, however, also creates greater difficulty in choosing the ones which are best for each circumstance. A good rule of

PHOTOGRAPHER: JULIUS SHULMAN

58. The kitchen.

59. The kitchen shown in Illustration 58 after it was made more convenient and attractive within the limitations of the existing structure and plumbing.

REMODELER: CHRIS CHOATE; PHOTOGRAPHER: JULIUS SHULMAN

thumb is to select the fewest but most versatile materials possible and limit oneself to them for the sake of unity of design. Patchwork quilts may be gay, but when a whole dwelling becomes one unrelated patchwork of different materials it is no longer gay but chaotic.

The Time Element

Architecture is a long-term investment. Even though most people no longer think of a home in terms of generations of their family living there, any dwelling is nevertheless going to be lived in by someone for the next fifty to one hundred years. Therefore it has to be a dwelling in which someone will want to live for fifty or one hundred years. A better investment is made when future needs have been planned for in a house.

Although most people can afford to buy a dress or suit and discard it in a year or two if they do not like it or it goes out of fashion, most people cannot afford to throw away a dwelling, so its design must be approached with a different point of view. Something "cute" or a fad of the moment may seem delightful now, but in each case one must consider how it will look ten or twenty years from now. There is no reason for good things to go out of style or become old-fashioned. Something that was truly useful and well designed a hundred or a thousand years ago can still be beautiful. The great buildings or furniture styles or any other objects of past civilizations may not fulfill our current needs, but they are certainly beautiful as an expression of the needs for which they were designed. When you consider that many of these old styles are enjoyed after hundreds or thousands of years, there is no reason for anything in our homes not to be worthwhile for our lifetimes as well as for future generations. To periodically replace the objects that surround us is expensive; it is much more economical to think of the dwelling and things in it with a long-range point of view.

It is true that there is usually the least money available when one first establishes a home. People feel that they can't afford to buy at this time the good things that they might be able to buy later. This is everyone's own decision, but it may be more satisfying to buy fewer good things as one can afford them and get along without other things until one is gradually able to afford the quality that will last.

Another attitude of our shifting culture is that if we don't like something later we can always sell it and get something better. But who wants to pay for your mistakes? Someone may have to accept them, but it is more difficult to make a profit on mistakes. If you have something truly worthwhile to offer, even if it may become inadequate for your needs later, someone else will be more willing to pay well for it. This will then enable you to replace it with something else worthwhile.

If the basic structure has unity and all subordinate parts are related, it need not become dull or go out of style. It also need not be elaborate or expensive in order to be convenient and comfortable to live in. Such a house may be simple and yet have movable and removable things in it which can be changed as often as one likes in order to create new interest and ornament. There are ample opportunities for enough ornament and change in any house to make it continually interesting. The simplicity of the pyramids of Giza have never been referred to as dull. The Taj Mahal, which is over three hundred years old, has never been called "old-fashioned" or "out of style." The great cost and inevitable length of time a building will be used demand that it be worthy of being used that long.

SPACE AND THREE-DIMENSIONAL FORMS

One of the basic differences between modern architecture and that which was done in the nineteenth century is the concept of three-dimensional space. In the last century the basic aim of the architect was to make the building "look good." Architectural students spent years learning to draw and apply the various "styles" to a structure. The beauty of the doorway had become more important to them than what happened inside. It is not that houses were not planned to be convenient, but it was the façade which assumed primary importance. This becomes apparent when one sees pictures of traditional houses. The pictures are always made of the front of the house and the main rooms. What happened in the back was generally not of great concern, nor was the plan of the house considered important enough to be shown either. Today almost any article about a modern house will show pictures of its various sides and a plan. These new houses are three-dimensional objects and it is the arrangement of the space within them that is the most important.

Frank Lloyd Wright expressed this idea as follows: "The reality of the building is in the space within."

Although he and later architects used this idea to create new forms and to open up the interior space as was not conceived previously, the idea is not a new one. In the sixth century B.C.—2,400 years ago—the Chinese philosopher Laotse wrote in *The Book of Tao,*

> *We mold clay into a vessel,*
> *But it is on the space where there is nothing*
> *that the utility of the vessel depends.*
> *We cut out doors and windows in the walls of a house,*
> *and from these empty spaces arises the utility of the house.*
> *Therefore, by the existence of things we profit,*
> *and by the non-existence of things we are served.*

Such an apparently simple idea forms the very core of modern architecture. A cup that has no space to hold anything would be of no use. A house that is a solid object without space inside in which to walk around would be equally useless. Yet, if it is the space inside a house that makes it useful, and is important, how is it possible that 99 percent of all houses

ARCHITECTS: SOLERI AND MILLS; PHOTOGRAPHER: JULIUS SHULMAN

60. This space is divided and limited where necessary in order to be most useful and satisfying.

built today contain cubes or rectangular spaces in them. Even if there is a slight variation formed by a sloping roof so that the rain will run off, this variation is still a far cry from the potential variety of possible shapes that could be built. Look at the variety of structures created by animals—shells, nests, webs, cocoons, beehives, etc. One can conclude that the box is not the only answer to creating structures and space.

A Room Need Not Be a Box

The cube or rectangle may be easier and sometimes cheaper to build, but to compare it again to a dress, it is probably easier to make a dress out of a gunnysack by cutting the appropriate holes for the head and arms, rather than by cutting and fitting material into the exact designed shape. However, we expect clothes to fit, so why not expect the spaces in which we live to fit our needs as well? There is nothing wrong with the cubes or rectangles, but there is something very wrong in thinking that we must limit ourselves exclusively to these shapes. Today with modern building techniques almost any imaginable space can be created by building around the space where necessary to limit it.

The essential challenge of modern architecture is concerned with limiting space in a most useful and satisfying manner. It is like designing a gigantic sculpture, not an image of a person or thing but an abstract three-dimensional form with the most possible conveniences for living built into it.

That a house is a three-dimensional object may seem obvious, since everyone knows it has length, width, and height. But how many houses are

61. A sculptured dwelling.

ARCHITECT: HERB GREENE; PHOTOGRAPHER: JULIUS SHULMAN

really designed as three-dimensional objects or use even a fraction of the potential three-dimensional forms now possible?

The reason most buildings today rely on such elementary shapes as the rectangle and cube is that most people are not trained to think of the space or the limiting forms around it in three dimensions. Children in nursery schools and kindergartens play with blocks and build imaginative three-dimensional forms, but soon thereafter they are directed to sit down at desks with paper, pencils, and books. From there on the intellectual world around them is represented in two dimensions. After twelve years of this kind of training and thinking it is hard to be able to think otherwise, or manipulate objects in relation to space. A second reason why so many buildings are not conceived as three-dimensional objects is that most people are used to seeing only floor plans of houses. When house plans are published, usually the floor plan alone is shown. The drawings of the walls, roof, and interior partitions are usually not shown; hence the relation of the vertical elements of design are not understood. Even a simple house cannot be represented by a single floor plan. (See Part VI.) By the time the roof structure, each wall, and all the different parts of the house are represented it requires at least ten good-sized sheets of drawings. Unfortunately, the building magazines must oversimplify the concept of the house for the sake of brevity, and so many things are misunderstood. It is true that the idea of the house is expressed in the plan. The plan also indicates how the space will be divided at the floor level, showing where the walls will be and where doors and windows will be placed. But do all walls look alike? Do all doors and windows need to be alike? Since the ways of limiting space in any particular direction are endless, it becomes apparent that a floor plan alone is inadequate where more dynamic concepts of space apply. If all walls, doors, and windows are thought of as inevitable blank surfaces rising vertically from specified places on the floor plan, with color or pattern as the only variable elements, this is hardly realizing the inherent potential of the available space. To limit the concept of the word "room" to something approximating the inside of a giant shoebox with holes cut in it for entry and air, or to limit our concept of the word "wall" to a blank surface painted pink or green, is like limiting yourself to the same food every day, or cultivating only one type of plant in your garden. Nothing is wrong with such specialization, but an uninteresting solution hardly makes the most of the possibilities. There are many ways of limiting space and each person should develop some understanding of these methods rather than being satisfied with the stereotyped dullness so often produced.

If you are unconvinced about the variety of forms that can enclose space, think back through history and look at what man has done in the past to enclose space: the conical tent or teepee, the dome-shaped igloo, the curved surfaces of the nomadic tent, and the more complex forms of the Gothic cathedral and Chinese pagoda. The variety of forms is endless. These were not developed in an effort to be different—they were solutions to the living requirements of their times and were produced with the material and techniques available.

PHOTOGRAPHER: JULIUS SHULMAN

62. A very simple, low-cost room. It is a totally enclosed box.

63. A room identical to that shown in Illustration 62 is permitted to open up to an even lower-cost space outdoors. The occupant is not trapped.

ARCHITECT: GORDON DRAKE; PHOTOGRAPHER: JULIUS SHULMAN

Indoor-Outdoor Space

The modern three-dimensional dwelling offers more flexible living by its varied use of space. Some of the areas can be totally enclosed for protection against the elements; some, such as the garden, can be totally open for use in good weather or to look out on. Also, various areas which can be changed from openness to partial openness or total enclosure can give greater flexibility as well as greater beauty to a house. This means that the house does not have to be totally enclosed with four walls shutting it tight as a drum from a totally exposed garden with no protection from the elements at all.

The traditional porch or veranda furnishes such indoor-outdoor living, but is often tacked onto the design of the house like a tail rather than as part of the whole scheme. In modern dwellings, partially open or partially closed areas are often the most pleasant part of the house.

64. A screened porch links this indoor and outdoor space.

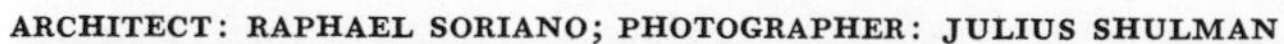
ARCHITECT: RAPHAEL SORIANO; PHOTOGRAPHER: JULIUS SHULMAN

ARCHITECT: RAPHAEL SORIANO; PHOTOGRAPHER: JULIUS SHULMAN

65. This kitchen opens onto a partially enclosed dining area.

Flexibility of Interior Space

Even though numerous divisions of space are required in a dwelling, it is not necessary that the space be boxed into cubicles side by side. In a three-dimensional dwelling some of the interior divisions sometimes need be only partial divisions. It is not necessary that blank walls totally divide all rooms, but where total division is necessary the solid wall material can be useful and serve other purposes as well as divide the space. It can be a place in which to store things—a closet, cabinet, or a bookshelf. It can also be a fireplace or an open area surrounded by glass. It can be made into a beautifully designed plane of almost any material such as brick, concrete block, wood, fabric, plastic, metal, etc. Again, the possibilities

66. No "interior decoration" is needed in this small apartment. High glass extends the room visually while the cabinets below give the adjacent room privacy. At the same time there is storage for dishes, linens, and books, and a buffet.

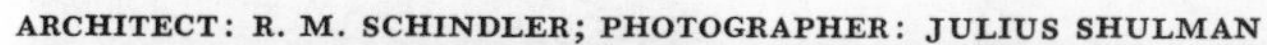

ARCHITECT: R. M. SCHINDLER; PHOTOGRAPHER: JULIUS SHULMAN

DESIGNER: J. R. DAVIDSON; PHOTOGRAPHER: JULIUS SHULMAN

67. Sliding panels give flexibility to this space.

are vast. If each partition, interior and exterior, is useful as well as ornamental, there is no reason for dullness or drabness or even added so-called "interior decoration." Each part of the structure in a modern three-dimensional dwelling will have more meaning because its structure will be more visibly functional and division of space will be used only where necessary.

Flexibility of space can be achieved now that there is hardware to make glass or solid walls which can slide easily. The need for numerous roof supports is eliminated with the use of new, stronger materials. This flexibility can also make less space serve more purposes, which means that less money will also go further.

A truly economical building need not imply a poorly put-together building of miserable materials, but rather a building with space used to its greatest advantage and with every piece of material used to serve as many functions as possible. For example, if a wall is holding up part of the roof it can also be used to support shelves or enclose part of a closet. This type of construction, combining several purposes, is going to cost more than a plain wall serving only the structural purpose, but in the end it will be more satisfactory and cost less than the combined costs of the plain wall plus the necessary shelves of a separate closet for storage. In this case the wall would serve two purposes. The cost of building per square foot is important, but more important is the usefulness of each square foot. (See Illustrations 54 and 55.)

Light

Another determining factor in the design of space is the amount of light that is needed for that space. Not only the amount of light but its distribution is important. People who build their homes usually say to their architect or builder, "How big is this room?" Although this is a fair question, this factual information can be misleading. Let us say that a bedroom measures 10 feet × 10 feet. These measurements might give you some idea of how the furniture could be fitted into this room, but the figures alone will have little relation to how attractive or how large the room can be made to appear. This amount of space could be either a dark, depressing, inadequate, box-shaped room that no one would want to live in, or it could be made into a truly delightful room with convenience and comfort built into it. For example, if one wall of the room is glass, the effect achieved will be that the space extends beyond the plane of the glass, thus giving the impression of a larger room. (See Illustrations 62 and 63.) If it is possible for the light to enter in from many places, such as between the wall and the roof, by having a small strip of glass inserted along the top of the wall, this will give the room a totally different feeling than if all the light entered through one window. The distribution of light eliminates a feeling of being trapped; it also diffuses the light, thereby producing a more pleasant atmosphere. The amount of light coming into a room is not as important as its distribution. This can be easily proven by placing a 300-watt lamp on one side of a

ARCHITECT: GORDON DRAKE; PHOTOGRAPHER: JULIUS SHULMAN

68. Soft, diffused light, both natural and artificial, comes from every direction into this tiny entry. Thus it is quite a different space than if it had a single light source.

room, and then replacing it with five 60-watt lamps distributed throughout the room. The whole effect of the room will be different despite the equivalent light output in each case. Statistics which deal with square footage of floor space or window areas, or the number of watts of light, or the ceiling height, or any other figures can be misleading. It is not the dimensions, the amount of light, or the size of the room that really counts, but rather how they are used.

To design three-dimensionally takes great skill and experience. It is not within the scope of this book to try to make a designer out of anyone, nor can this be accomplished by any book. It is essential, however, for everyone to have a better understanding of his environment and to better realize the potentials for better living which can be offered by modern design.

Since the designer's principal method of conveying his ideas is through drawings, it is necessary to be able to read these in order to better understand modern planning—be it a house, a civic center for your town, or a new cabinet for your apartment.

REPRESENTING THREE DIMENSIONS ON A TWO-DIMENSIONAL PAPER

The problems of communication between people in any field are many. This has been clearly recognized in the area of verbal communication, hence all grammar schools provide a basic knowledge of how to read and write words and where to look up spellings and definitions. One is also taught to interpret symbols and lines that convey specific meanings such as what a boy looks like, or the shape of a continent, or a mathematical relationship. Line drawings, maps, and charts are complex suggestions of things and ideas, but we have become so used to them that we hardly remember any more that we are interpreting very abstract symbols. A 1-inch wiggly black line that represents the silhouette of a boy can be shown to most four-year-old children and they will instantly recognize it as a boy. Yet there are almost no physical resemblances between this line and a real boy. A boy is not a head floating in space, a boy is not 1 inch high; he is not pure white with a black line around him, nor is he a two-dimensional flat object. All this line actually has in common with the boy is the similar shape of his silhouette which represents him from one viewpoint only.

It is remarkable that everyone can recognize a boy from such scanty evidence, and in the comic strips he is recognized even when his outline is not followed with any degree of accuracy. Depending on the particular shape of the mouth or eyes, the drawing can be made to express a great variety of moods and feelings. Yet, although what one sees in the comic strips is really not clearly expressed, it nevertheless is clearly understood by everyone, because the symbols are generally understood.

In architectural drawings almost the opposite is true. Here everything is precisely and clearly stated, but since many people have not seen this sort of statement before the crucial moment when they want to build something, it is difficult for them to understand. Suppose you want to have a new cabinet or some shelves built into your closet; you will have to indicate to someone by means of a drawing what you want. If you have a larger project in mind and have an architect design it for you, he will show you drawings in order to explain his ideas to you. If you cannot understand his ideas as you see them on paper, you will then be buying the most expensive thing in your life without knowing exactly what you are buying. Even if you don't plan to build anything yourself, your town may ask you to vote on its new civic center. How can you vote on this if you don't know what it is they plan to build?

One does not have to be an engineer to be able to interpret architectural drawings. A basic knowledge of what such drawings consist of will make them comprehensible to most laymen. The first thing about an architectural drawing that makes it easier to interpret than most drawings is that it is clearly labeled. The picture of the boy does not indicate which boy it is and what side of him you are seeing. When you look at the drawing of part of a house, for example, it is definitely stated at the bottom of the page or under the drawing exactly what house this is and what part of the house you are looking at (front, rear, side, top or "plan" view).

Scale

The scale of the drawing is the next thing to look for. This will indicate the actual size of all the objects drawn. Most pictures do not really show what the actual size of the objects represented are. The relative sizes of other objects may lead you to certain conclusions, but you have to figure this out for yourself. In any architectural drawing, however, it will indicate a specific scale. For example, a scale of 1 inch = 1 foot. This means that every linear inch on the paper represents or is equivalent to 1 linear foot. If the same scale (1″ = 1′0″) were indicated in the drawing of the boy's silhouette, then by interpretation this would mean that since his head measures 1 inch on paper, the boy's head actually measures 1 foot. There is no guesswork involved. Maps are also labeled with scale values, only in this case the scale represents such large distances that they must be drawn on a very small scale. A world map might thus be drawn at a scale of 1 inch = 500 miles, whereas a city map requires a larger scale in order to show smaller distances, as for example 1 inch = 1 mile or 1 inch = ½ mile.

Thus architectural scale seen on a drawing indicates the size of the drawing relative to the building. The word "scale" as used here has a somewhat different meaning from the way it has been used in previous chapters. The expressions "out of scale" or "in scale" are frequently used by designers to indicate whether the relative dimensions of objects, or their proportions, do not go well together (out of proportion) or do go well together (well proportioned). This usually means that the proportions are either adequate or inadequate. For example, a 240-pound man is not well

PHOTOGRAPHER: JULIUS SHULMAN

69. These windows, by an unknown architect are "in scale" with the dogs. Their friend, apparently a Great Dane, is taking a nap.

proportioned to a dainty rococo chair; he is therefore "out of scale" with it. But so is a 250-pound man. The exact relationship of the proportions are not important, but rather the general relationship. However, when the "scale" is indicated on a drawing, this is a statement of exact dimensions.

Preliminary Drawings

There are two types of architectural drawings. The "preliminary drawings" are a presentation of the idea. They are like the drawings on the envelope cover of a dress pattern, which show what the dress is going to look like. Architectural preliminary drawings show what the building will look like, but you cannot build anything from these drawings any more than you could make a dress from the pictures on the dress pattern envelope. The preliminary drawings of a house include only the plot plan, a house plan, elevations, and maybe a perspective or rendering. These drawings are usually done at a scale of ⅛ inch = 1 foot 0 inch which means that every inch on the paper will represent a dimension of 8 feet on the house.

Plot Plan

The plot plan relates the proposed building to the site. It will show the dimensions, elevations, and other important features of the property, and how the house will fit into them. In order to give an accurate picture of the ground elevations, a survey will be needed. It will show all irregularities of the slope and give the architect a better idea of how to adapt the house to the site. The survey is made by a surveyor who has special training and equipment to do this job in a few hours. To try to save on the cost of the survey can be a mistake that will cost far more than the survey would—if, for example, as a result the house is inadvertently built on someone else's property. Also, if the property is not level, the building must be specially designed to fit the irregular contours. To try to build without knowing exactly what these contours are is like trying to have someone make a dress or suit for you without telling them your exact measurements. It can be done; however, the chances of a good fit are poor. The contour lines on the plot plan will show where each particular elevation is on the site, and will look like an aerial view of a site that has been contour-plowed.

Not only the house but the location of driveway, outdoor living space, and other exterior features will be shown on this plan. The outdoor area can be just as valuable to a family as the space inside the dwelling, and in the warmer seasons of the year even more so. However, the full potential of this space cannot be realized if the entire plot is not planned. It is the entire property, not simply the building, that is one's dwelling. For example, a house is often plopped in the center of a relatively small lot, meaning that 10 feet of open space may be left on either side of it—and "left" is the appropriate term. This space is wasted area. Since it is too small to be really useful, it just exists. If this same house were moved 5 feet closer to one side of the lot, leaving only 5 feet of space on that side,

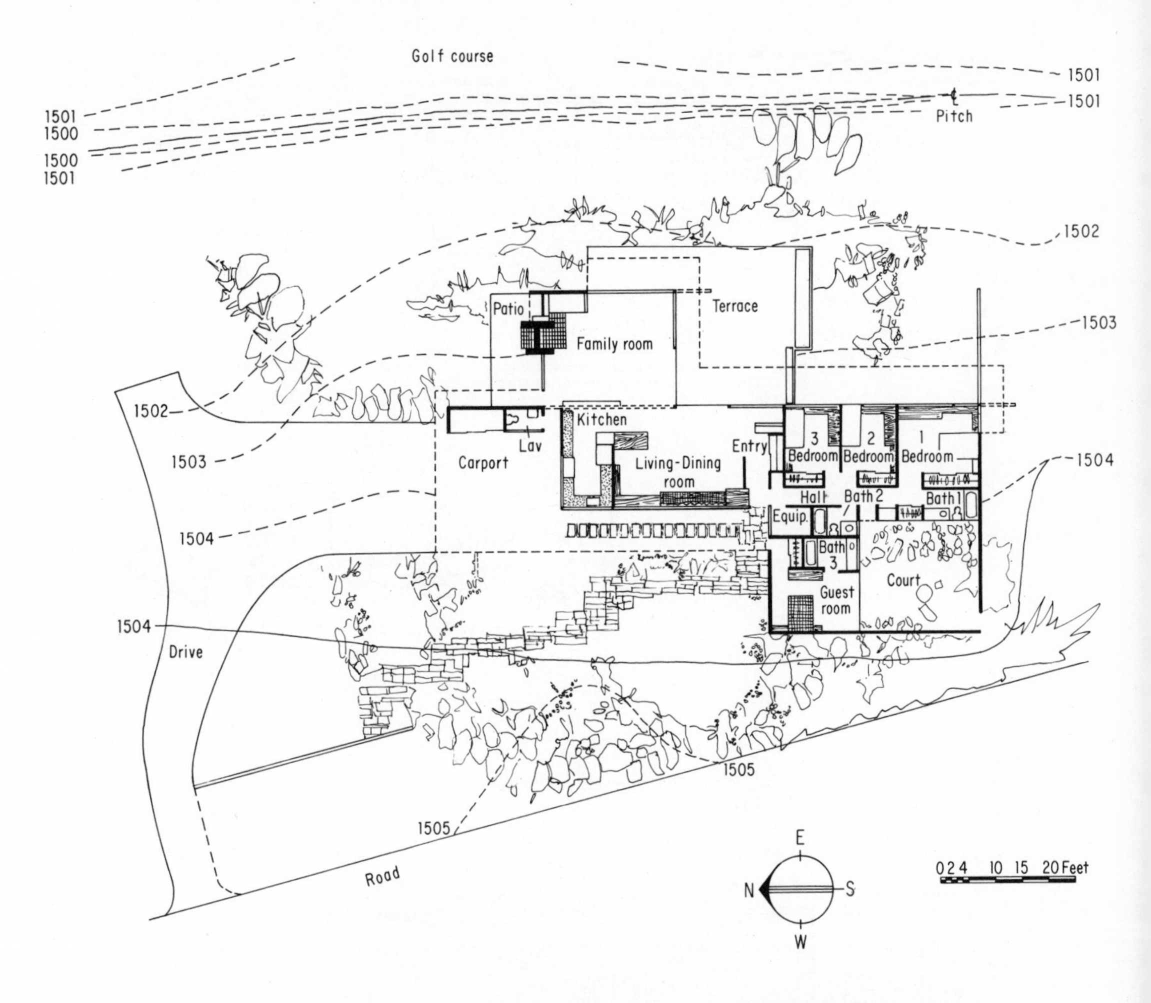

70. Plan and plot plan, showing how both indoor and outdoor space will be used. Curved dotted lines indicate ground elevations.

ARCHITECT: RICHARD NEUTRA; PHOTOGRAPHER: JULIUS SHULMAN

this would then make 15 feet available on the other side. The 5-foot space could still be planted with shrubs for some feeling of privacy, and the 15-foot space would then be large enough to become an outdoor room or even enclosed at a later date. Many different things could then be done with this better-planned exterior space when there is enough space to work with, but poor planning—or, as is more often the case, no planning—results in a waste of space. Therefore planning must start with the entire area clearly visible on a "plot plan." (See Part VII.)

Floor Plan

The floor plan may be combined with the plot plan or may be separate. It will show how the various rooms of the house are to be arranged and how large they will be. The relative sizes of the various areas can be seen

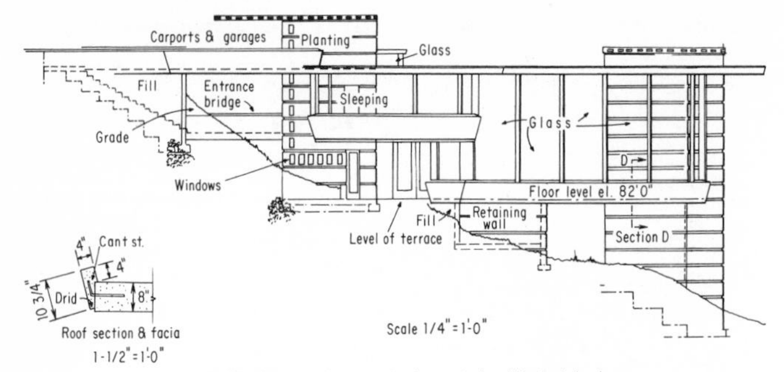

NOTE: These elevations are taken from actual architectural drawings but have been simplified so that they could be reproduced at such small scale.

Perspective from south

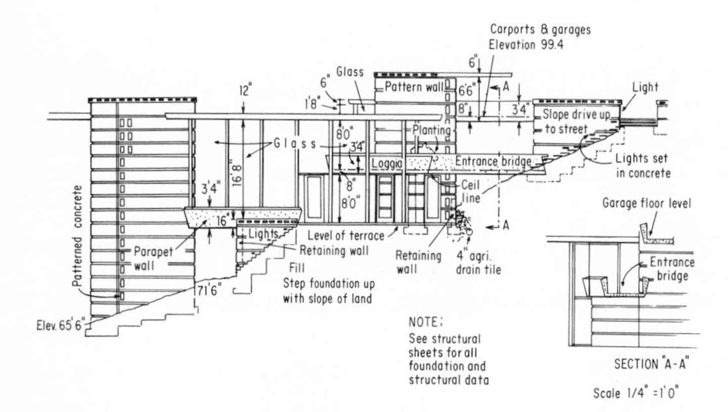

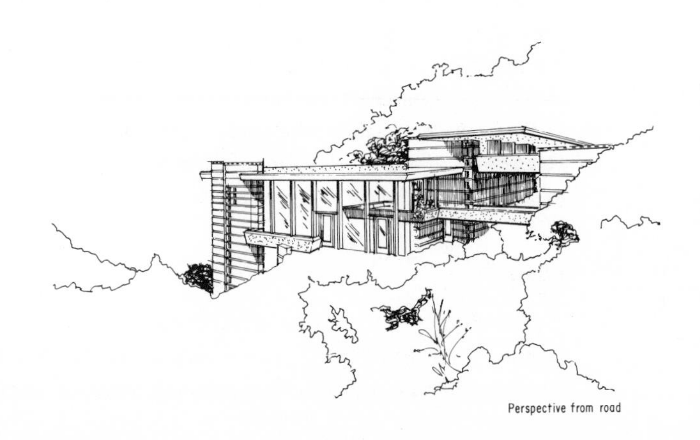

Perspective from road

at a glance, and the walls, doors, windows, and cabinets will be shown. Bathroom fixtures, fireplaces, and any built-in furniture can also be indicated in order to give the best possible idea of how these will fit into the dwelling. There should also be some notations as to what materials are going to be used for the structure.

A study of the floor plan will reveal much important information. For instance, if the first and biggest space you see on the plan is labeled "garage," the largest room in your house will be the place where you store your car or cars. If your living room is right in the center of the plan, it may be a convenient solution but most likely will not be a very peaceful one. If you find a long central hallway with no access to exterior light you will then know that it will be dark. Sometimes in order to achieve one advantage in a house something else has to be sacrificed, but now in the stages of the preliminary drawings is the time to realize the various possibilities and discuss them with your architect. Changes can be made on the preliminary drawings, but by the time a house is built it is either too late or too expensive to make changes.

This is the time to go through your list of requirements again and see if most of them have been satisfied. Some adjustments can then be made to satisfy any requirements that have been omitted.

Elevations

The elevation drawings will show many other important features of house design such as the placement and shape of doors and windows. Elevations are drawings of the outside walls of the structure in which all dimensions are drawn to scale. The house will not look like these drawings to the viewer, because the parts that are farther away will look smaller when they are seen by the eye or a camera. These drawings do show the dimensions of the walls as they will actually be built. On these drawings are designated the various construction materials that will be used and how they will go together. The shape of the roof will also become apparent. From the elevation drawings the height of everything can be measured. Usually at this point only the elevations of the outside walls will be shown, but if there is something of particular interest inside, such as a fireplace, this may also be indicated.

Perspective

The "perspective" or "rendering" is an artist's drawing of what the house will look like to the eye or camera. These drawings are usually made as attractive as possible in order to sell the idea. Often the dwelling is seen

71. Two elevations and two perspectives of the same house. Elevations show actual dimensions; perspectives show the way an object or house will look to the viewer.
DESIGNERS: DUNCOMBE AND DAVIDSON; PERSPECTIVES: JANE DUNCOMBE

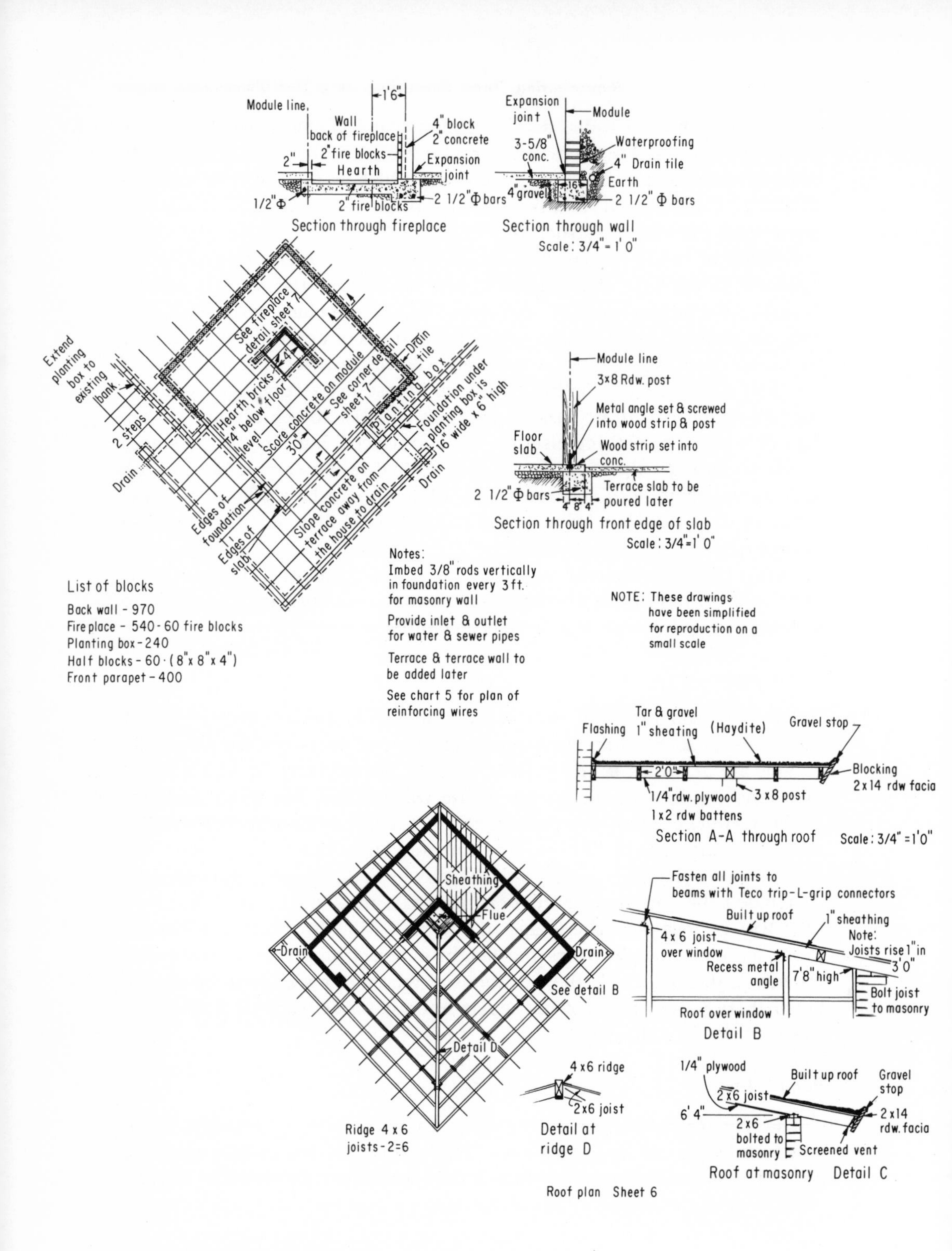

72. The foundation plan shows all the dimensions of the foundation and where and how the walls or posts are joined to it. The roof plan shows each piece of wood in its structure and how it is fastened to the walls or posts supporting it. These plans are drawn on a 3 × 3 module system.

ARCHITECTURE AND DRAWINGS: LOIS GOTTLIEB

through a grove of trees, making it look enchanting no matter what the architecture is. One must be careful to be sure one is buying the idea, the convenience, and the beauty of living, not the beauty of a picture done by a skillful draftsman. By the slightest distortion of the perspective, a good draftsman can make a small house look twice its size. Although these renderings are nice, it is really the plans and elevations that convey the true information and should be given the most attention.

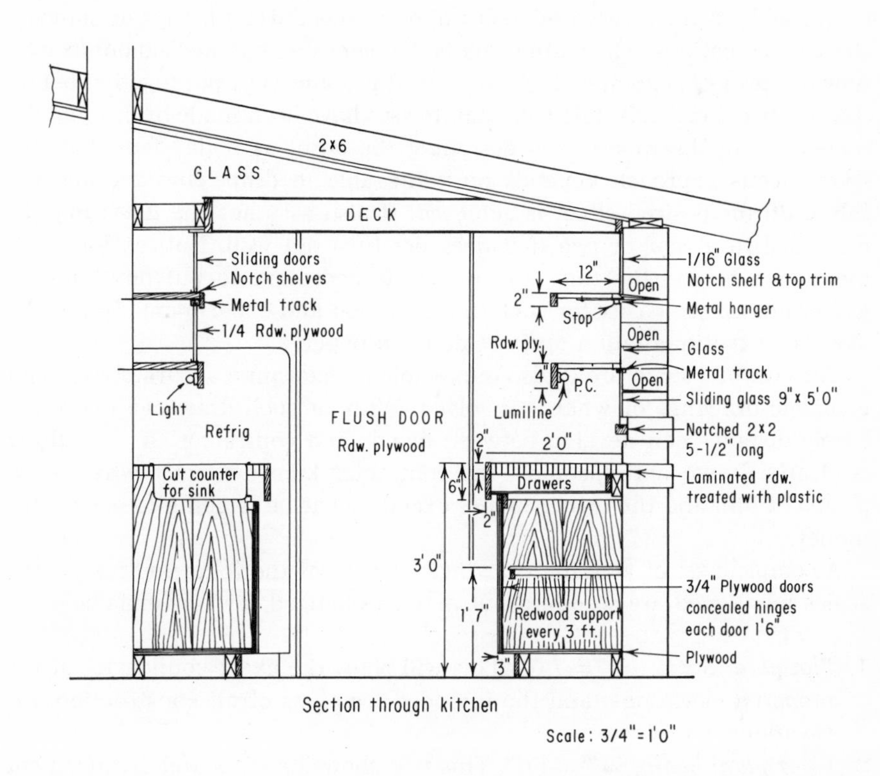

73. A section through a kitchen showing dimensions and construction of walls, roof, and cabinets.
ARCHITECTURE AND DRAWINGS: LOIS GOTTLIEB

Working Drawings

After the preliminary drawings are approved and everyone is satisfied that most of the requirements of the project have been met, a much more detailed set of drawings must be made before any actual construction can begin. It does not matter if the project is a civic center, a house, the remodeling of one room, or the building of a single cabinet; the procedure is the same. The preliminary drawings are intended only as the outline of the idea or the diagram of the way the project is going to look in general. Now the particulars of construction must be worked out. Exactly how each piece of material in the whole structure is going to fit together must be thought through. It is like a gigantic three-dimensional jigsaw puzzle. These drawings that show how it all fits together are called "working drawings." They are equivalent to the dress pattern, and from them the building can be built.

Working drawings for a house will require at least ten sheets of large paper and will have in conjunction with them a list of materials and directions for their assembly that are called "specifications." These are sometimes written as notes on the drawings or are sometimes on separate sheets or in booklet form. Every architectural office has different ways of showing these specifications. The main thing is that someone has worked out exactly how this project is going to look and how it is going to be put together before the construction starts. It is true that dresses have been made by draping the material over the wearer and designing the outfit as it develops, but this spontaneous approach depends on being able to drape and redrape the fabric till the desired effect is achieved. It also assumes the dress may be discarded in a year or two if it does not turn out well. But, as has been mentioned before, the time and materials necessary to put buildings together are far too costly for such manipulation and experimentation at the site. The experimentation must be done on paper.

The cost of a structure is also impossible to determine accurately without complete drawings of what is involved. Without such drawings many unhappy disputes can develop between owner and contractor. If everything is clearly drawn and specified, the contractor knows exactly what is expected of him and the owner knows exactly what he is going to get for his money.

A complete set of working drawings consists of the following items (the scales mentioned are standard but may be changed for convenience):

1. *Plot plan: Scale, ⅛″ = 1′0″.* This will show the exact boundaries of the property, elevations, and the intended locations of all construction, excavations, etc.
2. *Floor plan: Scale, ¼″ = 1′0″.* This will show the sizes and arrangement of all the rooms. It will show where the walls, doors, and any other vertical structures extending up from the floor will be. All built-in closets and cabinets will be outlined. The placement of all electrical outlets will probably be on this plan, otherwise all electrical wiring, connections, etc., will be shown on a separate plan. The outline of the roof will also appear on the floor plan as a dotted line. All necessary dimensions to insure proper construction will be shown.
3. *Elevations: Scale, ¼″ = 1′0″.* There will be as many elevations as there are sides of the house. They will show exactly what materials each wall will consist of, and how these materials will be fitted together. For example, if the house is made of concrete blocks, each block should be shown so that it will be clear exactly how the windows and doors will fit between these blocks. The same piece-by-piece clarification is necessary when wooden boards are to be used. There is no reason for the windows not to fit between the boards. If some of the boards have to be notched out around the windows, this may still insulate as well, but

there will be an impression that things don't fit together very neatly—sort of like a crooked hem on a skirt. This improper fitting together of materials doesn't really hurt anything, it just looks messy. Elevations should show all trim strips around the windows and doors. Such necessities as down spouts, plumbing and heating vents, and electric fixtures must be planned for and shown on these drawings or they are likely to be placed in a haphazard fashion, which though still fulfilling their functions will give the feeling that no one seems to care. If the materials shown in each elevation fit together to make a beautiful pattern, each side of the house will be beautiful to look at. If the design of the elevations look dull or ugly, so will the house. (Beware of a fancy front elevation and ugly side elevations. Every elevation should look good.)

4. *The foundation plan.* The exact size and shape of the foundation will be shown on this sheet. If the floor is to be made of concrete, details of its construction will be shown. The plumbing requirements and sewer lines are often shown on the foundation plan, as well as any other details at ground level.
5. *The roof plan.* Although the floors must be flat and level for obvious reasons, the roof can be constructed in any one of innumerable possible shapes. Not only can the shape of a roof be beautiful but the framework or structure supports can emphasize the beauty of its design. This framework must be carefully worked out and shown on a separate plan. The roof will also need some sort of waterproof covering and maybe a covering inside in the form of a ceiling. Both the roof as well as the ceiling can be beautiful if they are carefully designed, not just plopped on top of the walls like an old hat and forgotten. Let them be carefully placed like a new and delightful hat; one with shape, color, texture, and ornament—one with style. The connections with the walls, the finishing at the edges, and the waterproofing of the joints will be shown on this drawing.
6. *Sections.* A "section" is a drawing which shows in more detail how the construction materials fit together. In a section you can see what the inside of the structure will look like, as if the object were sliced through the middle with a giant knife, or like a section of an orange that has been cut in two. All the inner parts of the structure are shown. The specific details of a section depend on the place at which the object is cut into. If you cut an orange across the middle, the thickness of each segment is exposed. If you cut it from end to end, only two of the segments are shown, but in this case their length and over-all shape become apparent. The whole structure of an orange can therefore be shown in two sections. The inner construction of a cabinet can usually be explained in one section, whereas a house will take a number of sections to show clearly what the inside should be like at various points and how it will be put together. The experienced designer will know at which places to make these imaginary section cuts so as to show more clearly any complicated details of construction.
7. *Interior elevations.* These are drawings of the inside walls. Materials to be used and the placement of the openings on the walls are shown here.

8. *Details.* Detail drawings are the equivalent of photographic close-ups. For any place where there may be a doubt as to how two or more pieces of material will fit together, a more detailed drawing, larger in scale than the rest of the plans, shows in a precise diagram the method of construction. The exact scale, which can vary considerably, will be shown on the drawing. Exact dimensions of each part will also be indicated. (See Illustration 72.)
9. *Specifications.* These explanatory notes on the materials and construction of whatever is being built are as important as the drawings themselves. In the plans of a house, for example, you may see the drawing of a toilet. But what kind of toilet? Toilets can be bought for as little as $25 or as much as $150. Which do you want? What are you going to get? There are vast differences in prices and types. You may be very dissatisfied with the $25 toilet, or you may be equally unhappy to find that you have bought a $150 toilet when you could have been just as happy with one that cost $25. To plunge into an expensive building project without knowing exactly what you are getting is like a man calling a store and saying "Send out a size 38 suit—any kind will do." This probably never happens, and yet it is a common procedure to put thousands of dollars worth of material and equipment into a dwelling without the owner's knowledge of precisely what he is getting. Some very different grades of products cannot be distinguished one from the other even when you see them. Take, for instance, a tar and gravel roof. All that is visible is the gravel, which is the least important part of it. It is the quality of the underlying layers of tar and paper that make the difference in the length of time a roof will remain waterproof. Roofs are guaranteed by the companies that install them, and for very little more money you can have a "20-year guarantee" rather than a "10-year guarantee." This represents a substantial saving in the long-run maintenance of a house. However, unless your preferences are indicated in the specifications you will not know what quality of material you are getting.

   Specifications are important even in a small project. The same amount of labor is required whether one puts together poor-quality materials or fine-quality materials. A poor-quality object can cost almost as much as a fine-quality object and yet be worth only half as much and be half as beautiful. Even small items like hardware can either enhance or offset the advantages of using fine materials. Nothing is more irritating than a beautiful door or drawer that doesn't work properly. If an object does not fulfill its basic function, it is of little use. By having all these materials accurately specified you will know what you are getting and be able to make other choices before it is too late. Specifications also are a legal document and hold the builder responsible for his work.

The Need to Understand Architectural Drawings

If we believe that architecture is the result of an idea and the expression of this idea, and that it reflects our thinking and living, then we must realize that it is not a static element of our surroundings but an ever-changing one. As our lives and thinking change, so must the architecture around us if it is to continue to express our needs.

A tomb may be adequate for as long as five thousand years because no change in its function is ever required. Great cathedrals can still be used as they were built hundreds of years ago because there is so little change in the rituals practiced in them. Primitive tents and huts are practically the same as they were hundreds of years ago because the lives of the people living in them are almost the same as they were hundreds or thousands of years ago. However, nearly all other types of dwellings have changed and are constantly changing just as most of our lives change from generation to generation and from year to year.

Families expand and contract. They change their interests and activities. They change their needs. Either the environment must change to suit their changing needs or become a handicap. One's environment can become a strait jacket because it can gradually and sometimes unnoticeably begin to pressure a family from various obscure points. What was once a perfectly adequate dwelling can become inadequate or uncomfortable and even unbeautiful. Tensions between family members can grow and, as a result, conditions can become chaotic. Hanging a new picture on the wall, or putting a new ruffle on the curtain will not help in such situations. The changes must be more basic than these and be specifically directed toward alleviating the particular inadequacies of the situation.

Often minor architectural changes can make a great deal of difference. Sometimes one can walk into a store, buy something, and counteract the immediate inadequacies, but more likely one will come out far ahead if one is able to build something to meet the specific need. A new closet or cupboard so that it is possible to keep things stored more neatly; a new light so that it is possible to read more comfortably; a workshop, a sewing area, or a play area; all sorts of needs can be fulfilled to each individual's particular satisfaction and delight. Whether you can build it yourself or expect to get someone else to do the building, the best way to work out and convey the idea to yourself or the other person is through drawings. On paper you can explore numerous possibilities, and you can test out the various alternatives. This is the equivalent of draping and redraping the material on a model for a dress. Planning is the key to better design and environment. It must be done on paper, using the visual language of architectural drawings.

V

ORNAMENTATION AND SUBORDINATE FORMS

CONCEPTS OF ORNAMENTATION

Up to this point the material in this book has been primarily a discussion of architecture and the structure of the dwelling. This knowledge is necessary in order to understand how the ornament in the dwelling relates and is subordinate to the whole dwelling. Nevertheless, since most people will not build their own dwellings but live in an existing house or apartment, they are primarily concerned with these subordinate parts of their immediate environment.

This embellishment of an existing space in order to make it into a livable home is usually called "interior decorating" or "interior design." Although these terms are commonly used, they will not be used here because they often carry with them implications of what is "good taste" and "how things are done correctly." But who is to decide what is good taste, or what is correct? What may be appropriate, or suitable, or in good taste for one situation may not be for other similiar situations. One can cite examples and infer that the reader can adapt these ideas to his or her own needs, but this approach is not as valuable as suggesting a method for each person to ornament his or her own room based on his or her own individual needs.

Because something may be appropriate for a particular era or place does not mean that the same thing is necessarily appropriate for another era, place, person, or family. To cite an extreme example: it was undoubtedly considered very correct and in perfectly good taste for a Pharaoh of ancient Egypt to spend the wealth and manpower of an entire nation on a tomb for himself. Today, if a ruler of any country did such a thing it would be considered totally unacceptable and in poor taste. As a second example: within a home, an elderly couple may have a very elegant room in their Victorian mansion with delicate furniture covered in pale rose-colored satin. This room may be perfect for their needs; correct, in good taste, most useful, and representative of their life. If this same room were transplanted into a tract house for a young couple with five small children, it would then be totally out of place, in poor taste, unsuitable, and undoubtedly very soon ruined. Whether or not a room is appropriately decorated or designed can be discussed only in relation to the people and situation for which it is arranged. Generalizations which pertain to decorating one's home are rarely valid.

It is also possible to have too much good taste. There can be good taste and nothing else. One can create a room that is like a little stage set or a display in a department-store window. Everything is apparently arranged just right, but no one seems to live in this sterile setting. What is it that produces such a feeling in a room? The situation can be compared to a well-bound book filled with unrelated words or blank pages. Nothing seems to have been said, nothing has been expressed, nothing means anything; just a group of elegant meaningless words. The most elegant furnishings can also be meaningless. It is the meaningfulness that is of foremost importance. If a dwelling does not make a definite statement as to how the owner wants to live and what he is living for, all the good taste in the world will be dull and without significance. It must be meaningful to him, and if it is meaningful to him it will probably be meaningful and a delight to others, too. The impression which it makes on others should not become the prime objective since the others are not there most of the time. A home is not an exhibit. It is not a thing to be looked *at* like a stage set or store display. It is something to be lived *in*. Such considerations as how to make the room look larger are also of less importance than how to make the most use out of the space that actually exists. It is important to deal with realities, not effects. One's home must be made meaningful, useful, and beautiful instead of being made to look like something it is not.

One's needs will fall into two basic categories: physical and mental. Both are equally important. Most of the physical needs can be satisfied with the addition to the basic structure of various types of subordinate three-dimensional forms. Just as a house must be planned within its environment, so must any forms within the house be planned for or chosen to relate to the structure itself.

With regard to the interior needs, there will have to be some sort of forms to rest on; some for sitting, and some for lying. There will need to be surfaces to do things on, and equipment for temperature, light, and sound control. Storage spaces will also have to be provided for.

All this can be referred to as furniture; nevertheless, at the mention of words such as "chair," "table," or "desk," almost everyone finds it hard not to visualize his own concept of a chair, a table, or a desk. In planning for the most useful furnishings, one must start with the idea that certain three-dimensional forms will be necessary, and then determine the most appropriate shapes for them. With this analytical approach it is easier to create real comfort and beauty rather than fall into the pattern of "what is being done," or what is in "good taste." It is necessary to reexamine all family activities and to plan the furnishings of each room so as best to facilitate these activities. The first question to ask oneself is not, "What style of chair do I want?" but, "On what sort of object can I sit and relax most comfortably?"

Since a detailed analysis of specific equipment and forms for greater physical comfort is a large subject in itself, this will be discussed in a following chapter. First let us consider more of the broad possibilities and techniques of ornamentation.

Useful Ornament

To decorate a room is to incorporate into it equipment, comforts, and objects that will make it most useful and beautiful. In addition to physical needs everyone will want many things in their home that will stimulate the intellect or delight the spirit. Pictures, sculpture, and many other things are generally thought of only as decorations or ornaments, since their basic function is to appeal to the intellectual or emotional senses. However, there is no reason why necessities should not also be beautiful.

The concept of dividing ornamentation from the necessities of life is a relatively recent one in world history. This is due to the fact that wealth and surplus are required before man can afford to have objects that are purely ornamental. In primitive cultures all decoration serves either a physical purpose or has a spiritual significance. Most of us are delighted by the crafts of other countries, and yet most of these crafts are only the necessities of life made beautiful. In our culture we would never question the need for a given object that is "just an ornament." We ask no more of it. But this is not so in other cultures, and people who know these cultures know that in many places there is no such thing as "just an ornament."

Dr. Fredric Spiegelberg, Professor of Indian Civilization at Stanford University, tells how on a recent trip to Tibet he saw contraptions made of multicolored strings placed on the tops of the houses in Tibetan villages. The strings were wound over a wooden framework in beautiful patterns and looked a little like a cross between a kite and a television antenna. Since he knew there was no television in Tibet, he asked what these things were. He was told they were "just ornaments." If he had been told this in the United States there would be little reason to doubt it since most homes here have many things that are just ornaments. But knowing that the Far Eastern cultures produce no ornament that does not have use or significance, Dr. Spiegelberg's immediate reaction was, "Of course I knew that they were not telling me the truth, so I continued to try to find out what these things were." Ultimately, through much investigation, he found out

PHOTOGRAPHER: JULIUS SHULMAN

74. Two cans containing similar snacks. The one on the left is designed to be reused and attractive on a kitchen shelf. The right-hand one merely attracts attention.

that these were "ghost traps." Rather than ignoring ghosts as we do in our culture, or trying to frighten them away as some cultures do, the Tibetans put up these beautiful traps. When the Tibetan ghosts become trapped in these, the ghost and the trap are done away with by throwing them over a cliff. In the meantime, the trap is enjoyed aesthetically while it serves its significant purpose.

The ghost traps may seem a playful ornament to us, but to the Tibetans it was their functional purpose which stimulated such imaginative design. Often the necessary objects of our daily lives, though most useful, appeal to none of the senses and are so ugly that they must be hidden in cabinets when not in use. For example, such objects as packages of food, kitchen utensils, or cleaning equipment are manufactured by the thousands and are used in every American home. Yet there is almost no box or package that can be aesthetically enjoyed visually. To find a utensil or other piece of household equipment that is good-looking or pleasant to hold is almost impossible. If you are finally so lucky as to find a household necessity that is beautiful too, it will usually bear the label of another country. Household utensils are certainly just as useful as ghost traps, but there is, unfortunately, too little public concern with the aesthetic appearance of our daily necessities, otherwise there would be more concern by the manufacturers to make them beautiful. Mass-production methods cannot be blamed for this situation. Actually they should facilitate better design. To take the time and thought to design one object greatly increases the cost of production, but when the same object can be mass-produced millions of times the designing cost becomes negligible per item. If all the objects in our homes were beautiful as well as useful, our homes would not need additional decoration.

Informative Ornament

One often brings into his or her dwelling ornaments that are intended only to be interesting or informative. This type of intellectual ornament is usually two-dimensional and is made up of words, pictures, or symbols of

75. Passages from the Koran in elaborately carved Arabic lettering form part of the ornament on The Alhambra in Spain.

PHOTOGRAPHER: LOIS GOTTLIEB

some sort. Today such ornaments are usually framed and hung *on* the surface of the wall, while in the past there were almost always painted or carved directly *into* the wall. This informative ornament set into the walls is used little today in comparison with its use in past civilizations for the reason that paper and printing are cheap, plentiful, and easier to produce than carvings or paintings.

Informative signs appear on our commercial buildings but they are either a visual shriek for attention, or totally insignificant. (See Illustration 20.) The numbers or names which are used on most of our dwellings are also neither beautiful nor interesting aesthetically, although they could be.

Earliest man apparently took great delight in recording the events of his life on the walls of his cave. Centuries later, with the advent of the stone structures, the Egyptian, Mayan, Khmer, early Christian, and other architecture became relatively permanent and throughout the world the walls of buildings were covered with information and records of the life of the times. These early records and ideas were either painted on the walls, carved into stone, molded out of clay, or assembled into mosaics of tiny colored stones. Such pictures and symbols were obviously meant to inform,

76. Meaningfulness rather than "good taste" alone. A trip most significant to the owner is described on his home in Egypt.

PHOTOGRAPHER: LOIS GOTTLIEB

but they were nevertheless executed in as fine a manner as possible. As a result they are now regarded as works of art, and today there is a great awakening of interest in these arts of early civilizations. This informative ornamental work was often very elaborate, but it was rarely chaotic because it was part of the structure of the building and was kept subordinate to it. Unity of design was achieved by the use of a common material throughout as well as a common theme.

There are still a few places where informative murals and mosaics are done. In Mexico, many of the exterior as well as interior walls of the civic buildings depict important incidents taken from Mexican history. In Egypt it is the Moslem custom to paint the story of one's pilgrimage to Mecca over the entire front of one's house. Many of these paintings are not well done, but this is not important because they convey a significant message to the Moslem community. These ornamental wall decorations give a vitality and creative interest that "good taste" alone could not produce.

Although there are few people in this country who would want to paint such informative ornament on the front of their house, the inclination to express one's interests within one's surroundings is certainly a valid one. Any group of objects which have been of enough interest to collect can be attractively arranged on shelves, in cases, or on the walls in some way. Panels can be papered with maps or other significant printed matter. Whole walls have even been papered in wine bottle labels. If the labels happen to bring back some pleasant memories, this then is a more meaningful decoration than using wallpaper covered with pictures of cabbage roses.

Proportion

As in all design, proportion becomes an important part of ornamenting a dwelling. What is done, or in this case, what ornament is used on a wall is no more important than how it is arranged. For example, if one places a 1-foot × 2-foot picture on a wall that is 8 feet high × 10 feet across, the entire picture one sees is actually the 8 × 10-foot area, and the 1-foot × 2-foot picture is relatively so small in comparison to the total area that it becomes insignificant. The relationship between an object and its surroundings is of paramount importance. Painters and photographers can express the insignificance of man in contrast to nature or his dominating character by controlling the proportions of related objects in the picture. The movies show a tiny Foreign Legionnaire going off into an endless desert. Everyone knows that he is so small in comparison to the desert that his days are numbered. But the same Legionnaire can be shown dominating his surroundings in a close-up with no space around him. Here he is conquering the world. In other words, it is not the absolute size of an object or person, but the size in relationship to the environment that has meaning.

Proportional considerations must apply to any picture or other ornament that is being used to interest or inform. The significance of the picture is not only within itself, but in relation to the surrounding area. Small-size pictures or other small displays can be placed on a small wall or in a

ARCHITECT: RICHARD NEUTRA; PHOTOGRAPHER: JULIUS SHULMAN

77. A large picture placed on a large wall. Smaller pictures form a group on a smaller wall, and a tiny picture is part of an arrangement including flowers and sculpture.

group or to ornament the panel of a door or cabinet. The problem is not different from that of the relationship of house to site, room to house, or furniture to room; it is one of proportion.

There are no clear-cut rules of proportion. Just as each individual photographer has to make his own decision as to exactly how big that Legionnaire is going to be in the desert in order to convey his message, so must each person determine the size relationship of an ornament to a wall. The tiny picture on the large wall or the too-large picture overwhelming the small room can each convey an entirely different feeling than was intended if their relationship to their surroundings are not suitable.

Ornamenting the Structure

Not only must a home be embellished to satisfy human needs, but the physical structure of the building may also need to be enhanced by ornament.

PHOTOGRAPHER: JULIUS SHULMAN

78. Barren room. See the same room in Illustration 79.

79. Soft rugs, upholstery, books, and other ornaments embellish and make livable an otherwise stark room.

ARCHITECT: CHRIS CHOATE; PHOTOGRAPHER: JULIUS SHULMAN

Since the structure must of necessity be built of a hard material, it may convey a feeling within the dwelling of too much hardness or starkness. The surroundings may not only feel hard and look hard, but may also sound hard. Such unpleasant qualities can be counteracted with the addition of softer materials such as rugs, drapes, or cushions. Large blank wall and ceiling surfaces—particularly untextured ones—create a feeling of starkness. Blank walls and ceilings are very common today since they are less expensive to construct. They need embellishment of one sort or another.

Ornament for Cover or Accentuation

Another reason for ornamenting the structure is to cover up or accentuate something. Although one of the tenets of contemporary architecture is supposed to be that a building should be honest by revealing its structure, there can also be too much honesty. Often the subtlety of something not entirely exposed is more interesting or beautiful. If a framework or structure is beautiful enough, it can be honestly exposed. But, unfortunately, few are that beautiful or interesting. Such honest modern style demands expert

80. The elaborate lacing on this African quiver makes it beautiful and also fastens together the various parts.

PHOTOGRAPHER: ROBERT GOTTLIEB

craftsmanship as well, and since this is time-consuming and expensive it is not common in most buildings today. Rather than expose an unattractive structure, or poorly made joints, it is preferable to cover them up and embellish the dwelling in some way. These coverings can be done in a straightforward, uninteresting manner such as a patch, or they can be ornaments. Such applied ornaments are common to all the arts. The use of elaborate lacing on basketry or leather work in most primitive cultures is a good example. Not only are the two pieces of material put together, but the lacing becomes an ornament and also hides the joints. Hemstitching is another way to join two pieces of material and at the same time accentuate and ornament it.

All sorts of problems can be solved by making patches or trim strips into ornaments. Suppose a skirt gets a hole in it. To cover it with a single patch would make it look like a patch and most people would not want to wear it again. But suppose one appliquéd a series of equal-sized squares or any other repetitive motif around the skirt, then the section covering the hole would not be noticeable and the skirt design would become more interesting than before. All unattractive holes, joints, openings or shapes in a home can also be embellished into assets rather than left as liabilities. These covers or trims can become positive statements made to delight, rather than apologetic excuses for covering poor workmanship that most trim strips are.

By accentuating a blemish or joint in various ways (such as hemstitching), one can also create ornament. This type of embellishment can be compared to the application of cosmetics. The girl whose facial structure is fine and whose skin texture and coloring are perfect needs little or no make-up. She is the so-called "natural beauty," and if the visible structure of a dwelling is beautifully designed, it too will need little or no ornamentation to cover it up. If the features of a girl or the structure of a building are not beautiful, a little well-placed make-up or embellishment in order to accentuate certain lines or ideas can often be of great help. The basis of doing this sort of embellishment well is to keep in mind what one is embellishing. If a girl uses cosmetics well on her face in order to emphasize what is there, something is gained. If the cosmetics distort or hide what is there already, nothing is gained, only changed. It will usually become obvious that what one sees is a mask. The same principles of applied embellishment apply to architecture. Most buildings can be improved by emphasizing or adjusting what is there. And this approach should be thoroughly considered before one resorts to such a drastic change as tearing the building apart.

Unity Through Repetition and Variation

Ornament can also be used to give harmony and unity to unrelated parts of a structure by the addition of a common ornament to each of the parts. This method of using ornament is used in dress design. A navy blue skirt and a white blouse are not a related ensemble until some ornament—

ARCHITECT: LESTER WERTHEIMER; PHOTOGRAPHER: JULIUS SHULMAN

81. These battens not only cover the rough joints and nails at the edges of both the insulating boards and the wood but accentuate the joints to form an ornamental pattern. The horizontal trim strip at the top of the window carries a curtain track, protects the top of the curtain, and is a shelf for "pets."

maybe a red stripe—is added to both. Thus the two unrelated parts become a "two-piece" dress.

In the study of clothing design it is stressed that the various parts of an outfit must be related. This does not mean that there can be no contrast or diversity within the outfit, but it does mean that the contrast, diversity, or ornament must be subordinate to one idea if it is to be an ensemble rather than a casual assemblage of various articles of clothing. If the ornamental accessories match each other, they can unify the whole effect. No woman would wear pink shoes, yellow gloves, a pale blue hat, a beige purse, a flowered skirt, a plaid blouse, a rhinestone necklace, silver earrings, and a gold bracelet all at the same time; yet there are millions of homes today decorated with just such unrelated combinations of colors and other decorative patterns. Much of this ornament used in housing is designed to create diversity within the dwelling rather than unity. Yet if this diversity is valid, why shouldn't it be just as valid on the well-dressed woman?

The principal argument for such diversity of materials and colors in modern housing is that one cannot see all of it at the same time, whereas one can see the entire outfit of a woman in one glance. Such a woman would probably evoke some such comment as "What a mess!" whereas in the case of the dwelling various colors and unrelated ornaments are more easily accepted because one does not see them all at once. Although this is true so far as what is seen with the eyes, the mind does, in effect, retain the images and visualizes all these things at once. All visual impressions are retained in the mind and are related to preceding impressions. Our visual senses work like a movie camera. Unless you cover up the eyes the brain will keep on storing up visual impressions. Although the brain can store more impressions than one can see in a lifetime, there is nevertheless a limitation. Its filing system can comfortably handle only a relatively small amount of diverse impressions within a given length of time. If impressions repeat or relate to any previous impressions, they tend to fall into definite channels in the brain and the result is a feeling of peace and order. If, on the other hand, each visual impression is unrelated and disorganized, the brain gets confused.

In such cases the brain functions under greater tension and as a result one gets some sort of uneasy feeling of chaos or confusion. The more unrelated each impression is (that is, the less some central idea or theme is apparent), the more difficult it becomes to realize exactly what is wrong. This multiplies the uneasy feeling, and then one can either refrain from looking and hope the feeling will go away, or retreat and go for a ride in the country. Here it will seem more peaceful, since one will see what one expects to see. "If nature is repetitious we can make predictions. If it changes according to 'Natural law' we can make even more predictions." * This quality of repetition which makes things recognizable gives most people a secure feeling, and it should be used within the dwelling as it is in nature outside. The chaos of a carnival can be exhilarating for a short time; but for day-in, day-out living, no one can maintain this pitch of

* Quoted from an unpublished paper by Dr. Malcolm Sowers.

DESIGNER: CHARLES EAMES; PHOTOGRAPHER: JULIUS SHULMAN

82. The bold structure of this house makes a unifying framework for the many activities and varied possessions of its owners.

excitement or continue to store up such an endless stream of unrelated impressions.

Subordinate Diversity

It is not that a constant sameness or endless repetition should become the aim. This would be too dull, just as the steady beating of a drum becomes dull if there is not some variation within the rhythmic pattern. A unified theme can be created with continuity and repetition, and interest can be created simultaneously with variation and contrast which is subordinate to the major theme.

The kaleidoscope furnishes one of the simplest and most beautiful visual examples of combining both repetition and variation of a singular motive. Here a jumble of broken glass fragments is meaningless until the mirrors within the tube repeat this image and change its position until it forms a circle or hexagon and a beautiful design. (See frontispiece.)

The same principles relate to all arts and apply to ornamenting the home as well. In order to be comfortable a household needs hundreds of diverse objects, each of which is more different from the other than the pieces of glass in a kaleidoscope. The skill and art of interior designing is to fit these diverse household objects into some larger more understandable pattern which will also be useful and comfortable. This is difficult to achieve since no other art combines so many problems of practicality and aesthetics to such an extent. Nevertheless it is worth one's effort to consider the ways in which decoration can help to unify a dwelling.

Ideally the structure of the well-designed building will be a bold unified concept such as the simple circular arrangement of kaleidoscope segments. Within such a structure many different things can exist together so that even a somewhat jumbled interior will be subordinately related to the larger organization of the structure. Unfortunately this ideal situation does not exist everywhere, but almost any dwelling can have some unifying factor such as having the same wall surface or similar furnishings in all of the rooms. Either wood or masonry walls can form a neutral background for any subordinate decoration, or a wall can be painted a neutral color that will go with anything. It is not that there is anything wrong with brighter colors, but since most people cannot afford to redecorate too often, it is best to choose a background color for the walls that will be pleasant to live with for a long time.

Furniture can help to unify the dwelling by having a common theme or style, such as the same kind of wood, or the same cover material. Couches can then be accented with beautiful pillows of different fabrics; tables can be ornamented with flowers, dishes, cigarette boxes, ash trays, coasters, or whatever is useful and desired. Desks can be embellished with books and stationery items. There are numerous articles that are necessary which can be used to embellish any room. One need never be overly concerned that by keeping the furniture related and simple will make the room uninterest-

PHOTOGRAPH: PHOTO SOUISSI (COURTESY SERVICE GENERAL DE L'INFORMATION, MOROCCO)

83. Integral ornament is built into and is part of the structure, object, or fabric.

ing. Actually such underlying unity will make it more interesting because it will then be possible to see other smaller objects that are of interest. Interior ornament can thus be used to create simplicity even though it is usually thought of as something fancy.

TECHNIQUES OF ORNAMENTATION

Although the reasons for ornament are many, and the varieties of ornament are unlimited, this quality that beautifies can be developed in only two ways:

1. Integral ornament. The pattern or design is developed out of the form of the structure itself as an essential part of it.
2. Applied ornament. The pattern or design is placed on the building or object after the basic structure is complete.

Clear-cut examples which illustrate these differences can be seen in different fabrics. The Scotch tartan is an example of integral ornament. The plaid pattern is woven into it so that the design develops out of the particular placement of the different-colored threads that make up the cloth.

Other fabric designs can be created within the material itself by crossing the threads over and under each other in various patterns. These ornamental patterns cannot be removed without destroying the fabric itself. Thus the ornament is an integral part of its structure.

On the other hand, applied ornament is seen on embroidered or printed fabrics where the pattern is put on after the cloth is woven. These ornaments could be cut or bleached off the material and the structure of the material would remain unchanged. This type of ornament is not an essential part of the fabric, but is applied after the structure of the fabric is complete.

These divisions of ornament can be applied to architecture as well.

Integral Ornament

Integral ornament in architecture can be divided into three categories:

1. Architecture in which the whole building is designed as a piece of sculpture.
2. Architecture in which the basic supporting members of the building form the ornament.
3. Architecture in which the placement of the subordinate but necessary parts of the building create a pattern.

PHOTOGRAPHER: J. BELIN (COURTESY SERVICE GENERAL DE L'INFORMATION, MOROCCO)

84. Applied ornament is added to a completed structure, object, or fabric.

Many buildings have ornament that could fit into more than one of these three categories, and many buildings have both integral and applied ornament. By dividing all ornament into specific categories it will be possible to analyze and better understand how ornament is developed and the possibilities of using it to the fullest advantage in one's own dwelling.

Architecture As Sculpture

There are numerous well-known examples of architecture in which the whole structure forms a gigantic piece of sculpture. The pyramids of Egypt, the pagodas of China, and the temples of Bangkok were all designed for much more than pure physical efficiency. Today vast concrete shell structures are also designed not only to shelter man but to uplift his spirit with their elegant forms. It is interesting to note that the buildings which have most fascinated and inspired men over the centuries have been designed as sculptures in addition to serving their particular physical function. Frank Lloyd Wright's "Falling Water" is one of the outstanding contemporary examples. (See Illustration 4.) Such an example may represent large and expensive architecture, but large size or high cost are not necessary. Gournah village in Egypt was built with very limited funds and materials. The architect, Hassan Fathi took the only material available to him, the desert earth, and had it made into mud block (adobe). With this he sculptured a village. It is not the materials but their form that constitutes the ornament. Wood, concrete blocks, canvas, or any material can be made into a significant form.

85. Sculpture in concrete.

ARCHITECT: ARTHUR LAVAGLINO; PHOTOGRAPHER: JULIUS SHULMAN

The Building Framework as Ornament

The second category of integrally ornamented architecture is exemplified by the Gothic cathedrals. In these structures the form of the framework is ornamental. Here the columns and ribs of the roof are left exposed and embellish the structure while they also support the building.

In the field of housing, the original English Half-Timber style was an outgrowth of the same ornamental concept. The beauty of these buildings resulting from the patterns formed by the structural timbers is integral ornament. But later, when these patterns were no longer part of the real structure but were appliquéd onto the surface of the outside walls as false indications of a nonexistent structure, the integral ornament was gone and the applied ornament was false. (See Illustrations 38 and 39.)

The ornamental beamed ceiling, so popular today, also develops out of the structure and is integral ornament.

The Arrangement of Building Materials as Ornament

The third category of integral ornamented architecture is the most common variety. This ornament develops from the arrangement of the component parts or pieces of material that make up a building. Within a masonry building there are thousands of bricks, blocks, or stones. These individual building units can be fitted together to form a plain unornamental wall or they can be arranged into a pattern. The materials of a wooden building can be handled in the same manner. Boards can be nailed together in a number of different ways to make beautiful patterns and at the same time provide shelter. (See Illustration 138.)

Doors, windows, skylights, vents, or any other openings needed for convenience can also be arranged into ornamental features of a building's design. This arrangement is not a matter of cost. It rarely costs more to put a window or door in one place rather than another. It is a matter of planning, and of starting with the idea that if you are going to have a door or a window, it might just as well relate to the design of the entire structure, and at the same time fulfill its functional requirement. The wonderful stained-glass windows of Chartres Cathedral built in France in the thirteenth century rely totally on the placement of the openings and the glass. One could imagine that if the pieces of colored glass were put in haphazardly without making a pattern they would not be particularly beautiful.

86. The ribs of this revolving dome are also the dominant pattern and ornament of this room.
ARCHITECT: PAOLO SOLERI; PHOTOGRAPHER: JULIUS SHULMAN

ARCHITECT: LLOYD WRIGHT; PHOTOGRAPHER: JULIUS SHULMAN

87. Both the structure and the glass patterns create the design of this chapel.

88. Both the patterns within the blocks and the total arrangement of the blocks ornament this dwelling built in 1924.

ARCHITECT: FRANK LLOYD WRIGHT; PHOTOGRAPHER: JULIUS SHULMAN

Other subordinate parts of the dwelling, such as hardware or built-in lights, also might just as well look like they were placed carefully rather than just plopped anywhere. This equipment can be just as ornamental to a building as buttons or jewelry are to a dress. Even outside, garden walls, paving, or any other necessary parts of the garden can also become ornaments by arranging the materials used in this area into a pattern. In short, any part of one's dwelling can be developed into something ornamental and at the same time serve its useful or structural function.

Applied Ornament

The development of integral ornament as part of the structure itself is most often the job of an architect, but everyone has the opportunity to apply some ornament to his or her own dwelling. If the dwelling is being rented, any ornament added will probably have to be impermanently attached to an existing surface. However, there are many ways applied ornament can be used to create beauty without changing the original structure.

The cheapest and most commonly used applied ornament is color. Any surface can have color added or changed by the application of stain or paint, or by the addition of a veneer.

Stain

Stain is a pigment or dye that penetrates into a surface so that the texture of the surface will show. Thus wood can be stained and the grain will still show, or concrete and concrete blocks can be stained and the rough texture will still be visible. Stain, therefore, will only change the color of a surface; it does not cover the existing surface, but will accentuate its texture. In the case of wood, the texture becomes accentuated because the softer grain absorbs more stain and becomes darker and more distinct.

Paint

Paint is a heavy opaque substance that totally covers up a surface. Paint changes the texture of a surface as well as the color, forming a smooth, plain surface that gives little or no clue to what is underneath. If a surface is unattractive, paint is certainly the simplest way to cover it up. Unfortunately, sometimes the most beautiful and expensive wood surfaces are painted over.

One should be cautious, however, about overrating the importance of color in the dwelling. There is no question that a fresh coat of paint will clean and brighten things up just as a fresh dress will brighten a girl's spirit, but a fresh dress will never make an ugly girl look beautiful, neither can fresh paint or color in the dwelling basically change it. It can make rooms look fresher and cleaner, lighter or darker, bigger or smaller, warmer or cooler, gayer or duller; it can heighten or minimize many effects, but it will change only *in degree* that which is there. If a room is a pink box and is repainted blue, it becomes a blue box. One may like a blue box better; a blue box may go well with one's furniture; a blue box may remind one of the sky, or it may feel cooler. There may be many reasons to change the color of this room, but it is still the same box. To paraphrase Gertrude Stein, a box is a box is a box, or a room is a room is a room. Color is of relatively little importance in relation to the structure itself. Paint can be a most valuable ornament, but it is only an ornament. It can only embellish what is already there.

If change is desired, it is often very difficult to achieve the color one has in mind. Color can be as full of optical illusions as the size of a room. A 1-inch × 2-inch color sample may look like a delicate fleshtone, whereas 500 square feet of wall area (the area in a small room) covered with the same color may appear "shocking pink." It is impossible without great experience to choose the color you visualize with only a tiny sample from which to judge. If it is possible to match the color sample to some large existing surface the results will be more predictable. One can also plan on using several coats of paint and thereby be able to vary the color of the second coat if one is unsatisfied with the first coat.

Unfortunately, the question of color choices must remain unanswered in a text. Color preference is a very personal thing and has intangible psychological implications for all people. The only guide one can rely on is practice and experience. Each family's dwelling is therefore an individual problem, since each family is going to establish its own atmosphere. Books have tried to formulate color combinations; many rules are set up whereby certain colors are said to blend, or not to blend, with other colors. Such rules, however scientific in their reasoning, just don't work. A rose may be a rose, and a room may be the same room no matter what color you paint it; but all orange is not the same orange, at least not on two different walls of different homes, in different environments. In a cold northern climate a soft or muted orange wall may be warm and cheerful, whereas in the heat of the desert an orange room would appear brighter and could accentuate the feeling of heat so much that it would be impossible to stay in the room.

It used to be considered shocking to put red next to purple, or one shade of red next to another shade of red. But although the fuchsia blossom has one predominant color, it has many subordinate shades of reds and purples. Even the way light hits a color makes a difference. The qualities and relative intensities of color, as well as their proportions, can make the subtle difference between beautiful coloring and garishness.

Transparent Finishes

If only the texture is to be changed and the color left as is, there are numerous clear oils, lacquers, and plastics that can be applied. These transparent products form a waterproof and durable surface without losing the original color or ornamental pattern of the surface material they cover. Any good paint store will have information as to which of the many protective products is best for a particular situation.

Veneers

A veneer is another ornament that can be applied to a surface and change both its color and texture. A veneer is often thought of as a thin sheet of wood, but it can also be a thin sheet of any other material such as paper, fabric, plastic, glass, or even a thin layer of stone. A veneer is simply an applied material that serves as a covering or skin. Since any of these solid veneers are a good deal more expensive than the liquid products that can be brushed or sprayed on, veneers should be used only where they will definitely do something for the surface that cannot be as satisfactorily accomplished with a liquid.

Wood paneling is often misused simply because it is usually considered "elegant." Many people feel that a study or den or "family room" deserves wood paneling. But just as a rose can be out of place in a vegetable garden, so can the wood-paneled room be out of place if it does not relate to the rest of the house.

Any of the applied colors, stains, or veneers can be beautiful, but a much more important consideration than the material itself is how it relates to what is around it. If you will recall the description of the woman with all the different unrelated pieces of clothing, accessories, and jewelry, we may even assume that each item she had on was something really fine in itself. Yet no matter how beautiful or expensive each part of her outfit is, the total effect will not be beautiful. The trouble with the modern veneer materials is that there are too many from which to choose. They all have virtues and advantages which makes them tempting to use. The same variety is available in clothes, but since most of us are fortunate enough to be able to afford many outfits within a lifetime, one can make more choices. But since most of us live in only one dwelling at a time, it becomes more necessary to limit our desires for variety. An attempt to be elegant in one room, gay in the second, practical in the third, and contrasty in the fourth will end up in chaos. If many different surface materials and colors are to be used in one dwelling, there must be some strong framework or unifying structural pattern to relate this variety. Unless there are specific reasons for using more than two or three different surface materials in a dwelling, one can be assured of better success by limiting one's choice of materials.

Wallpaper particularly must be chosen with caution since most of it is profusely patterned. A room can quickly become a visual patchwork without the charm of the quilt. Truly beautiful patchwork quilts are put together so that the different pieces of material form a larger design, even though the pattern within each piece of fabric is unrelated to the next. This is similar to the kaleidoscope effect.

There are many other veneers that can cover surfaces to add color, texture, or design patterns. The new synthetic products have specialized uses since they are usually waterproof and indestructible from many points of view, but their very number make them more difficult to select. Too many synthetics can be a detriment in the disguise of a blessing if not used with care.

Other Two-Dimensional Ornament

Other types of applied ornament include such things as pictures, mirrors, drapes, rugs, and anything applied to part of the total area rather than the entire surface. These objects also need to relate to the whole area rather than being stuck around like postage stamps. (See Illustration 77.)

A good many objects appliquéd onto walls or floors do have a practical use even though they might be thought of primarily as an ornament. A decorative mirror would be entirely out of place if it were hung higher than anyone's head. So would a picture or bulletin board that is inconvenient to see and so becomes more of an irritation than a joy. Rugs are ornaments as well as sound deadeners. They help to create both visual and actual warmth. But since they are walked on, one must consider what they will look like after a few thousand footprints have been made on them. The most beautiful light-colored rug may be fine when first used, but after a sandwich or an hors d'oeuvre or two have been dropped on it what then! Light rugs can be cleaned or be put away and used for only special occasions. However, the more delicate things one has in a home, the more irritation is caused by trying to protect them. Plain light-colored surfaces that are not so vulnerable to dirt and abuse as is a rug can be used in many places in a room.

Draperies are another ornamental addition which has practical use as well. Draperies control light and create privacy when necessary; however there is no reason for a drapery to hang in front of a window when it is drawn back and cut out some of the light. In most cases the drape can just as easily hang in front of the wall when folded. Draperies do not necessarily have to be divided into two parts and pulled back on both sides of the window, they can draw back on one side only. It is a question of what works best for each individual case.

There are two points to consider when placing functional ornament in the dwelling: On the one hand the object must be looked at as an ornament subordinate to the total room or dwelling; on the other hand it must be regarded in relation to its own use. A successful ornamental design succeeds in both areas. Sometimes compromises are necessary, but the solution that fulfills both aesthetic and functional needs with the least compromise is the best one. If a compromise is too great, it may be necessary to revise the whole idea. One must proceed on the assumption that it is almost always possible to make an ornament applied to a dwelling serve the function it was intended for, while at the same time contribute an attractive embellishment to the home.

This certainly holds true of almost any three-dimensional applied ornament as well. With the exception of decorative sculpture, all objects in a home have some use as well as decorative value. If they are thought of as a subordinate part of the structure of the dwelling and relate to it in some way, it will be just that much easier to perceive the total environment of the dwelling as one unified entity. Comfort and beauty can be one and the same.

COMFORT AND BEAUTY COMBINED

How many homes have a really adequate place to wrap a package, or a place to comfortably sew a button on a shirt! Very few. And yet how can these things be overlooked when it is impossible to run a household without these activities? Arrangements for such so-called mundane activities are necessary for comfort, and they can be made beautiful.

When people speak of "decorating their homes," they imply creating both comfort and beauty, but then such words as "style," "elegance," "fancy," or even "cute" enter the picture and often obliterate such basic needs as a place to sew or wrap a package.

A young couple may spend all their extra money for the year to come by purchasing a $400 bedroom suite on the time-payment plan. They may feel elegant for the moment, but they may also be left without money for many other necessary comforts. Their real need was for a comfortable place to lie down plus some storage space for clothes. Such essentials can be obtained for half the price or less and there will be money left over for other necessities.

If one's living requirements and the equipment that goes with them are listed, one can understand the real needs rather than succumb to the persuasions of custom or fashion. Often the most mundane but important needs are taken for granted, whereas specialized needs receive first consideration.

For instance, if a member of the family is a pianist, the need for a piano will often be more clear than the amount of equipment it takes to read a book comfortably. More people read books than play the piano, yet it is not at all uncommon to find an "elegantly furnished home" with a piano but no comfortable places in which to read. The style may be authentic early American or slick "modern" with furniture designed by the best designers, but if most of the people living there cannot comfortably do the things they enjoy doing in the home this elegance will be only a pretty stage set. If a dwelling is to fulfill the needs and be comfortable for everyday living then the following requirements will have to be clearly recognized and properly provided for:

1. Shelter and privacy
2. Temperature control
3. Light control
4. Seating
5. Space for reclining
6. Necessary horizontal surfaces
7. Storage

Most needs will fall into one of these categories and many activities will need equipment from a number of the categories. To this list specialized needs should be added. In cross-checking the list, it will be seen that some items can be combined and thus be satisfied with one object. For example,

ARCHITECTS: BUFF, STRAUB, AND HENSMAN; PHOTOGRAPHER: JULIUS SHULMAN

89. This wall provides shelter, storage, a buffet counter, and lighting—and it is beautiful.

if there is a need to divide a space in two in order to create more privacy within the dwelling, and there is also a need for more storage space, a cabinet may do both jobs at once. Each category can be analyzed in the following manner.

Shelter and Privacy from the Outside

The most basic function of a dwelling is to create shelter and privacy. The physical shelter is created by a roof and walls that will keep the rain off one's head and the cold out. But there is a need to have a feeling of shelter that demands more of our dwellings. A glass box can be made to satisfy all of one's needs for physical shelter, but there are very few people who would feel sheltered in one. A single iron post and a few wires can be made to hold up a roof, and yet most people would not feel sheltered and protected by such a construction even if they were shown all the engineering data that proved it would stand up for a hundred years. Shelter must satisfy a physiological feeling of protection, a feeling that there is something solid around one. Shelter must also include a feeling of comfort and warmth. A prison cell certainly provides plenty of shelter, but it is a hard and stark kind of shelter that is hardly comforting. The soft and warm feeling that forms an essential part of shelter is achieved primarily by the subordinate parts of a structure and its embellishments. (See Illustrations 78 and 79.)

Glass is considered a basic element of a modern house, but if all privacy is lost by its use, the glass is not enhancing the house but is detracting from it.

With more and more glass being used in modern buildings, privacy must be achieved through the use of some material that will enclose an area when the openness of the glass walls is not wanted. In most instances windows or glass walls will need to be covered some of the time. These coverings can be beautiful ornaments both when drawn over the window and when they are pushed back and not in use.

In deciding on a particular covering for a window area it is important to know exactly what one is trying to achieve. If privacy is desired, then privacy from what? From the neighbors, from people in the garden, from the street, from the sun? It is easier to know what type of barrier to put up if one knows what is being blocked out. If there is a need to control the light coming through the window, this may be combined with some control of privacy. If there is a need for deadening the sound of a room or a need for a softer feeling, a soft-textured fabric can accomplish both these things at once. Even temperature can be controlled simultaneously with privacy by using a fabric made of special insulating material. Only by a careful analysis of all requirements will it become evident which type of window covering is most suitable. Whatever covering is decided on can be made into an ornament for the entire room.

Draperies

The cloth drapery is the most commonly used covering for a glass wall. Draperies work easily and well, and they can be reasonable or as expensive as one wants them to be. In addition to forming a soft contrast to the hard walls of a room, they can deaden or soften the sound. With an infinite variety of colors, patterns, or textures available, draperies can be very attractive. (See Illustration 89.)

Panels

Another way of covering glass walls is to use some sort of sliding panel. Sliding panels have been used in Japan for centuries and are adapted to many of the Western needs. The original shoji panels used in Japan were usually made out of paper, but modern translucent plastics give much the same effect and are a great deal more durable.

Since sliding panels must be lightweight in order to work easily, they

ARCHITECT: WILLIAM STEPHENSON; PHOTOGRAPHER: JULIUS SHULMAN

90. Japanese shoji.

are usually braced with crosspieces to give them sturdiness. In Japan the crosspieces of the shoji panels usually form an all-over pattern of rectangles, however any pattern will do which braces the panel. It need not be an all-over pattern, and the covering materials need not be translucent like paper or plastic. Many materials would be equally suitable. A heavier opaque material such as wood can also be used if adequate hardware is installed for the panel to hang from or roll on.

ARCHITECT: PAUL STERLING HOAG; PHOTOGRAPHER: JULIUS SHULMAN

91. A series of painted panels form louvers which cut down the glare from the ocean.

Louvers

The louver is another sheltering device which can be used over a glass wall or window. This device is made up of a series of boards or strips of any material with intermediate slots through which light enters. One can easily see out through a louver but it is more difficult to see in. The size of the louver strips will depend on the amount of light and privacy needed.

ARCHITECT: GREGORY AIN; PHOTOGRAPHER: JULIUS SHULMAN

92. Small-scale louvers protect paintings and books from direct sun.

Some louver systems are constructed so large, with panels measuring 2 or 3 feet deep, that they take on the proportion of a fin. Other louvers are more like the venetian blind and have strips 1 or 2 inches wide. No matter what the size, the principal function of the louver is the same—to filter the outside light.

The venetian blind uses this louver principle plus the advantage of being adjustable so that the angles of the slats can be varied and the entire blind can be raised or lowered at will. There are now similar devices that have the slats arranged vertically instead of horizontally. Some varieties can be used on the inside of the window, some on the outside. The choice here depends on what the greatest need is, how much one wants to spend, and how permanent the arrangement is to be. If one feels that some texture

93. A louvered fence and bamboo give both terrace and glass-walled rooms privacy from the street.

ARCHITECT: RICK FARBER; PHOTOGRAPHER: JULIUS SHULMAN

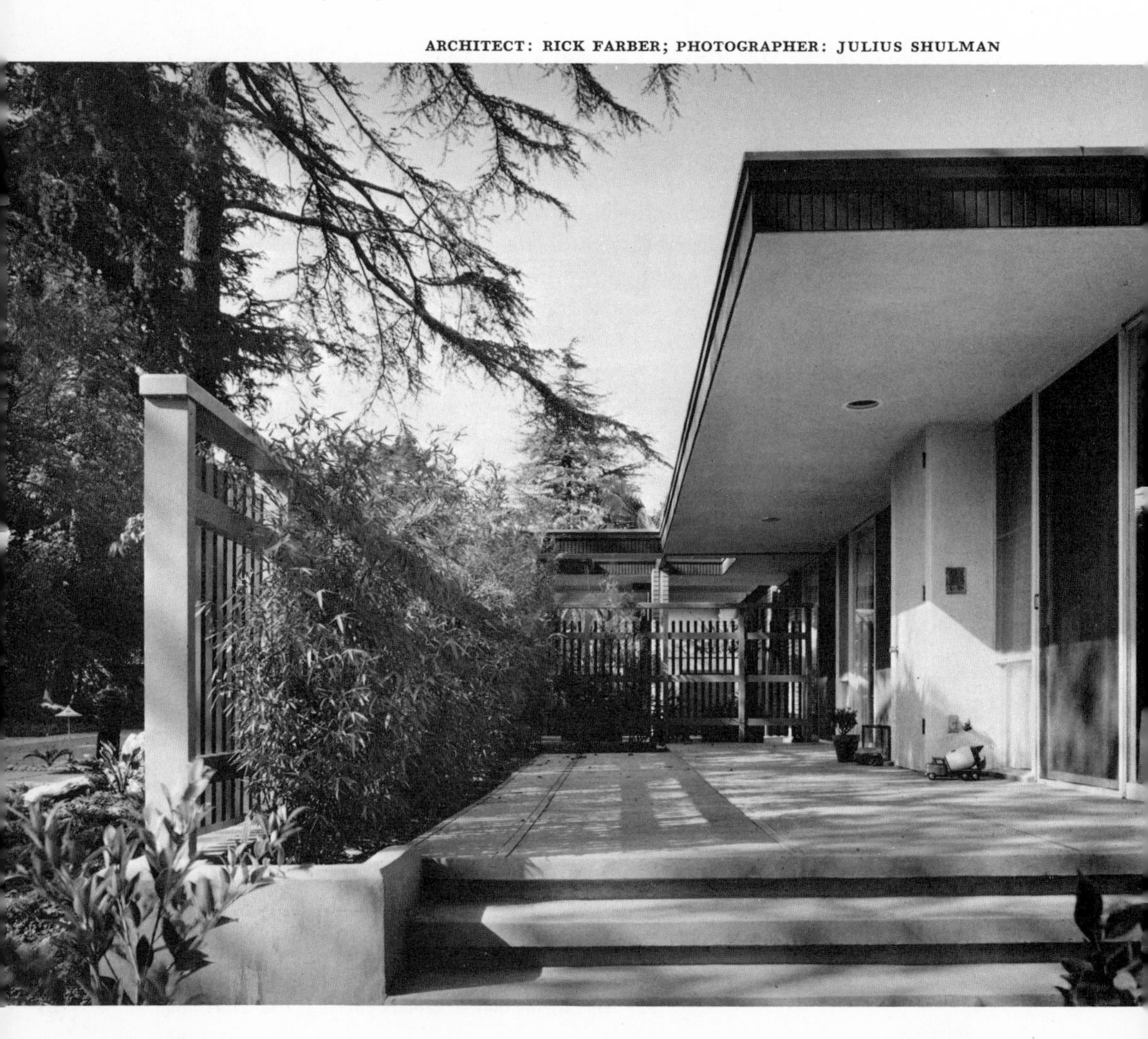

such as wood will enhance the room, to use this material in a louver system may be better than to cover an already existing and adequate wall area with wood paneling. If there is a need for color in a room, these window coverings furnish splendid opportunities for coloring. However one decides to cover the window, the covering can become as ornamental as an abstract picture on the wall. If a solid panel is used it might even have a picture incorporated into its design pattern, thus forming a natural mat and frame for the picture. (See Illustration 94.)

Planting

Another method of creating privacy in connection with glass walls is to put up some sort of barrier on the outside. On a ground floor, plants can be used for this purpose. The planting could even be arranged so that one could see out and yet not be seen.

Privacy Within the Dwelling

In addition to shelter and privacy from the outside, a dwelling must also give privacy to each member of the family and to the various activities within the dwelling. Adequate solutions to present-day needs are becoming more necessary because dwellings are becoming more compact as building costs rise. Since one space is often used for several activities, it has become more necessary to arrange the dwelling for greater flexibility. As a result of efforts toward increased flexibility, and also to make smaller spaces seem larger, many new dwellings have an "open plan." This type of dwelling usually has as few partitions as possible. This does increase both the flexibility of movement and the feeling of greater spaciousness; however, unless some sort of partial or total partitions are arranged for in "open plan" dwellings, privacy can be lost. As has been discussed, these partitions can take the form of sliding panels, storage walls, shelves, or some other piece of furniture. In creating privacy in "open plan" houses of limited space it is desirable that as many needs be incorporated into one object as possible. Blank walls, therefore, become extravagant wastes of space in smaller dwellings of this type. (See Illustrations 66 and 67.)

Not only is there a need for privacy of the individual, but some objects and activities also require a certain amount of seclusion. A kitchen full of unwashed dishes after a dinner is not attractive no matter how neat the housekeeping or how beautiful the dishes. The informal, open kitchen may be fine before the meal, but afterward some division should be provided for separating the kitchen area from the living or dining areas. There is nothing more time consuming and demanding of one's patience than the dwelling that must be kept perpetually neat. At times one should be able to close off a mess and not have to look at it. Sewing and many other crafts when in process can make a room look very disorganized and unpleasant to be in. Arranging for the clutter of such activities is as important a part of decorating as adding actual ornament. Good design is not only the result of the addition of ornament, but must provide for the absence of chaos as well.

ARCHITECT: GORDON DRAKE; PHOTOGRAPHER: JULIUS SHULMAN

94. Simple shelves and attractive dishes create sufficient privacy for the kitchen to conceal unwashed dishes and yet do not separate the person cooking from the rest of the group.

Privacy Within the Garden

Outside areas of a dwelling also require planning for privacy if they are to be of much use. The walled garden or "patio" of Latin America creates an outdoor living area which can be used for eating and other family activities. The front lawn seen on most residential streets today may make a pretty street scene, but it is practically useless for the family activities because of the lack of privacy. With land as valuable as it is in most cities or suburbs, it is a shame to own space that cannot be used to its full advantage. Not only is this wasted front space not private enough to be of use to its owner, but it is too private to be used by the public. In many countries the streets are enhanced by a park area in the center that is set aside for public use. With this arrangement everyone can enjoy the trees and grass for walking or other activities that require no privacy, and their upkeep is

PHOTOGRAPHER: JULIUS SHULMAN

95. The Latin American "patio" creates both sheltered and open space for outdoor living that is usable because it is private.

96. An outdoor room in a modern idiom.

ARCHITECTS: JONES AND EMMONS; PHOTOGRAPHER: JULIUS SHULMAN

provided for by the city. (See Illustration 15.) In the meantime the walled-in patio area common to these countries functions as part of the dwelling since they furnish true privacy. Such space can also be achieved by modern planning and in a modern idiom.

Temperature Control

Temperature control is usually not thought of as a part of interior decorating. Yet there are few places that do not get too hot or too cold at some time of the year. Most people must, therefore, provide ways to control the temperature inside their dwellings. Window arrangement, roof overhangs, insulation, and mechanical heating systems are all part of temperature control and part of the visual design as well.

Orientation and Solar Heating

The way the structure of the dwelling is designed to adapt to the prevailing climate is more important than the type of heating system in it. Solar heat can be used to the greatest advantage by orienting the open areas and windows of the dwelling toward the south so that the low winter sun will come in. And by protecting these windows with a roof overhang, the high summer sun will be kept out of the rooms. Louvers, awnings, trellises, and other devices can also aid in controlling the amount of solar heat which enters the dwelling. (See Illustrations 91, 92, and 93.)

Insulating the Structure

If the dwelling is properly insulated, the least amount of artificial heat or cold will be necessary. The greatest heat loss is through the roof and walls. These can be insulated with a number of very economical products. They act as blankets and stop the heat or cold from coming through, or they reflect the heat with metal foils. The method of construction of the building will determine which type of insulation can most easily and economically be used, and the initial cost will be offset by lower heating bills and greater comfort. (See Illustration 81.)

An air space such as a hollow wall, an attic, or a basement will also act as an insulator. On this same principle "blanket insulation" is effective because it has millions of tiny air spaces within it.

Large roof overhangs also insulate a house from the sun by providing an area of shade around it. The roof not only protects the walls and windows but gives one a feeling of shelter, shade, and coolness that the best air conditioner cannot seem to achieve.

Heating and Air-Conditioning Systems

Added control of interior temperatures can be accomplished with mechanical systems. The choice of system will depend not only on climatic

DESIGNER: CLIFF MAY; PHOTOGRAPHER: JULIUS SHULMAN

97. Heavy walls and deep roof overhangs help control temperature.

conditions but on the way the dwelling is constructed and the amount of money to be spent.

There are two ways in which a dwelling can be heated:

1. *Convection* heating systems heat air in a furnace and fill the dwelling with it. Warm-air gravity systems or forced-air furnace systems work on this principle.

2. *Radiant* heating systems heat a large object or surface which, in turn, radiates its heat through the air to other objects or people. The air itself is not necessarily heated. Pipes to convey hot water or electric wires can be imbedded in the floor, walls, or ceiling to radiate heat.

There are various heating systems which combine both these methods of producing heat, and all must be properly designed to fit the particular dwelling in question by a heating engineer or the manufacturer of the equipment.

Although the mechanics of these systems must be worked out by an engineer, the parts of them that show, such as the vents, should be placed so as to be part of the design of the house. At least 98 percent of such vents in houses are just plopped anywhere. They are considered necessities and as such, not objects worthy of any aesthetic consideration. To compare this to clothing design again; buttons on a suit are just as necessary and yet they are always carefully placed in a neat row. A good tailor knows that buttons can become attractive ornaments, and there is no reason why air vents cannot also be thought of in the same way. (See Illustration 107.)

Since radiant heating systems are not usually visible, they are not an aesthetic problem, but it is possible that even this type of heat could also be produced in beautiful forms. Attractive radiant blankets are already made, and elegant drapes or fine tapestries, too, could radiate warmth.

If individual heating units have been selected or added to separate rooms, there is little that can be done to enhance their appareance, since they have been designed at a factory. Nevertheless they will be quite handsome if placed in an orderly fashion, giving the effect of being planned rather than plopped.

Fireplaces

While today's mechanical heating systems are thought of as only utilitarian, the opposite is generally true of present-day fireplaces. Many of today's fireplaces are regarded as attractive ornaments with little concern for the amount of heat they produce.

Contrast the typical modern fireplaces with the Early Colonial fireplaces which were the central feature of the house. The Colonial fireplace was massive so that there would be plenty of room for a large fire. There was a large hearth so that there would be no fire hazard from flying sparks, and it had cooking equipment because it served as the kitchen stove. These early fireplaces are still attractive not because they were 6 inches bigger or smaller, or because of the color or the texture of the finish, but because of their feeling of generous warmth. It is apparent that they were well used and were the center of the household.

Compare this with the neat little brick or marble-faced box that sits outside many a living room in most homes today. One of its sides is open to the room and it is possible to see the fire through this opening, but little heat comes out. One can't toast more than a marshmallow there. If a spark or

99. This gracious Colonial fireplace, open to the room, gives heat and is useful for cooking.

PHOTOGRAPHER: JULIUS SHULMAN

98. Despite the "rustic" used brick, this fireplace does not give one the feeling of wanting to toast even a marshmallow.

KITCHEN FROM THE HOUSE OF THE MILLER OF MILLBACH, PENNSYLVANIA, 1752. PHILADELPHIA MUSEUM OF ART

puff of smoke comes out it is a near disaster for all the freshly painted and polished materials around. Although the fire is nice and the fireplace itself proclaimed to be "in good taste," it bears little relation to its original self. It is only costume jewelry.

In order for a fireplace to be of worth, it must give a good amount of heat. This may seem obvious, but since so many give so little heat, it is apparently not so obvious. Efficient fireplace design can be accomplished only by allowing for a big enough opening into the room to let some of the heat enter. It may be better to think of the fire as sitting in the room on noncombustible material which will be undamaged by soot; it will also need a hood and opening above for the smoke to escape. If one enjoys barbecuing, what better place to cook sauce! There is no reason why these two uses for fire cannot be combined. (See Illustration 133.)

100. A bedroom-sitting room made more comfortable by the addition of a simple metal fireplace.

ARCHITECT: BOYD GEORGI; PHOTOGRAPHER: JULIUS SHULMAN

Another type of fireplace is the metal stove. Although these stoves are often considered primarily ornaments, they do radiate a good deal of heat. If one is remodeling a house they are by far the easiest and cheapest form of fire container to install.

Light Control

Some aspects of natural light and its effects on interior space have been discussed in the chapter, "Space and Three-Dimensional Forms." Although this is not usually considered part of interior designing or ornament, it is all-important in the broad aim of creating more beautiful space. It does not matter how fancy or expensive the furniture or what subtle colors are in the room. Without adequate light it will be gloomy, and any ornament that is added to the decor is not going to show to any great advantage.

The structure of a rented dwelling cannot usually be changed, but if one owns his own dwelling it is usually not too difficult or costly to cut an additional window into a wall or even replace a solid door with one of glass. A hundred dollars spent on more outside light may be a much better investment than the same money spent on fancy furniture. If the view is nice, a window that will permit it to be seen is as fine an ornament as any picture. (See Part VI.)

Artificial Light

Artificial light is just as important to any dwelling as natural light. Adequate lighting can be achieved today due to the efficiency of the modern electric bulb; however to light a room attractively is one of the most difficult problems of design. Built-in lighting is the most satisfactory from many points of view, but since it adds considerably to the initial cost of a dwelling, it is not used frequently. Therefore almost any place one moves into will need some additional artificial lighting.

In providing artificial lighting for a room, the first consideration is how the room is to be used and what areas need more light. Most rooms will need some general illumination. For such purposes diffused light is better. As with natural light from the windows, it is not the amount of light in the room that is important but how it is arranged. One central fixture with bright lights can, by contrast, create dark and gloomy corners. Centralization of lighting is economical, but it just does not adequately light more than a small room. Rooms can be more evenly lit with more, smaller bulbs spread throughout the room.

Lighting Each Room

For special activities such as reading, cooking, or sewing, special concentrated lighting is of great importance. The following paragraphs explain the kind of lighting most suitable to the various rooms within a dwelling:

ARCHITECTS: KENNETH AND ROBERT GORDON; PHOTOGRAPHER: JULIUS SHULMAN

101. A large living room with ample diffused light plus concentrated light near seats.

102. Glass tubes diffuse but eliminate none of the light from the bulbs inside them. Candles and a few branches form the ornament for the table.

ARCHITECTS: CRITES AND MC CONNELL; PHOTOGRAPHER: JULIUS SHULMAN

THE LIVING ROOM

Since the living room is probably the largest and most generally used room in the house, it will need the most lights. Soft, diffused light will be needed for general purposes and concentrated spots of light should be provided for reading, card playing, studying, or whatever other activities take place in the room.

THE DINING ROOM

Since the dining room has a specific purpose, the planning for lighting is relatively easy. Eating requires only general illumination, but if a dining table is to be used for activities other than eating then a higher concentration of light may be desirable. In either case there will no doubt need to be light directly above the table. Candles on the table are festive, and can be bought for very little in a wonderful variety of colors and shapes. These make beautiful and fascinating ornaments for a dining table or any other room.

THE KITCHEN

In addition to the general illumination needed in a kitchen a high concentration of light must be provided for the counters. If all the light comes only from the ceiling so that one's head is between it and the food, at least

103. Light where needed—at the counter level.

ARCHITECTS: KILLINGSWORTH, BRADY, AND ASSOCIATES; PHOTOGRAPHER: JULIUS SHULMAN

ARCHITECTS: SKINNER AND TERNSTON; PHOTOGRAPHER: JULIUS SHULMAN

104. Adjustable lights focus on pictures and light entire length of this hall.

half of this light will never penetrate to the counter where it is needed. If there are shelves or cabinets above the counters, it is easy as well as very practical to add tubes of light under them. If there is nothing above the counters, the addition of a shelf about 3 inches wide with a facia about 2½ inches deep will be enough to hold the tubes of light and deflect the rays downward to the work surface.

HALLWAYS AND STAIRWAYS

These constitute as specialized a lighting problem as the kitchen. In a square room a central light can radiate evenly in all directions. Since hallways are usually long and narrow, one light will not illuminate it evenly. For hallways and stairways to be pleasant at night, they must be lighted every few feet. No place is more dismal than a dark hallway. This has certainly been exploited by moviemakers who so often use an improperly lit hall as a set for frightening or pathetic scenes. The stairway presents the same illumination problem, plus a need for safety precautions. The surest way of focusing one's attention on the stairs and thus avoiding accidents is to put a small light every few feet at the level of the treads.

UTILITY AREAS, WORKSHOPS, ETC.

These specialized areas require more concentrated light near the work surfaces just as in the kitchen. Often such work areas are thought of as unimportant and are inadequately lit. But since it has been proved that people work more safely and efficiently under good lighting conditions, providing adequate illumination for these activities will, in the long run, save time and energy.

BATHROOMS

A bathroom is usually small enough so that one ceiling light fixture will adequately illuminate the whole room. But if this room is being used for shaving or putting on make-up, either the main light must be placed so that it is not above and behind one's head or supplementary lighting must be added to illuminate the mirror area.

BEDROOMS

Bedrooms also require general illumination plus some additional lights placed at a dresser or bedside table. If more than one person uses the room and one is a "reader in bed," a fixture can be arranged so that all the light rays are concentrated on the book and will not illuminate the rest of the room. (This will be further discussed in the following section.)

Control of Light Rays

When considering these special lighting needs one must think not only of the placement of the bulb but the direction of the light rays. There are shielding devices which can either diffuse the rays or concentrate them

ARCHITECT: RAYMOND KAPPE; PHOTOGRAPHER: JULIUS SHULMAN

105. Light where needed—near mirror.

toward one spot. A so-called "indirect light" is one which has something beneath or in front of it so that the bulb is not seen. Such indirect lighting is often reflected off the walls or ceilings. These large surfaces act as diffusers and spread the light rays out into a soft glow more evenly distributed over the entire room. The opposite effect is achieved with a reflector such as in a flashlight or automobile headlight. In such fixtures a small bulb has a large reflector behind it which directs all the rays in one direction. This reflecting principle can be used to increase the concentration of light onto reading or work areas. There are also many lighting fixtures which combine diffused light with direct light.

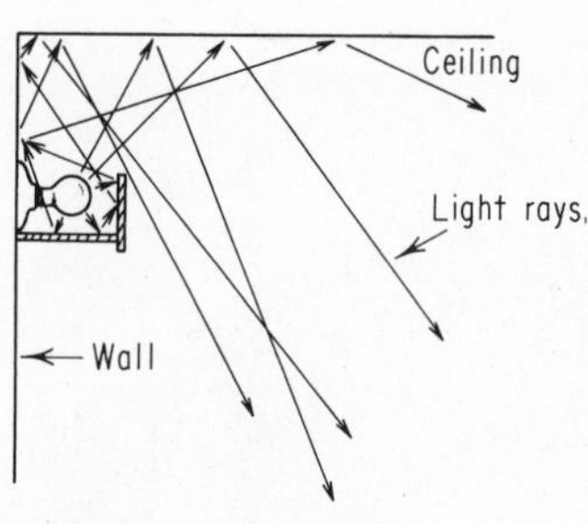

Indirect light reflected from ceiling

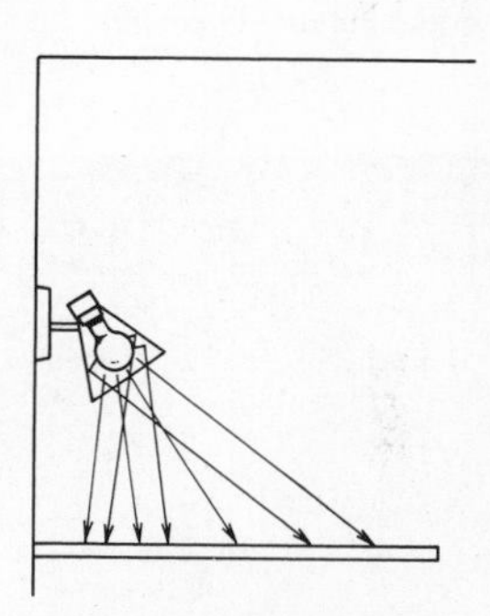

Both direct and reflected rays concentrated into one area

106. Indirect and concentrated rays of light. The direction of the rays is as important as the placement of the light.
DIAGRAM: LOIS GOTTLIEB

With such a variety of lighting available today it is apparent that the naked bulb hanging from the center of the ceiling is too crude a solution of the problem for real comfort. The lamp with the ruffled shade that traps most of the light inside it is an equally inefficient way to light up a room, a book, or anything else. Specific light must be provided for each room and activity.

Fixtures

It is the fixture and the way it directs the light that makes it both useful and an ornament. There are essentially three types of support for a bulb: (1) fixtures that hang from the ceiling, (2) fixtures that extend out from a wall, and (3) fixtures that are supported from below.

For general illumination a ceiling fixture has many advantages; it is out of the way, it can't be knocked over, and the whole ceiling can act as a reflecting surface, especially if it is a light color. Ceiling fixtures can be large enough to give a great deal of light from one source. The greatest difficulty in design is making them large enough. Since the ceiling fixture is usually the only single ornament on a large ceiling surface, it must relate in proportion to the entire surface. If it is too small in proportion to the ceiling it will look more like a pimple rather than part of a design. When designing a ceiling fixture that is to hang low over a dining or other table, it should be hung so that it can be raised if it becomes necessary to move the table.

107. Grill over heating vent extends to encase electric wires for light fixture. The total arrangement makes a handsome ornament on the ceiling.

ARCHITECT: JOHN SJOBERG; PHOTOGRAPHER: JULIUS SHULMAN

Many ceiling fixtures give only indirect light by shining the light up onto the ceiling. Unless there is plenty of other direct light in the room, central indirect lighting will not be enough for general purposes. Indirect light can be beautiful, but it demands a great deal more light output from the source if it is to be successful. In most cases a ceiling fixture is expected to give a good amount of light. If so, the bottom of it should be made of some translucent material which will diffuse the light so that there will not be a glare from the bulb.

When a ceiling is being built, light fixtures can easily be recessed into the ceiling surface. Such recessed light fixtures are made of metal boxes with reflectors built in which reflect all the light downward. These boxes can be arranged to form a definite ceiling design just as one might appliqué a pattern of white squares or circles around the bottom of a skirt. Recessed light boxes are very efficient, very cheap, and easy to install before the ceiling surface is finished. If it is impossible to cut into the existing ceiling surface, a similar effect can be achieved by using a series of simple fixtures that are made to be fixed onto the surface of a ceiling or wall. (See Illustration 104.)

If the light is needed to illuminate an area close to the wall, it will probably be most convenient to support the fixture from the wall. Just as a ceiling fixture must be designed as part of the ceiling, so must a wall fixture become a subordinate part of the wall. There will have to be support for the bulb and also some kind of diffusing material and a reflector in front of it. If the rays are reflected back onto the wall the light will be indirect and become softer. If more light is needed below the fixture, a reflector placed above it will deflect all the light down. (See Illustration 106.) This will create a shadow area above the fixture, so that area of space may then need some additional light from this or another source. Often dark shadowy areas are disturbing and give the room a more dismal look than a general over-all low intensity of light. Another way to think of wall lighting is to think of it as a ribbon or band of light rather than as a spot of light. (See Illustration 101.) The strip of lighting over a kitchen counter is such a design. (See Illustration 103.) One can even construct a high translucent shelf of ground glass or a plastic material with lights placed above it. This will make a pleasing and useful light deck. (See Illustration 105.)

Any number of lights can be attached to a wall, and by covering them with glass or plastic strips a beautiful as well as functional lighting arrangement can be created. The translucent coverings can have ornamental patterns in front of them which will become silhouetted when the lights are turned on. The possibilities for ornament are numerous on either ceiling or wall fixtures. They can be placed so that there are spaces left for flower arrangements. A beautiful piece of china or sculpture can be enhanced by careful illumination or a picture or tapestry or any other wall ornament can be highlighted.

Lighting fixtures can be supported either from the floor or any other surface such as a table. Though lamps which are supported from below are often in the way and can easily be toppled over, there is sometimes no other way to get the light where it is needed.

ARCHITECTS: BUFF, STRAUB, AND HENSMAN; PHOTOGRAPHER: JULIUS SHULMAN

108. Strips of wood at right angles to tubes of light form a decorative pattern of light.

In planning for interior lighting, the first decision concerns where the light is needed and from what surface it is going to be supported. Then the actual form of the support can be the next consideration. Obviously almost any rigid frame will support the bulb and shade, but it should be attractive as well as functional and relate to the rest of the ornament in the room. The only other requirement is that there must be a place for the electric cord to run through the support to the bulb. Most light fixtures sold today have long forgotten that their principal function is to support. Looked at in these terms of actual function, it seems irrelevant for a bulb to be growing out of the head of a plaster horse or a Spanish dancer. There is nothing wrong with horses or Spanish dancers, but if the piece of sculpture is considered something fine it should be appropriately displayed without a light bulb coming out of the top of its head. Even if one is a horse lover, it will not increase one's feeling for horses to put a shade that looks like a ridiculous hat on the horse's head. It is one thing to shine light on a piece of sculpture in order to show it to best advantage; it is something else to deride a piece of sculpture by making a lamp out of it. Even the commonly used flower vase has little relation to a light bulb since its shape was designed to hold water, not run a wire through.

A base for a lamp can be a sculptured design, but its form must be related to the bulb and shade as part of the whole design. They are no longer separate entities, but part of one whole object.

The design of the lampshade is crucial to the functioning of the lamp. If a light is placed away from the walls or ceiling, it will either need a shade all around it to diffuse the rays, or one on one side, above, or below it to direct the rays in a particular direction. If a light is intended for general illumination the shade must be as translucent as possible. It can have any sort of ornament that will not hinder greatly or block out the light. This may also seem obvious, but the stores are full of shades that look very pretty and yet blot out most of the light. The most usual shade is constructed in the form of a circle that is open top and bottom. Actually shades can be made into any shape of translucent box. All sides can be translucent and give out light, or some of the sides or the top can be made of a solid material that will prevent the light from going in certain directions. Again, one's specific needs determine the design or selection of a fixture.

Seating

In the United States and most Western countries people expect to sit on something at about the level of their knees with the lower portion of their legs extending down to the floor. We take this for granted and assume that there is no other way. All our houses are well equipped with things on which to sit in this position. There may be some question as to whether or not this is the most comfortable position for all sedentary activities, since more than half of the people in the world do not sit this way.

In the Middle East, for instance, the idea of sitting off the floor is foreign to most people. The sewing machines sold there are especially equipped with hand controls rather than foot pedals so that the people sewing with them can sit on the floor with their feet under them. In order to comfortably turn the potter's wheel with their feet, the potters of Morocco dig a hole in the ground and set the wheel into it. They can then sit on the ground and put their feet into the hole to turn the wheel. For them this is more natural than lifting their bodies off the ground.

In other countries people sit off the ground, but have their feet tucked up under them. One sees the tremendous seats which are the thrones of the kings or sultans of some countries. These were made to be sat on with the ruler's feet up under him.

The Japanese people prefer to sit on their knees with their feet behind them, so, instead of chairs, they have cushions and low tables to go with this kneeling position. (See Illustration 90.)

In planning one's seating requirements one should first recognize that there are various ways to sit, and then decide how one wants to sit for various activities. If one is happy to sit on the floor for some activities there is little problem. For extra comfort some cushions can be beautiful ornaments as well as useful. Even if one is accustomed to using chairs, a few extra cushions around will add a comfortable feeling to a room. Cushions are useful as well for children or extra guests.

If one wants to be up off the floor, various structural solutions must be provided. Seating structures are subordinate forms to the rest of the room and should relate to the room and each other as much as possible. Since people will probably want to sit differently for different activities, several types of seating arrangements must be provided.

The Hassock

The simplest type of seat is an enlarged and glorified cushion called a hassock. The originals in the Middle East were huge, lavishly ornamented leather pillows solidly stuffed with grass. (The word hassock means "thick clump of grass.") In Europe, where there was more wood, people raised themselves from the floor with wooden stools. Today most seating arrangements are an outgrowth of these ideas. The softness of the hassock has been combined with the wooden leg supports of the stool to form many types of attractive seats.

For economy you cannot beat a hassock or a stool. It is also a seat that anyone can make for himself. A simple wooden frame upholstered with cotton or foam rubber and covered over with fabric can become a comfortable seat and an attractive ornament in any room. The questions to ask yourself when making or buying one are, "Is it comfortable?" "Does it go with the room and the other furniture?" "Is it in scale with the other furniture and the rest of the dwelling?" and "Does it serve any particular need that is required of it?" For instance, if space is a problem, can it be easily stored or stacked? Or, if it must be moved, is it easy to pick up?

The Chair

A more complex type of seat is the chair. This not only raises the body off the floor but supports the back and sometimes the arms. Since a chair comes in contact with more parts of the body, it must be designed to fit the contours of the body, and if the chair is to relate to the room, it must have an architectural quality as well. Some chairs are designed to be very architectural; that is they are structurally designed with straight lines of the room, and therefore go well with it. But many architectural chairs are pretty hard on the body. Other chairs are very comfortably designed only to fit the contours of the body, but these often have no visual or structural relation to the room or the other furniture in it. In order to satisfy both the interests of comfort and design, compromises usually have to be made. A material which offers both comfort and architectural lines is foam rubber. It is not only comfortable to sit on, but when not in use retains a rectilinear architectural form.

The Couch

The most flexible seating arrangement for the dwelling is the long couch on which the most people can be accommodated in the least space. It is also possible to sit on a couch with your feet up under you or to use it for lying down. The couch can be either a structure by itself or it can be built in against the wall thus economizing on available space.

The couch is also the most ideal solution for an economical arrangement. The advantages here are similar to those of a multiple dwelling. One structure is usable for many people. The couch is also an ideal structure in that almost anyone can make his own. A couch need only be comprised of an elongated hassock with pillows or bolsters against the wall. The wall of the room can thus be used as the back of the seat and save an additional cost. The only disadvantage of the couch is that it cannot be easily moved, or provide as much arm support as a chair.

Combining Various Types and Styles of Seating

Any home will need several different types of seats. For eating or some other activity at a table or desk, the seat should be high enough for the sitter to reach the table surface comfortably and yet low enough at the arm rests for the seat to slide under the table when not in use. If there is a back to the seat it should be vertical enough to give the necessary support. Some saving on the number of chairs needed can be attained if the dining chairs and the desk chairs are the same. Then they can be used together when needed for entertaining. Other types of chairs in the dwelling require special forms; also a lounging chair needs to be lower, with a more reclining back, and possible supports for the arms; and children need smaller chairs to fit them. All seats should be selected for the definite purpose for which they will be used.

Since every household will require a number of different types of seats, there will be diversity and contrast in their styles. Therefore, in the interest of unity, some method of relating these chairs one to another should be devised. If all these seats are made with a similar scale and structural method, they will seem unified rather than a jumble of unrelated things in the dwelling. If all the upholstery is the same, there is unity, or if any other ornamental part of these seats is repeated, a common theme will be created.

As to the use of older furniture styles in a modern dwelling, many people are concerned that they will not fit in with a modern dwelling; or vice versa, that a contemporary chair cannot fit into a traditional house. If interior

ARCHITECT: HAROLD BISSNER; PHOTOGRAPHER: JULIUS SHULMAN

109. Traditional European furniture, pre-Columbian Mexican ornaments, and modern chairs go well together here because each piece is in itself well designed and heavy in scale. Even though they are from three different centuries and civilizations, there is no confusion.

furnishings of another era do not fit the style of a house it is not because the styles are different; it is because the ideas or the scale of the style is different. Beautiful objects of many styles can be carefully combined and related to each other to create a beautiful room. It is true that the more diverse the origin of the pieces, the more difficult this is to do successfully, but it can be done if one looks for the unifying factors in each piece.

If one has a new house with heavy, exposed woodwork in it, a delicate antique rococo chair will be entirely out of place. The age of the furniture is not the conflicting element here, but rather the scale of the chair as compared to the structure of the house. Older, heavier-scaled chairs dating from the Gothic era will most likely be more suitable for a heavy-scaled structure of this kind. Conversely, contemporary furniture can relate to an older-style house providing there is a relation in scale or visual character. It is obvious that a modern tubular steel or plastic chair will look like a wrong note in a Georgian or Mediterranean house. Again, stylistic conflict here is not due to their ages but rather to the different materials and methods of construction. There are many heavy-scaled wooden contemporary chairs that would be both beautiful and comfortable in such a setting.

Putting together different-style objects is like making up an invitation list for a party. If all the guests are the same age and come from similar backgrounds the chances are that they will have much in common to talk about and will get along well. If, on the other hand, one invites a group of people of various ages and from different places, the party will turn out a good deal better if these people have a common interest. Such unrelated groups can be brought together, but must be chosen with greater care. The same discretion must be used in choosing physical objects for a room. Although it is much simpler to keep all furnishings in the same style, it is not necessary to do so unless one is creating the style of a particular civilization or time, such as a Colonial room or a Swedish modern. In these cases the theme is historical rather than merely visual.

Quality of Materials and Construction

The quality of a chair is an important criterion of its value. A poorly built chair is no economy. Although quality is desirable in all furniture, it is most necessary in chairs. There is no other piece of furniture that must absorb so great an amount of stress and strain. It is remarkable that a 20-pound chair holds together at all considering that it is expected to support a 200-pound man. This strength can be more appreciated if one imagines a boulder, weighing ten times more than a house, falling through the roof. This is about what happens to a chair when a 200-pound man sits on it. We ask a great deal of a chair, but a good one will last a lifetime. This does not mean that money need be spent on something fancy—just good material and sound construction.

The other part of a chair that should be sturdy is the upholstery. Since the cost of reupholstering a chair can be almost as much as the cost of buying a new one, a few extra dollars spent on the original fabric will buy material that will last longer and look better. Chair upholstery gets hard use and is not the place for a delicate fabric.

Space for Reclining or Sleeping

In the United States the mention of the word "sleep" will immediately make most people associate it with the word "bed," and a bed is usually thought of as a spring and mattress supported on a frame or bedstead. This may be a perfectly comfortable and adequate way to sleep, but again it is not the only way.

In many tropical countries people sleep in hammocks so that the air can circulate all around them. In Japan, people sleep on mats which are rolled up in the daytime and put out of the way. Various types of folding beds have been made which can fold into cabinets or closets during the day. Just as in the selection of other furniture, there is more to consider when providing a place to sleep than just going out and buying a bedspring, mattress, and frame. Some considerations are:

When a couple is furnishing a household, the bedroom furnishings are usually the first things they buy. This is also the time when there are many things to buy and not enough money with which to buy them. The choice of a very simple sleeping arrangement may be worthwhile in such cases. To be able to distinguish between simple sleeping comfort and an unncessarily elaborate bedstead is essential.

Frames for Beds

A large bed will probably be the biggest piece of furniture in the house. Unless one has a very large room especially for it, it may be better to minimize its size rather than accentuate it with a larger-than-necessary framework. The spring and mattress alone are big enough so that oversize frameworks are not needed. Conventional bed frameworks often look like a tall man wearing elevator shoes. The canopied bed, for instance, is scaled to fit into a 20- × 30-foot palace bedroom and in such a large room it can look elegant. In a 10- × 12-foot room it will look overpowering and be out of scale. The size of a bed must be considered in relation to the room size.

A supporting framework is necessary to keep the mattress up off the floor, but this can be easily made in smaller dimensions. A low frame built to block solidly the space between the springs and the floor will keep socks and other stray objects from accumulating underneath. If the bed has to be moved when being made up it will be much easier to do so if wheels or casters are attached to the frame.

Headboard

Since most beds are placed so that the heads of them are against the wall, headboards are generally provided to protect the wall. These are usually made of wood and can be easily ornamented any way one likes. Since a headboard is primarily needed to lean against, a padded headboard of attractive material will provide great comfort. The fabric can be matched to the spread or complement the color. Another way of solving the need for a headboard is to put a bolster against the wall. This makes the bed comfortable for sitting as well as for lying.

Sometimes storage space near the bed is of prime importance. Headboards can be built to incorporate either shelves or little cabinets into them.

DESIGNER: J. R. DAVIDSON; PHOTOGRAPHER: JULIUS SHULMAN

110. This bed has not been put against the wall. Its headboard provides comfort with lights, radio, switches, plugs, and storage.

Footboards

Footboards can be an ornament or can provide a storage place for blankets. However, with the larger-sized blankets that will tuck in and stay in place, a footboard is no longer necessary. If there is ample space in the room for this, it is fine; otherwise it is an item that can be eliminated without great loss.

The Spread

The selection of a bedspread is important since it is the biggest area of the bed and the first thing one sees. If the bed is used only at night and the spread is then removed, any fabric that goes with the other furnishings in the room will look well. If the bed is going to be used as a seat during the

ARCHITECT: RICHARD NEUTRA; PHOTOGRAPHER: JULIUS SHULMAN

111. A simple room for sleeping and dressing. Note that the foot board has been replaced with storage cabinets.

day, the fabric must also be sturdy and a serviceable color. Because bed covers are not tacked in place, the fabric must be firm enough so that it will not muss easily. The color of the spread is a personal choice, but one should realize that a brilliantly colored or highly patterned spread is going to make the bed seem larger than it would with a softer or duller color. Because a bedspread covers a large area it is difficult to choose the color from a small swatch. Colors that look very subtle may look quite different on such large areas.

Uses of the "Bedroom"

The conventional bedroom is usually thought of as a special room in which to put a bed and to be used only for sleeping. Most people also dress and undress there, but in many homes this room is hardly used at all during the day. In today's housing situation with space at such a premium, families are willing to give the bed a less dominant role in the bedroom so that there is space in the room for daytime activities. Each person must first decide how he is going to use the bedroom. This decision will then influence the choice of beds.

Since so many people are now using bedrooms as studies or sitting rooms during the day, beds are being used more like couches. With the long side of the bed and the bolsters or pillows placed against the wall, the bed can be turned into a long couch. With casters on the frame a bed can easily slip under a shelf or some cabinets. This arrangement lessens the width of the bed, making it more comfortable to sit on as well as providing additional storage facility.

The main thing to be aware of is that a bedroom of about 10 × 12 feet costs between $1,000 and $2,000 to build. If the room is well arranged, the money will be well spent.

112. A combination bedroom-study. This room can be used both during the day and at night.

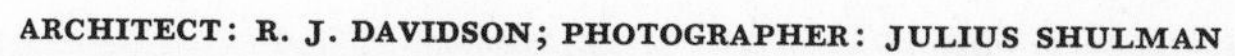

ARCHITECT: R. J. DAVIDSON; PHOTOGRAPHER: JULIUS SHULMAN

Horizontal Surfaces

Just as a place to lie down must look comfortable in order to be inviting, so must a horizontal surface give the impression that is is adequately suited to its purpose in order to look well. Fine wood and intricate carving around the edge of a counter may be impressive and good for ornamental purposes, but it is a large flat work surface on top that makes this space usable.

Most activities carried on in a home need a flat surface to do them on. Food preparation, eating, making things, writing, and just putting things down all require adequate surface space.

Height and Size of Surfaces

The dimensions needed for any surface area will be determined by how it is to be used. The height of a surface will have to be about 36 inches, if one is going to stand up while working at it, and this average height should be adjusted to suit the person who is actually going to use it. A tall man's work bench may be much more comfortable at a 40-inch height. A short woman will find it less troublesome to see over the rim of a pot if her stove is 32 inches high. At a certain age a child's play table may be most useful at a 20-inch height, and this will have to be raised periodically if it is to continue to be usable.

Surfaces intended for sitting at will be most comfortable at a height of about 28 inches. Again, this can vary with people and the types of activity. When planning for such an activity as typing, a lower work surface than normal will be more comfortable since the actual working surface is raised to the level of the typewriter keys.

Another important factor to consider is the size of the surface, which will have to be adequate or it will not be of much use. Many desks modeled in an elegant, traditional style with beautiful wood and fine carving provide only enough space to write a letter. At the time such desks were designed—one or two hundred years ago—letter writing was just about all they were used for and they served this purpose well. However, larger desk surfaces are necessary today because of more complex interests as well as more varied household activities. (See Illustration 112.) One need not spend a great deal of money for a large desk; an 8-foot length of plywood or even a flat plywood veneer door can serve the same purpose. With a trim facia added around the edge and appropriate storage drawers or shelves to support the surface, a very useful work space can be created. It will look appropriate because it will give the impression of being adequate for its needs.

Surface Materials

For some activities special surfaces are required. This need not mean an expensive or fancy material. Sometimes the least expensive material will be the most serviceable. A child's play table, for example, is obviously going to take a beating. Therefore, an inexpensive surface that can be replaced every once in a while for several dollars will be the most care-free

ARCHITECTS: KENNETH AND ROBERT GORDON; PHOTOGRAPHER: JULIUS SHULMAN

113. This work surface can be kept clear and usable because it has convenient storage with it.

and the best for the purpose. There are many types of wood and building board to be found in any lumber company that are cheap enough and could also be used for some adult work surfaces as well. Such surfaces will not have the elegance and beauty of polished walnut, but because they will not be destroyed by wear they will be more useful.

For more elegant counters and surfaces there are now a number of types of material. Each has advantages and disadvantages. No one material is perfect for everything, and should be selected with this limitation in mind.

The impossible cannot be expected from them. Some of the advantages and disadvantages of the various materials are as follows:

Resilient Materials

Linoleum, rubber tile, and sheet vinyls are attractive, resilient materials that are available in all colors and patterns. There are heavy ones made for floor coverings and there are lightweight ones made for upholstery or luggage. These may all be glued over plywood to make a waterproof surface.

They cannot be used as a surface on which to cut materials, and will be permanently scarred if burned. They should be put onto the surface with the fewest joints possible, and can be coved if desired. They are probably the least expensive surfaces for counters and tables, and are useful for kitchen surfaces since they are soft, quiet, and easy on dishes.

Decorative Hard-Surface Plastic Laminates

These synthetic surfaces are probably used more than any other counter surface today. The variety of colors and patterns is unlimited and they are relatively carefree. But these too can be cut into or burned, and once scarred cannot be repaired. They can be edged with metal strips or "self edged."

Ceramic Tile

Ceramic tile is another beautifully colored material which has the advantage of being totally heatproof and can be used as a base for cutting materials. However, its greatest disadvantage is the many joints which do in time fill with dirt and eventually crumble. Tile surfaces are noisy and hard on dishes, but with withstand hot pots and pans.

Terrazzo and Polished Concrete

These hard surfaces have not been used indoors as much as tile, but do have some of the advantages of tile without the disadvantage of the joints. Concrete surfaces are also well suited for outdoor surfaces and can be poured at the same time other floor slabs are poured.

Stainless Steel

A stainless-steel counter is an expensive and almost indestructable surface. This surface is of great advantage in the kitchen since sinks and stoves can be incorporated into it, and the dirt-collecting joints can be avoided. Stainless steel is also resilient enough to be easy on dishes.

Wood

Although wood is often neglected in favor of more "modern" synthetics, it is still one of the most serviceable and beautiful materials available. If treated with a clear liquid plastic it can be made to resist heat, stains, and water. The greatest advantage of a wood surface is that if something does happen to it, the finish can be sanded off and reapplied.

Wood surfaces also have the advantage of being able to match the wood furniture and cabinets of the living area. In a small house with an open plan this can do much to help the continuity of design and eliminates an unrelated kitchen. (See Illustration 135.)

The need to maintain a unity of design throughout the dwelling should be kept in mind when selecting counter surfaces. Since there are so many to choose from, it is easy to be tempted by all of them and create a patchwork result in the dwelling.

Storage

Adequate storage space must be provided for the equipment to go with all activities and work surfaces. These surfaces can be easily transformed from a work surface into storage space piled high with stuff if conveniently arranged storage space is lacking. A well-designed room must be orderly and the best housekeeper cannot keep order without proper storage space. (See Illustration 113.)

This storage space must not only exist, but it must be where it can be reached. In most kitchens more than half of the cupboard space is above 6 feet. This is about as high as the average woman can conveniently reach, and any shelves higher should be considered of value for only occasionally used things.

Organized storage must be planned for all activities. (See Part IV.) It is first necessary to list the equipment which is to be stored before making any decision as to what the equipment will be stored in. Some articles will fit best into drawers, others are most conveniently placed on shelves or in cabinets if you don't want to see them. Some equipment can be conveniently placed in baskets or in bins. Any one of these storage facilities can become a fine addition to a room and provide some ornament as well. Even a series of storage boxes can become beautiful when painted or papered.

The size of the drawers or shelves is important if one intends to make the most use of the storage space. For example, a drawer for sweaters probably needs to be 6 inches deep, whereas two 3-inch-deep drawers will be far more satisfactory for blouses. Shelf spaces for glasses need be only about 6 inches apart, and any additional spacing is only wasted. Adjustable shelves which can be varied in height are certainly the most versatile solution, but with a little planning any shelves or drawers can be more efficiently spaced.

A more efficient use of closet space can provide additional comfort and convenience. Where skirts and jackets hang in clothes closets, the space below them is often wasted. This waste can easily be corrected by lowering the pole about two feet so that the skirts and jackets hang almost to the floor. If this is done there will be enough space above for two or three more shelves. This will provide as much storage room as a good-sized chest of

DESIGNER: GRETA GROSSMAN; PHOTOGRAPHER: JULIUS SHULMAN

114. Attractive food containers placed in an often wasted space above the counter where they are easy to see and reach.

drawers. If space is efficiently planned to accommodate the various things one owns, it eliminates piling. With one's things in some sort of order and with a few attractive boxes on the shelves, a closet can be an attractive area in the dwelling rather than something to be hidden behind a door.

Perhaps the main reason why so many of our household things are hidden behind doors is that almost everything we buy in the United States comes in disposable containers. In many ways these paper and plastic containers are convenient, but due to their convenience they have practically replaced permanent containers. To illustrate this point, the kitchen cabinet is the best example: here most food items are not only packaged

DESIGNER: CLIFF MAY; PHOTOGRAPHER: JULIUS SHULMAN

115. Well-planned closets and shelves keep this children's room in order.

but display their own advertisements. To open most kitchen cabinets is to be faced with dozens of tiny billboards all at once, all competing with each other for your attention. The visual impression is one of chaos and ugliness. Although many food items can only be preserved in their packaging, many others can be transferred to more permanent and more beautiful containers. It is possible to find all sorts of beautiful food containers made of metal, wood, or glass. A row of any one of these on a shelf will enhance the appearance of any kitchen. (See Illustrations 74 and 114.)

Summary and Example

Summarizing the main points thus far presented in this chapter, the following requirements must be adequately provided for in order to make a dwelling comfortable:

1. Shelter and privacy
2. Temperature control
3. Light control
4. Seating
5. Space for reclining
6. Necessary horizontal surfaces
7. Storage space

Although each of these requirements has been discussed separately, in actual practice one activity will most likely combine several or all of these needs.

As an example, the following development of a design for a reading area will illustrate how all of these needs are involved and can be provided for.

A Reading Area

This design is not based on a traditional or preconceived "style" but is developed out of its particular needs. This piece of furniture may not be something everyone would want or like, but it (as well as other examples in this text) is not shown here as a criterion of what is good for everyone, but simply to illustrate the results of a type of thinking or analysis of a problem.

Consider a piece of furniture designed to be comfortable and attractive in a living room. It is to be for a person who enjoys reading in the evening. Sometimes this person likes to sit, and sometimes to lie down. Occasionally he may want to have something to eat or drink while reading, and he may want a storage place for his extra books or magazines. Light and some provision for extra warmth will be needed as well. This one activity will therefore combine all the requirements of comfort. How can these requirements be most conveniently combined?

1. A seat
2. A place to lie down

3. A certain amount of privacy
4. A surface to put food or drink
5. A storage space for books, magazines, etc.
6. A light
7. Extra warmth

The solution to a design problem is different from the answer to a mathematics problem in that there is not "the answer," there is "an answer." The design is one of an unlimited number of possible solutions for any particular set of requirements. There can be as many answers as there are designers solving the problem. Each one, no doubt, has slightly different values and different feelings about the situation and the materials to be used, so each will arrive ultimately at a different conclusion.

To make choices is sometimes difficult if there are too many things from which to choose. To narrow down the possible choices by recognizing certain limitations makes the choice easier. The waiter who comes along with a list of twenty different ice cream flavors sometimes leaves the customer speechless. If he says, "Chocolate or vanilla?" most people can quickly decide. It is the same with furniture. If one analyzes the possibilities, the choices can usually be made more easily.

1–2. A CHAIR AND A PLACE TO LIE DOWN

Since this piece of furniture to be designed for a reading area is to accommodate a person who either wants to sit or lie down, a chair will not do. Neither will a bed or hassock. The only type of furniture that will be comfortable for both is a couch. Immediately the solution to the problem is narrowed down to a couch of some sort. But where will it be located and what special features or accessories will it need to be completely comfortable?

3. PRIVACY

If this reading area is to be in a living room, there will most likely be other members of the family there doing other things, too, so for this reason an out-of-the-way spot would be the logical choice to insure some privacy and seclusion. The total arrangement of the room and its relation to the whole dwelling will naturally influence this decision, but in most cases it would be safe to say that a corner of the room is a good place to put a couch for reading.

4–5. A SURFACE FOR FOOD OR DRINK AND BOOK STORAGE

The next on the list of requirements is for a place to put things. This would probably be most convenient adjacent to the couch. If it is a sofa with arms and a back, a table at the end or a low table in front of the seat would be adequate. If the couch does not have arms, a shelf built at one of the ends can be an arm rest as well as a place on which to put things. In some cases it may be possible to build a shelf all along the back of the couch. Although there are numerous possibilities, probably the most convenient is the space at the end of the couch, since this is the most easily reached.

The space below the end-shelf can also provide any necessary storage; a shelf for books, a cabinet for pillows or blankets, or whatever is needed. There is no reason for this space underneath to go to waste when it can be used to store equipment that will make this reading area more convenient.

6. LIGHT

With the books and other objects to be stored planned for, the next concern is light. General illumination in the room will not be sufficient for reading. Reading requires direct light placed close to the reader. The light can be diffused with frosted glass or plastic or any light-colored, translucent shade, which does not prevent the rays from shining directly on to the book. A reading light must be so arranged that the reader's head or book does not come between the light source and the pages. A floor lamp, in order to be used for reading, would have to be placed at the end or behind the couch. If the couch is in a corner or there is some furniture at the end, a floor lamp will not work. A table lamp on the end table or shelf will probably be all right but it takes up space which could be used for other things. If it is possible to attach the lamp to the wall or hang it overhead from the ceiling, it will probably be the most convenient and out-of-the-way place.

7. EXTRA WARMTH

The last consideration in developing design for the reading area is to provide for extra warmth. When one sits or lies still this is often needed, and a beautiful afghan kept on the couch can supply it and at the same time be a colorful and decorative ornament.

This example of creating a design for a specific activity illustrates what Frank Lloyd Wright meant when he said, "Form and function are one." The couch and accessories are not what they are because of a whim, or because they are just pretty that way, or because someone made them that way three hundred years ago and it is considered good taste to stick with it. The couch and its subordinate parts were so designed because in this way it is both comfortable and useful. These are more important criteria of good design than whether or not it will "look good."

There is no formula which can define what "looks good." Fortunately the world is a more fascinating place because different people have different ideas of what "looks good." The she toad looks good to the he toad. The Ubangi tribe in Africa thinks it looks good for a woman's lips to protrude 3 or 4 inches. The Chinese used to consider it a sign of beauty for a woman to have feet about 4 or 5 inches long. Such aesthetic judgments are not based on invisible rules or a right way of doing things, but on the meaning of these customs. The Chinese woman whose feet were bound as a child to keep them from growing had this done to make it difficult for her to walk, and thus indicate that she was provided with many servants and did not have to work. Now that working is considered worthwhile for Chinese women, this custom has been abolished. Bound feet no longer "look good."

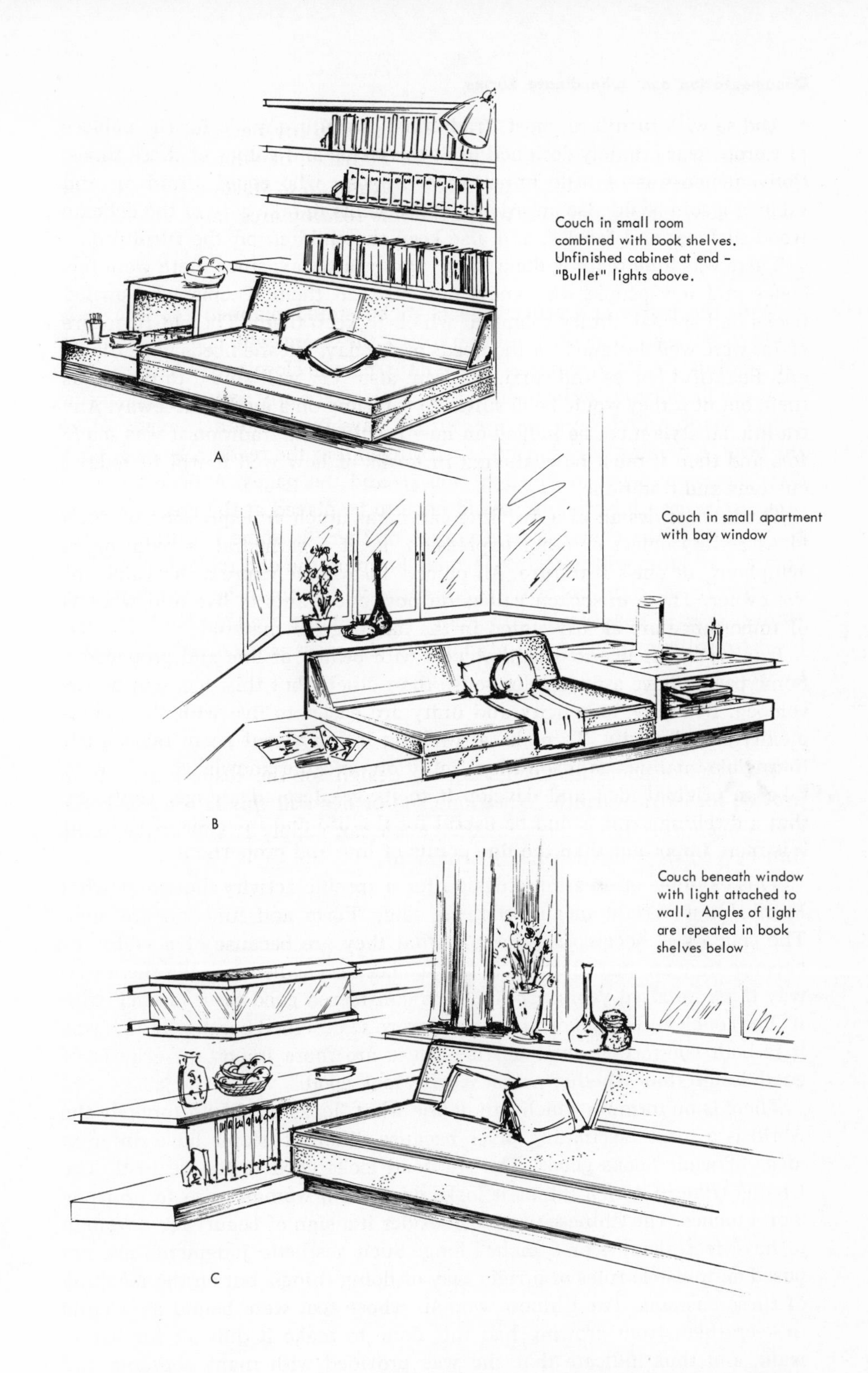

116. A reading area equipped for sitting or living with convenient storage, light, and heat.

DRAWING: LOIS GOTTLIEB

And so with furniture, most "traditional" furniture made for the palaces of Europe was ornately designed to fit the needs and values of those times. Convenience was of little importance. Anyone who could afford an end table or a sofa could also afford enough servants to take care of the delicate wood surfaces and fabrics, and also keep the children off the furniture.

There was little reading done in the parlor, anyway, since there were few books and few people who knew how to read them. People who owned books had special library rooms in which to keep them. The old furniture styles were well designed for the needs of the day, but the needs were different. Beautiful horses and carriages were also very well suited to the needs then, but now they would be ill suited to traveling on a modern freeway. Any traditional style must be judged on how it suited the tradition it was made for, and then it must be evaluated in terms of how well it will fit today's customs and traditions.

The interior design of a dwelling can be as much an expression of one's ideas as any object or other expression, be it a cathedral, a painting, a symphony, or one's furniture. All objects in a home express the values of the owner. These unspoken values on how one wants to live and what is of importance are clearly stated in the language of materials.

It takes experience to design objects with beauty of line and proportion. Some people have a finer color sense than others, but this, too, can be developed. Basically, simplicity and unity are easier to live with than complexity and diversity. To make a dwelling into a visual poem takes such intangible qualities as inspiration, intuition, and the knowledge of how to take an original idea and develop it to its greatest advantage. However, that a dwelling express and be useful for the life and interests of those in it is more important than the fine points of line and proportion.

VI

THE DEVELOPMENT OF A PLAN AND A HOME

INTRODUCTION

The kind of house that will make each owner most satisfied is the right house for him even though it may seem strange to others. There is the story of a modern house designed by a well-known architect that had the bathroom in the bedroom area. Many people concluded from this that modern architecture was indeed very strange. It is true that most people would not want this sort of arrangement, but the owner in this case did. The advantage of the modern house lies in its great flexibility. Almost anything can be done and done well. There may be limitations as to space or money, but, in general, more needs can be satisfied with the versatile building methods possible today than ever before.

In contemporary architecture there are diverse methods of doing things which produce a wide variety of results. People often conclude that a modern house looks like a square box, or a modern house is cold concrete, or a modern house has a low ceiling. It may have all these things, it also need not have any of them. Actually, a contemporary house is one that is designed to fit the special needs of the owner. The formulas of past ages have been discarded and new flexibility of design has replaced these formulas. There is no longer "the way" to do things. There are a multitude of ways, and each situation demands its own way to solve each set of requirements.

The traditional house, on the other hand, is designed by fitting one's particular needs into certain prescribed shapes and behind facades that are representative of the tradition one is copying. Although there are many beautiful homes designed this way, the designs are based on research into the past rather than a new search in the present. Most dwellings now are at least partially representative of "contemporary architecture." There is almost no kitchen or bathroom that is not built with the most modern equipment incorporated in it, and the apartment or multiple dwelling is definitely a development of our age. Even certain elements of the most standard tract house are also an outgrowth of modern technology and assembly-line methods, and the arrangement of the rooms is to some extent based on the need of the family. Unfortunately, this type of thinking has not, in most cases, been carried much further. Often the attempts to make an exterior attractive still rely on such reminiscences of the past as shutters that don't shut or gables that don't enclose anything.

If one wants a Spanish style house it is essential to have a tile roof or wood balconies or white stucco or it is not a Spanish style house. If one is going to have a Colonial house it has to be relatively symmetrical and have small windows or it just isn't a Colonial house. But a contemporary house can have whatever materials and forms one likes that will best suit the situation.

It is true that certain clichés have developed in contemporary architecture just as they have in other styles, so now certain forms and details are often thought of as "modern." But there is no reason why these standard ideas must be used over and over again.

The following three plans of contemporary dwellings are used to illustrate the versatility of contemporary planning. These dwellings are not to be judged by whether or not you would want any of them yourself, but to what extent the needs of the person they were made for have been fulfilled, and at the same time beauty of form has been created. The examples have also been chosen with cost in mind. Wonderful homes can be designed for $100,000, but this hardly relates to what most people will ever have. Unfortunately, many of these lavish houses dominate architectural and other home magazines, with the result that many people feel that they would like to have fine contemporary architecture, but cannot afford it. Therefore the following examples show what can be done by trained designers within the means of most people.

The first house was produced by remodeling a low-cost tract house. The minor modifications made in it greatly increased its usefulness and space. The result is certainly not great architecture, but often one has little choice but to work with what is available and remodel it to best fit one's own needs. This remodeling project shows that often the difference between inadequacy and comfort is not great.

The second house is part of a tract. It was designed to be built and sold. In other words, it was designed to be most appropriate for an "average family" and built at a low cost. However, within this cost and other limitations it was well designed.

The third house is an example of what can be done with a minimum of space. It is a highly specialized house designed for a particular client and site. It is used to indicate that even the smallest house can benefit from thoughtful design.

A REMODELED TRACT HOUSE

The Allotment of Space

The tract house used as an example here was bought in 1963 for $16,000. This house had four bedrooms and two baths, an adequate living room, and a good-sized kitchen. The greatest drawback so far as the present owner was concerned was the lack of dining space. There was a space at the end of the kitchen large enough for four people to eat, but no more. Although the brochure advertising this tract claimed that this model was made for "formal entertaining," it did not explain how this was to be done.

Each lot in this tract was more than adequate in size, and since the area was slightly hilly, the land had been graded so as to put each house on a different level and thus assure some privacy. This much of the planning was good. Unfortunately, there seemed to be little further thought as to how the outdoor space was to be used. All these houses were merely plunked into the middle of each lot with a large lawn sloping down toward the street in front. This front slope, though good for drainage, and pleasant to drive past, is difficult really to make much use of, and involves a good deal of work and expense to maintain. The remaining side areas between the houses were also difficult to use since they were large enough to require a good deal of planting and maintenance, but at the same time, too small to do anything with.

The outdoor area in back of this particular tract house was fenced and private, so it was already usable for outside activities. The main thing lacking was some transitional area. In this dwelling one was either inside or outside. When inside, one was totally enclosed. Although there were doors and windows, each room was a box. You could peek out of the windows, but there was no feeling that there was any connection between the inside and the outside. In other words, there was no flow of space between the inside and outside areas. When you were outside of this house, you were totally outside. There was no partial shelter in the outside space at all. This situation was particularly unfortunate because in this part of the country the climate was pleasant most of the year. With totally enclosed space so expensive, very much cheaper, partially enclosed space could be used and enjoyed to great advantage. Also, due to the hot summer sun, the lack of partial shade outside made the garden area almost unusable.

In the case of this tract house, the buyer was purchasing almost 8,000 square feet of total space, of which only 1,300 square feet were inside the house. This was the space allotment planned for living, plus an additional

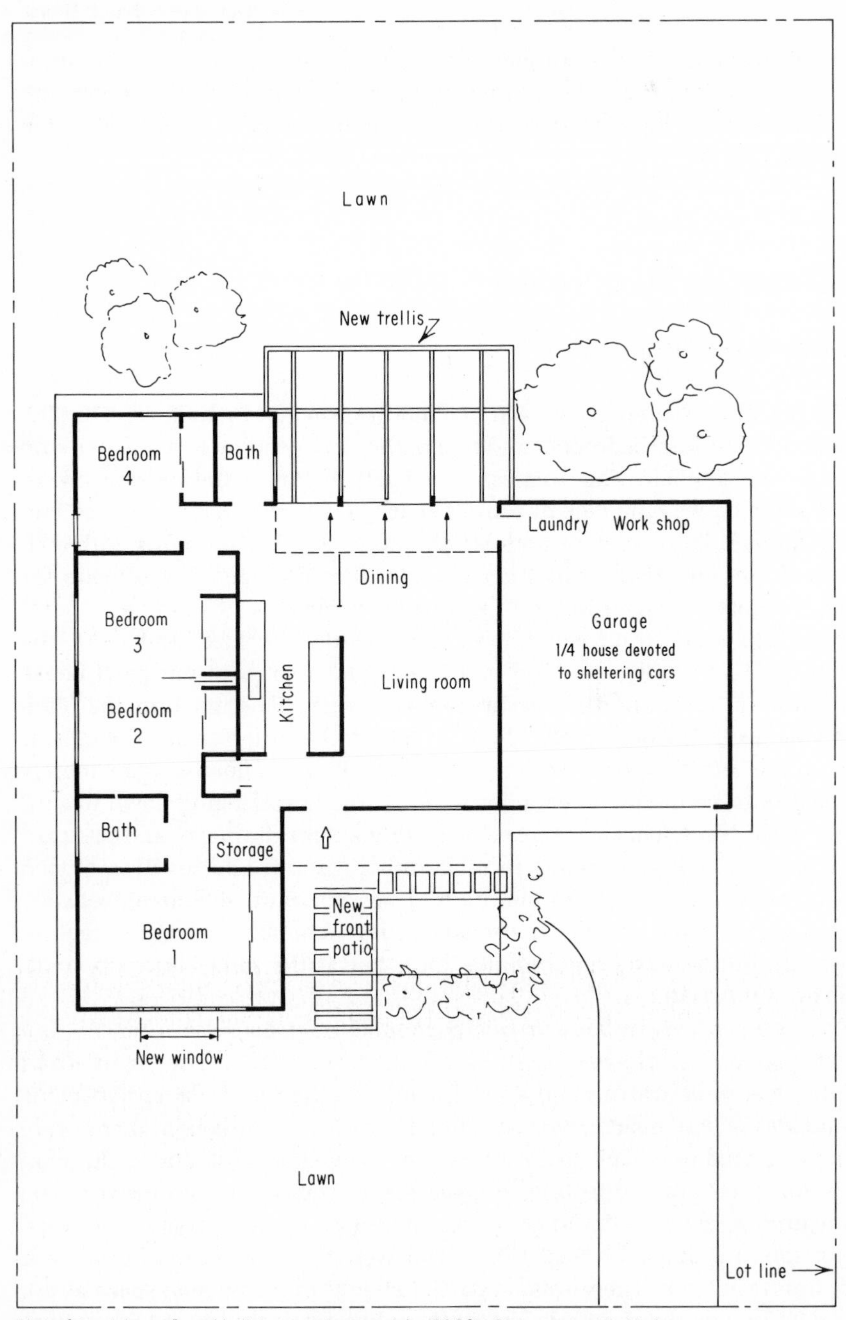

117. Plot plan of tract house indicating changes. Note that both the front and back thirds of the lot are unplanned.
DRAWING: LOIS GOTTLIEB

large area for the storage of two cars. In other words, about two-thirds of this 8,000-square-foot lot was something left over rather than something planned for. This typical layout for tracts is hardly an economic approach to the use of land and space. In tract building, where one of the decisive factors is economy, it is all the more necessary to plan for the maximum use of all available space. (See Illustration 49.)

With regard to the space allotment inside the house, the basic floor plan was quite good. From a small entry hall one could either turn right into the living room, go straight ahead into the kitchen, or turn left to the bedrooms and baths. The inside planning was efficiently handled in that there was hardly an inch of wasted space. There was also much convenience and privacy provided within this small house considering the total amount of space available. This tract house had a minimum of false details since so little money had been spent on ornament.

However, since the "style" or façade was supposed to be "California ranch," it was equipped with "shutters" that weren't supposed to shut, and a type of "fence" often used around ranches to close in the livestock. This fence, however, placed 2 feet from the house, was useless since the hundred acres between the house and the fence on which to keep the livestock was lacking. This fence was also open at both ends so that even a kitten could not be kept inside this structure.

118. Front of tract house. Note new bedroom window and added terrace and trellis.

PHOTOGRAPHER: FRED BAUMAN

The front entry veranda also imitated the California ranch style. Verandas of the original ranches were generously designed for outdoor living (see Illustration 35), but in this tract house it was only wide enough to be used as a corridor. The roof section over the veranda was supported by posts every few feet which were structurally unnecessary since the overhanging area was so small. The posts and the fence were a further nuisance because they blocked this small corridor from the rest of the outdoor space around it.

Remodeling Decisions

1. *Veranda*

A decision was made to increase the living space of the dwelling by creating an outdoor room in front. This was accomplished by removing the fence, shifting the position of the posts on the veranda to the ends of it so that nothing intervened with the outward flow of space, and pouring additional concrete in this outside area to create a more usable rectangle. This was shaded by extending a trellis outwards from the roof in two directions. This trellis also supported the existing, but sadly drooping, bougainvillaea. Plants were placed around the edge of the rectangular concrete area to give this space some privacy from the street. The space was furnished with a low table and little seats and became both an outdoor playroom for children and a true veranda for sitting, having a snack, or entertaining.

2. *The Interior Changes*

Although the arrangement of the interior rooms was good, there was no continuity of the space. Each room was an individual box with a door and a window or two for some light. The different colors of these rooms made for little relation between them. Fortunately no money had been spent on wood paneling or wall paper, so there was at least unity of wall material. All the walls were of plaster and could easily be repainted alike to bring about a further unity within the house. The rubber-tile floors also were unrelated from one room to the next because various-colored tiles were used, but nothing could be done about this.

3. *Bedroom*

All the bedrooms had large closets, but they were equipped only for hanging clothes. Because closet shelves were needed, each closet was partitioned into two halves and one of the halves was filled with shelves for folded things, toys, etc. The master bedroom was a good size—"auditorium sized" the brochures said—so this could be used as a study in the daytime. The major problem, however, with the bedroom was that it had insufficient light. The two small windows in this room made it dark and gloomy. By removing the whole wall area between these two windows and inserting a large piece of glass all across, the room was opened up. In addition, this large window area gave a beautiful view of some nearby mountains. Venetian blinds were installed to control the direct early morning sun and provide privacy when necessary. (See Illustrations 117 and 118.)

4. *Kitchen*

Although the kitchen was large and equipped with nice wood cabinets, at least half the wall space over the sink counter had no cabinets or shelves. The cabinets looked large, but since half of the shelf space in them was above most women's reach, these high shelves were not convenient. The overhead kitchen light was adequate for general illumination but it did not provide light where it was most needed. One's head was always between it and the sink counter when working there. Shelves with lights underneath them were added in front of the sink area to illuminate this work area. Handsome jars were then placed on these shelves to store food attractively.

119. Added shelves make kitchen more convenient. Lighting was built in along entire length of new low ceiling.

REMODELER: LOIS GOTTLIEB; PHOTOGRAPHER: FRED BAUMAN

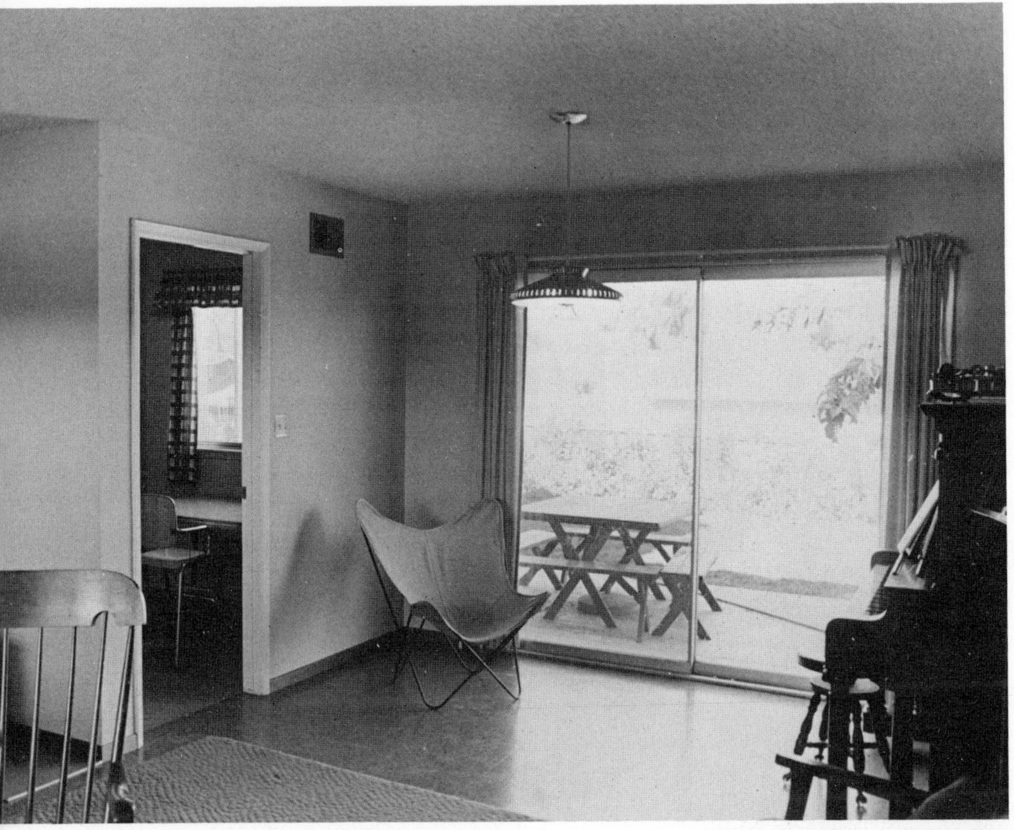

PHOTOGRAPHER: FRED BAUMAN

120. Living and dining areas divided for "formal entertaining."

5. *Dining Area*

As was previously mentioned, the most inadequate part of the house was the dining area. This 7 × 8-foot space allocated for such a purpose would hold no more than a card table. Although there was supposedly a "separate dining area" formally separated from the living room, it was ridiculous to assume that formality could be achieved in such cramped quarters. In order to overcome this situation, the formality of separate rooms was cast aside in favor of a more spacious informality where it would at least become physically possible to comfortably seat a dozen people if necessary. It became obvious that the walls between living and dining areas had to be removed. (See Illustration 117.)

Since the roof-supporting beam along the back of the house was not over the back wall of the living and dining rooms, but outside, 3 feet beyond it, no major structural changes were required to move the back wall out the 3 feet underneath this beam. The wall was not holding up anything where it was, and it could be removed easily. A glass wall placed underneath the

REMODELER: LOIS GOTTLIEB; PHOTOGRAPHER: FRED BAUMAN

121. Dividing wall removed and exterior wall extended out 3 feet. There is no longer pretense of formality, but there is space.

beam extended the room another 3 feet, and also increased the interior light and provided a flow of space out toward the back garden. A low ceiling was installed to cover up the rough edges where the top of the wall had been torn out. Indirect lighting for the interior was built into this low ceiling which provided general, even illumination.

6. *Back Patio*

Although this house had a back patio area, it was not very comfortable because it was exposed to the hot sun. What this area needed was a feeling of partial shelter in an outdoor room. A trellis was extended out, continuing the lines of the low living-room ceiling. The framework of the trellis defined an outdoor space, supported lights in the evening, and framed the view of the garden and valley beyond. The actual cost of this outdoor, partially sheltered living area was under $50 for labor and materials. In this way one is buying very usable space for less than 20 cents per square foot rather than paying over $10 per square foot for interior space. Even though this sheltered patio could not be used all the time, it could be used and enjoyed enough of the time in the year to warrant this small expenditure. (See Illustration 121.)

It is interesting to note that the remodeling changes made in this house simplified it in many ways. The house could have been originally built this way at no additional cost. It is no more expensive to put up a glass wall than a stud wall covered with plaster and paint. The wood used for the shutters on this house could have been used to greater advantage for extra shelves. The elaborate "ranch" fencing must have cost as much as the trellis and this money could have paid for an outdoor room for summer living. Money is better spent making the most out of what one has rather than trying to create an illusion of formality or of a ranch.

A TRACT HOUSE

This tract house was planned to satisfy the requirements of an "average" family who needed three bedrooms, and had to have it at an absolutely minimum cost. It was designed to be a pleasant environment within the

122. A tract house built for $13,000. The style developed from the needs of living rather than being a false front.

ARCHITECT: JOHN KEWELL; PHOTOGRAPHER: JULIUS SHULMAN

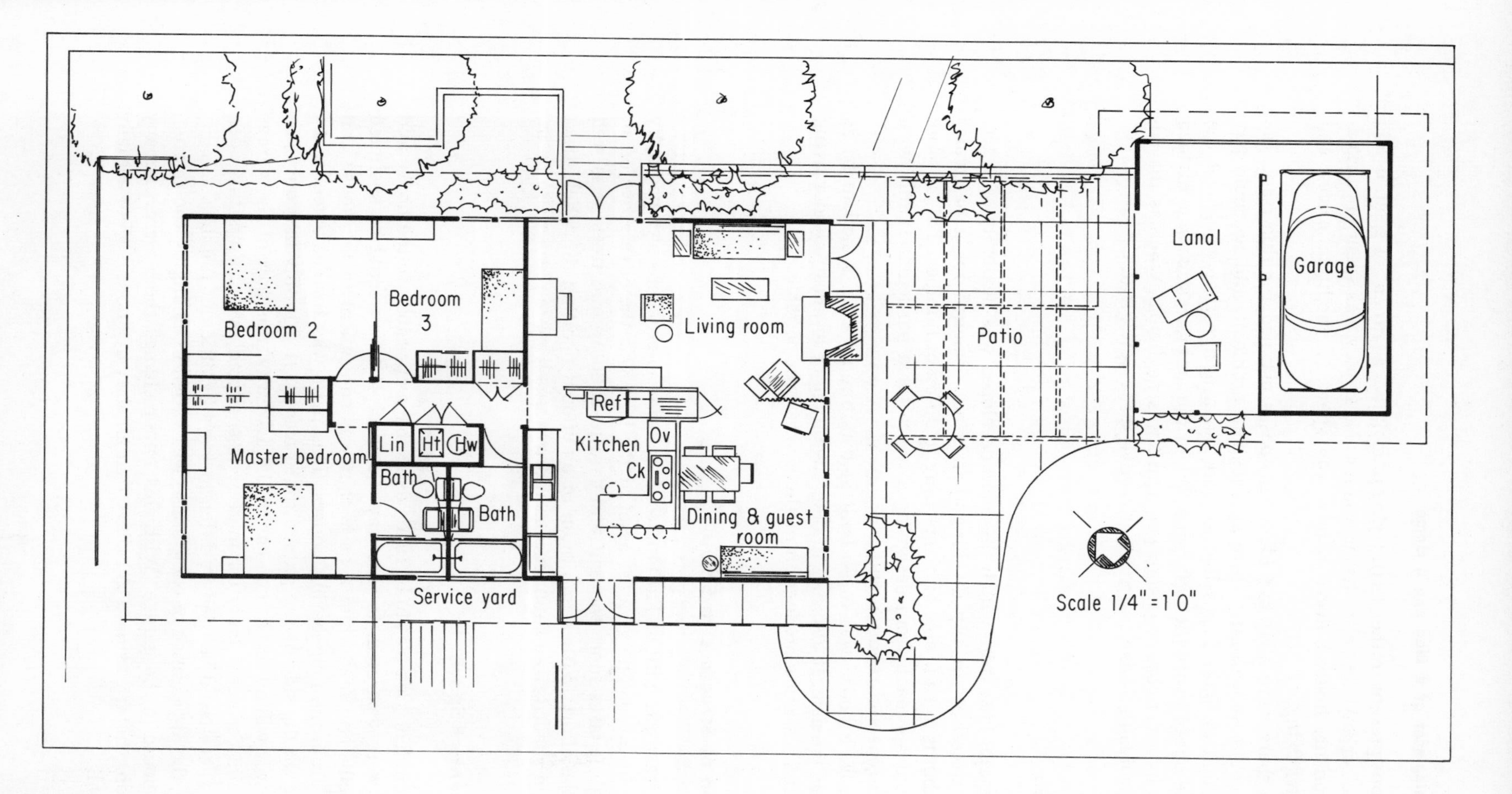

123. The simple, very flexible plan designed to use both indoor and outdoor space to the fullest and preserve existing trees.
ARCHITECT: JOHN KEWELL

limitations present, rather than trying to look like a "ranch" or a bit of "old England," or anything else that it was not. No money was spent on tacked-on ornament; instead every penny was spent to facilitate easier and pleasanter living.

Since there were sixty-five identical houses planned for this tract, the builder could well afford to hire an excellent architect, and he could pay him enough to make it possible to work out a design that would get the most use out of every inch of space. When the architect's fee was divided by sixty-five, the cost of design per house was negligible, whereas the advantages of both usable and more attractive space were great.

The Idea

The major idea from which this plan developed was flexibility of space. This is necessary in any dwelling that is not designed for a particular family, but is to be usable and appealing to different families. This is quite a different approach from designing a house for a particular family with special needs and requirements.

Since each house was to be built at a minimum cost, it had to be as simple as possible. It also had to take advantage of low-cost outdoor living space, and use mass-production methods wherever possible.

Relation of Structure to Site

This tract was built on flat land so there were no problems of topography or view involved. The greatest asset of the land was the olive grove on it. Although it takes more thought and care to build around trees, it is well worth the effort. With a minimum of additional planting the whole tract was soon shaded from summer sun and was much more pleasant to be in.

Allotment of Space

The outdoor area was to be made as usable as possible, so the house and garage were separated. In this way the space between could be sheltered by a trellis and made into a patio that was convenient to the house and private from the neighboring houses. This patio was further extended by opening up the side of the garage that faced it. If a family had only one car, or was willing to put one car in the driveway, this part of the garage then could become a lanai for more semi-sheltered living. Thus this open garage space could be used in different ways by different families.

Also, the appearance of each house was varied by changing the relation of the house to the garage. With this minor change there were so many variations that it was hard to believe that all sixty-five houses were actually identical.

ARCHITECT: JOHN KEWELL; PHOTOGRAPHER: JULIUS SHULMAN

124. The house and garage with the trellis between form an outdoor room.

Inside the house about half of the space was allotted for family activities in the living, dining, and kitchen areas. The other half was reserved for the more private areas of bedrooms and baths.

All space allotted for living was kept in one good-sized area. It was not cut up into parlors, or family rooms, or entries. If necessary, these divisions could be installed later by the owners, but to begin with each owner was

ARCHITECT: JOHN KEWELL; PHOTOGRAPHER: JULIUS SHULMAN

125. One side of the garage is open and can be used as a lanai.

provided with one good-sized room which he could arrange as he pleased. An entry, for instance, is pleasant to have and gives the living room more privacy. However, when a house is small, one cannot afford to cut it up more than absolutely necessary in order to achieve a sort of false formality that does not really exist anyway.

The dining room in this minimum house was larger than many of those in more expensive houses. One could entertain twelve people for dinner there, and it could be open to the living room or closed off from it. This dining room was also arranged to be large enough to put a couch in, and to be accessible through the kitchen to the bath so it could be used as a guest room.

The kitchen counter was planned to be a space for either food preparation or eating. It was open to both living and dining areas, but from neither room could the messiness of food preparation be seen.

From the kitchen one could go directly into the minimum-sized hall which led to the bedrooms and baths. The children's rooms were separated by sliding panels which could be opened to form one big playroom during the day or could be closed at night for greater privacy in each room.

126. Living and dining areas.

ARCHITECT: JOHN KEWELL; PHOTOGRAPHER: JULIUS SHULMAN

ARCHITECT: JOHN KEWELL; PHOTOGRAPHER: JULIUS SHULMAN

127. An open yet private kitchen with handsome cabinets.

Materials and Prefabrication

The materials of the house were simple, but of good quality. The primary materials were plaster, wood trim, and brick which where necessary for the fireplace and at the ground level for planting areas. The inside of the house was enhanced with well-designed wood cabinets and wardrobe units which were prefabricated and used instead of stud-wall partitions where possible.

Since the need for economy made the simplest shape most desirable, the house was planned in a rectangle. Nevertheless the rooms did not feel like boxes because the walls were designed as panels which did not go around the corners so as to produce a closed-in feeling. In every room the eye was permitted to continue outside through glass on at least one wall. This was made possible by the specially milled floor-to-ceiling windows. These windows presented one of the cost problems that the architect had to work out. The standard "stock sash" which is used in almost all houses to frame

ARCHITECT: JOHN KEWELL; PHOTOGRAPHER: JULIUS SHULMAN

128. Floor-to-ceiling windows and sliding panels between rooms give the minimum spaces in this house an open quality.

the windows was not large enough to give the open quality desired here. The architect discussed this problem with the manufacturer of these frames, and found out that the machinery for making them could be reset to produce any needed dimension for $40. Although this is expensive for one window, when this amount is divided by the number of windows required for all of the sixty-five houses, the cost is negligible. Thus the true economy of tract construction could be taken advantage of. These full-length doors and windows made it possible to open up these tract houses. With standard window frames these same houses would have easily been the proverbial "box."

The thoughtful use of space in this house even provided usable space over the toilet. A special bathroom fixture was designed in three sections. A flat section over the sink for a mirror and small shelf, a center section for a medicine cabinet, and a deep section over the toilet for towels. Since this whole unit was prefabricated it was quickly attached to the wall of the bath as a finished unit.

The key to real economy in tract or mass-production housing is the repetition and prefabrication where possible of well-designed parts to form a house. These parts must not only be designed to work in one place, but must be flexible enough to work in as many places as possible in each house. With this approach the tract builder can offer the public more and better quality for the money rather than a shoddy product made to sell because of a few fancy gadgets. The proof of this is that the houses of the tract shown in this example all sold without publicity or advertising.

A WEEKEND HOUSE

Preliminary Decisions

The owner of this house was a single man who lived in a city apartment but had a magnificent piece of property overlooking the Pacific Ocean, forest-covered foothills, and valley farmlands. He wanted a weekend house that would enable him to "hear the rain on the roof" and, in general, to partake of the beauties of this countryside. These were his only requests.

The nature of this site as well as the fact that it was to be a weekend house for one person, immediately set up certain requirements. Not too much money was to be spent on it. The house did not have to be very big. On the other hand, the site was covered with tremendous trees, so the scale of the house had to be planned as large as possible in order to relate to this environment. The solution, therefore, seemed to call for a small low-cost house, but as large in scale as possible.

Given any area, it can be broken up into smaller areas, strung out into longer, leaner space, or kept in one lump as much as possible. The decision to achieve as large a scale as possible made it desirable to concentrate all the space in one massive square. Other factors also helped to reinforce this decision. For economic reasons, it is better to build one compact form rather than the same number of square feet that are more spread out, be-

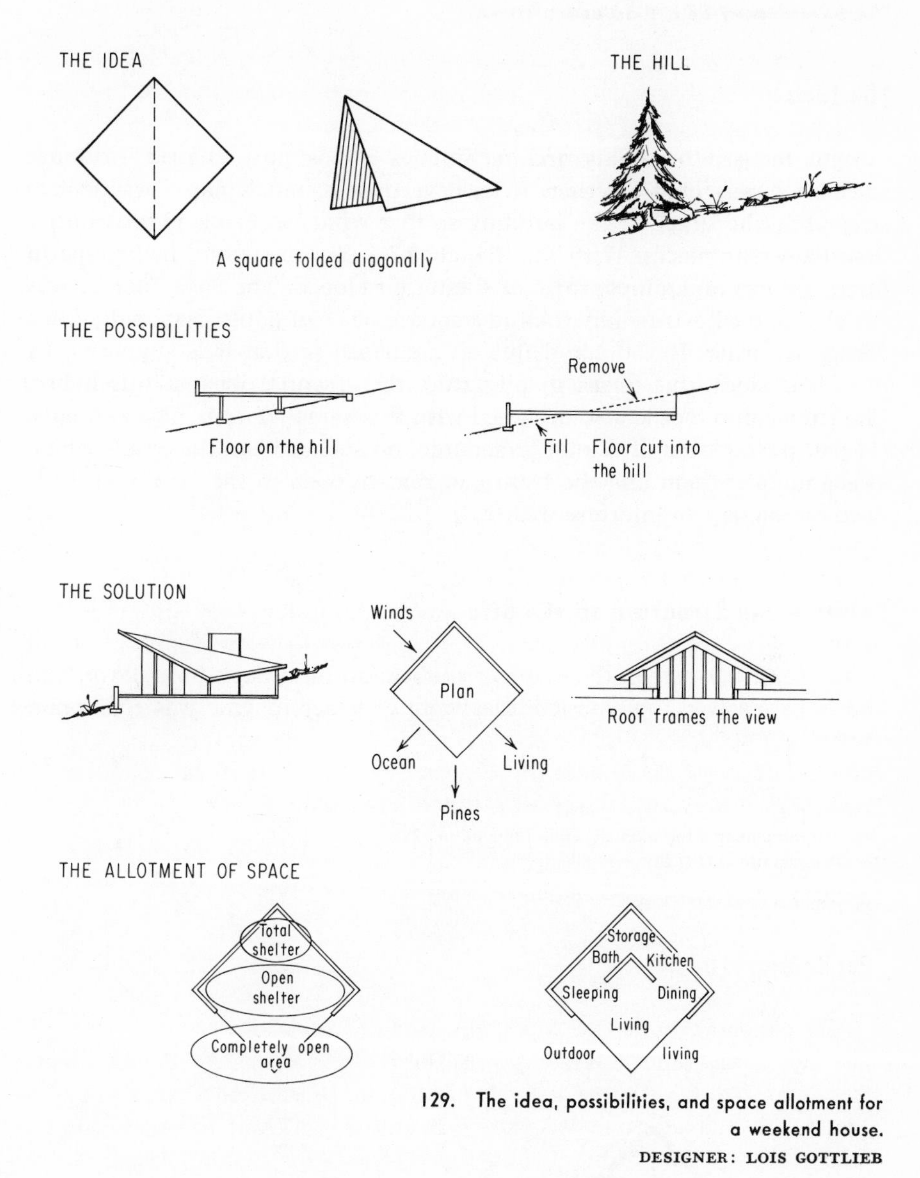

129. The idea, possibilities, and space allotment for a weekend house.
DESIGNER: LOIS GOTTLIEB

cause the more compact form requires less wall area. In the case of this house it was more convenient to have the various areas within the dwelling close together, since there was no need to plan for much privacy or particular formality of living in a weekend house for one person.

Another requirement determined by the site was the need for a feeling of great shelter. Since the house was to be on the crest of a high hill, this exposure to both the ocean and the inland valley meant exposure to the winds and rains of the locality. Thus, people living in this area not only had to feel sheltered, but the structures of their houses had to be strongly built to be able to withstand the severities of the climate.

The Idea

With modern materials and techniques almost any shaped structure can be securely held together. It is, nevertheless, much more practical to streamline the shape of the building so that winds will flow over it rather than blow it to pieces. With the thought of a square streamlined shape in mind, an idea of a simple form of shelter developed. The basic idea of this design can be illustrated by folding a square piece of paper diagonally from corner to corner. If you stand this on a surface so that it is supported by two of its sides, this forms in miniature the essential idea of this house. The simple pup tent is also designed with this same concept. The two back sides of the pup tent give total protection and shelter from the winds which sweep up over them and the front can remain open to the view with little need for support to interfere with it.

Relating the Structure to the Site

The conflict between the slope of the site and the need for a level floor had to be resolved. Two possibilities were considered: One was to support

130. Development of the plan shown in Illustration 129.
DESIGNER: LOIS GOTTLIEB

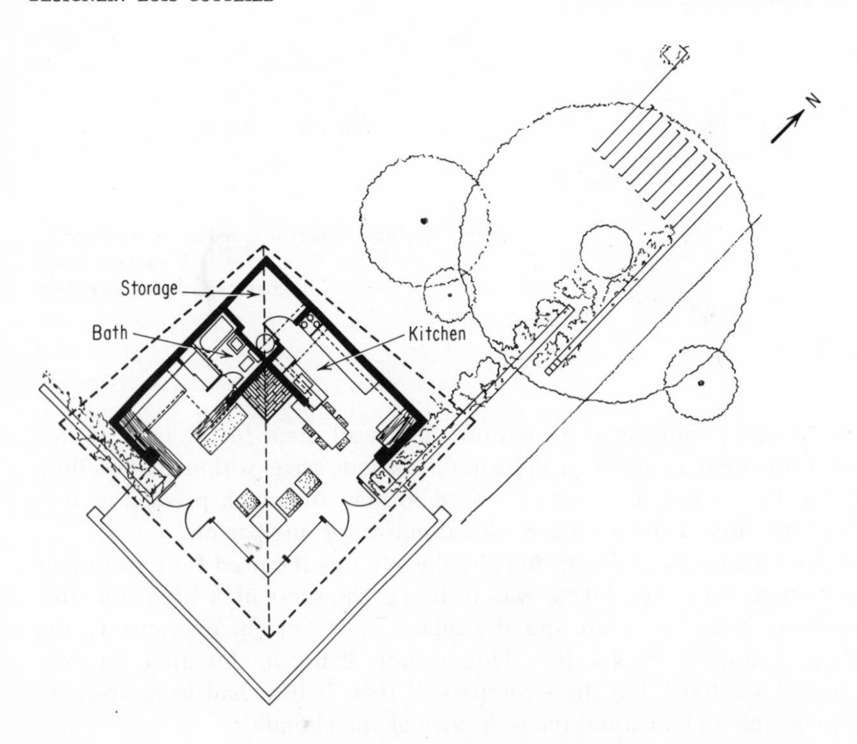

a raised floor on the existing slope, and the second possibility was to excavate and cut a flat surface into the slope. Years ago the first choice would have been easier, since it used to be more difficult to dig such a big hole and also to waterproof it. But now a bulldozer can cut a flat area in a few hours and waterproofing is more easily accomplished with modern materials. Furthermore, the second solution was ideally suited to the site because the back of the house would then be underground and further protected from the wind. Also the excavated earth could be dumped and leveled in front of the house to form a terrace at almost no additional cost. Still another advantage of using the excavation method was that it made it possible to walk directly out onto the hill rather than being at a higher level. Since the whole idea of the house was to enable the owner to enjoy the most contact with the surroundings, this advantage was important.

The plan of the house was so oriented as to take full advantage of the beautiful view. The diagonal axis of the structure was therefore laid out along the crest of the hill. This placed one of the front walls facing the ocean and the other facing towards the valley inland. The point at which the walls met looked out at a grove of Bishop pines with a range of hills beyond.

As the roof had been designed to frame this front view, the supporting posts were held back from the corner so that they too framed rather than cut through this central view. The two planes of glass then came together and were mitered and glued.

Space Allotment

Within this three-dimensional structure, space for various needs was planned. Part of the space was planned to be sheltered and secluded. Another part sheltered but left open to the view. And the remaining part left completely open to relate the house as much as possible to the natural surroundings.

Since this front area of the house had the view and little privacy, this was the obvious place for the living area. The back part against the hill could house the more secluded areas such as the sleeping area, bath, storage room, and kitchen. The fireplace could be used to divide the back utility areas from the living-room area. This completed the total allotment of space for each activity. The next task was to work out the actual dimensions of the different rooms so that they could accommodate such things as a bed, refrigerator, and stove.

In order to organize the space more easily and set up a rhythmic pattern, this house was designed on a unit system. A 3-foot × 3-foot module appeared to fit best since the total space seemed to divide itself most efficiently on this unit. The more commonly used 4-foot square module was discarded as it proved to be too big a unit for such a small house.

After more experimenting with the interior dimensions it was decided that all necessary parts of the dwelling could be comfortably fitted into a 24-foot square. This would be large enough to be spacious and yet small enough to be easily spanned by the roof. The fireplace thus seemed well placed and could cut off the back 2½ modules, or 7½ feet, for the width of the kitchen, bath, and storage. Although in plan this looks simple and obvious, several weeks were spent juggling these utility areas around like a jigsaw puzzle so that the least space would be taken away from the main living area while still leaving enough space for these smaller areas to be convenient and adequate.

Choice of Materials

The main building material was concrete and concrete block. Concrete was suitable in that a concrete floor slab could be poured directly onto the flat ground more easily and cheaply than anything else. Concrete is also indestructible and is easy to take care of. The fact that the two back walls would be against the hill and had to be waterproofed led to the choice of concrete block, inexpensive as well as attractive and readily available in the area. Concrete block is also fireproof, strong, and heavy enough to withstand the pressures of the wind and roof pushing down on it.

Warm colors were chosen for the concrete and block materials to give a pleasant feeling in the cold climate of the site. Rough block textures also seemed appropriate since they would not show the dust and are maintenance-free as well. There is nothing more discouraging than arriving for a restful weekend and having to start cleaning immediately. A waxed and polished concrete floor also shows little dust and can easily be washed off when necessary. It was stained a terra-cotta color and scored on the 3-foot module lines.

In order to expose the beautiful views, the two front walls were made of glass. For the glass frames and the other trim and furnishings of the house, the native redwood was used. Redwood also has the advantage of being weather- and insect-resistant.

The dividing walls for the more secluded rooms were built of redwood over a stud construction so that the plumbing and electricity could easily be run through them.

Since the bath and the kitchen were actually so much a part of the rest of the dwelling and so little separated, they were designed to feel like a part of it. Both were of the same concrete and redwood as the rest of the house. Thus the kitchen, in particular, blended into the living area and although it was only 10 feet from the entry door, there was no feeling that one was almost walking into the kitchen upon entering.

The material used on the roof was also important since the top of the roof was the first part of the house to be seen from the parking and entry area. An earth-colored gravel was used which blended with the landscape, and the edge of the roof was covered all around with a large redwood facia which extended far enough above the roof to act as a rain gutter as well.

Further planning was done to keep the roof uncluttered. The placement of the various vent pipes from the plumbing may seem like a small concern in designing a house, but it is really important. It is just as important as not having a bunch of safety pins showing on a dress or not cutting off the ends of the thread at the seams. Unfortunately, so many roofs are bristling with various vents that many people accept it as inevitable, but it isn't. It does take planning so that these pipes can either be concealed or somehow relate to the whole roof design. In this case particularly, the vents sticking up from a toilet or sink would destroy some of the glamour of the first impression of the house. By placing all the plumbing adjacent to the back chimney wall, all the vents could be kept concealed by running them up through the holes in the blocks of the chimney.

Subordinate Features of Design

The remaining considerations of planning the design were concerned with the many subordinate parts to the structure to make it a place in which someone could live comfortably. (See Illustration 130.)

131. Weekend house grows out of the hill.

DESIGNER: LOIS GOTTLIEB; PHOTOGRAPHER: MORLEY BAER

Since the back wall of the house was to be below ground level and the front of it completely open, there had to be a transition to relate the two areas. Some provision also had to be made so that the earth behind the back wall wouldn't wash out. The back wall was therefore brought around the corner 6 feet on either side to increase privacy and stability of the design. Planting boxes were then wrapped around these side walls so as to effect a more gradual transition to the natural surroundings and to retain the earth.

The planting box on the entrance side was extended back to lead into the series of steps which came down from the parking area. These steps, the first architectural feature one saw upon arriving, led one visually as well as physically to the house itself.

Just as the steps formed an extension to the house design, the terrace floor was an extension of the living-room floor, and the ceiling of the interior extended beyond the glass walls to form a partial shelter for the terrace. In good weather the front French doors could be opened so that the indoor and outdoor areas became one related area.

This house shows how a limited space can be designed to give the impression and usefulness of a larger space. The 16 square feet of area allotted to the enclosed living room on the plan actually extends beyond the limits of the glass walls, thus forming a larger area. The space in this house is limited, but it is not a box.

To further clarify what was done to create comfort and beauty, the subordinate parts of the house will be discussed in terms of the seven categories listed in the previous chapter.

1. *Shelter and Privacy*

Shelter was provided by the structure itself, and total privacy from the outside was achieved with inexpensive sackcloth drapes which could be drawn across both glass walls.

Inside, the utility areas of the dwelling were given enough privacy by extending the walls of the fireplace on each side. Additional seclusion was provided for the bathroom by putting a closet between it and the sleeping area. This also created a tiny entry hall for the bath. The kitchen sink was placed against the back of the fireplace and with a minimum of privacy for the kitchen it was possible for the person doing the cooking to visit with any guests and at the same time not expose the dirty dishes to the living area.

The sleeping area was also given only a bare minimum of privacy by having the back of the couch divide it from the main part of the living room. A dwelling for a family would have to have many more provisions for privacy than this house has, but for one person this was adequate.

2. *Temperature Control*

The main structure of the house was built to control the temperature as much as possible. The heavy masonry walls against the earth insulated the

DESIGNER: LOIS GOTTLIEB; PHOTOGRAPHER: MORLEY BAER

132. Spaciousness in a house 24 feet square.

back. The glass facing the south let in the winter sun, but the large roof overhang shielded the inside from the high summer sun. Additional insulation was provided in the roof and by the drapes when they were drawn.

Summer heat is almost never a problem in this area of the country, but it does get cold enough to need additional warmth in the winter. The central fireplace gave off a good deal of heat since it was sitting in the room rather than in a box outside it. And since the fireplace was designed to be a barbecue, it was set a step down from the floor so that one could sit on the step and cook. For automatic control of additional warmth the reinforcing wires in the slab floor were connected to a low-voltage electrical circuit, and to a clock which turned on the electric heat morning and evening.

DESIGNER: LOIS GOTTLIEB; PHOTOGRAPHER: MORLEY BAER

133. The central fireplace for warmth and for cooking. Fire actually sits in the corner of the room. Hood collects smoke, but most of the heat radiates out. Grate reflects roof structure.

3. *Light Control*

The sunlight coming through the front glass walls had to be controlled, so the drapes which were made in separate sections could be moved anywhere the light was too bright. The utility areas got a soft and diffused light through a number of openings in the wall where blocks had been left out and covered with panels of sliding glass.

At night, over-all illumination for the living area came from triangular boxes in the center of the ceiling. Additional indirect lighting came from above, decks extending out from the tops of the doors and the closet. Kitchen counters are provided with illumination by strips of light under the shelves above them. The desk and piano got light from a series of built-in lights set in the concrete blocks. Every other block had been left out to provide space for these lights. The two couches had direct lights above them for reading. Outdoor lighting came from two more ceiling-light boxes in the roof which extended the pattern of the indoor lights. The planting boxes were also provided with lighting to help light the terrace. Ornamental shadow patterns are produced where a series of blocks protrude from the wall.

There are approximately forty light bulbs in this small house. Although

134. Many small lights built into the structure of the house create soft patterns of illumination in the evening.

DESIGNER: LOIS GOTTLIEB; PHOTOGRAPHER: MORLEY BAER

hardly efficient in terms of light per socket, this number of lights were required to create a soft, over-all illumination rather than a few glaring spots of light surrounded by many dark shadows.

Lighting may easily be considered the greatest extravagance of this house, but actually no more was spent on it than one might spend on some other type of ornament such as a good painting or a piece of sculpture, or good plumbing. It is certainly more efficient and cheaper to build an outhouse over a septic tank than bother with interior toilets and complex plumbing, but almost no one would consider buying a dwelling without these. On the other hand, most dwellings are sold with little or inadequate lighting. Although lighting can be added at a later time, the results are never as satisfactory and are more expensive in the end.

4. *Seating*

In order to economize on the space, the separation between the living and sleeping areas of this dwelling formed a seat as well as a partial wall. It was arranged so that one could enjoy both the view and the fireplace while sitting there. The other living-room seating was composed of simple canvas chairs that could be easily taken outside when the weather permitted. (See Illustration 132.)

Wood and foam-rubber hassocks were used around the dining table. These could also be moved to other areas at any time. The fireplace also provided an additional seating arrangement. Pillows could be put on the floor next to the hearth, and with one's feet on the lower level of the hearth, this was comfortable for just sitting or toasting a marshmallow. (See Illustration 133.)

5. *Space for Reclining*

The sleeping area of the house had a twin-sized bed that could be made up to form a couch in the daytime, and the spread and pillows were of a heavy fabric that could be sat upon and not wrinkled. The seat next to the fireplace was made exactly the length of a bed so that it, too, could be used for sleeping or reclining.

6. *Horizontal Surfaces*

The kitchen counter, dining table, and desk were all the same laminated redwood treated with a wood hardener. They were like polished and stained butcher blocks, and took any reasonable wear well.

The desk was placed next to the bed so that it could also be used as a bedside table, and the top was hinged so that one end could lift up and open a cabinet for a phonograph beneath. The kitchen counter extended far enough into the dining area to act as a buffet as well as a work counter.

DESIGNER: LOIS GOTTLIEB; PHOTOGRAPHER: MORLEY BAER

135. The redwood kitchen was treated as part of the living area.

7. *Storage*

Each activity planned for in this dwelling had the storage space for the necessary equipment close at hand. The sleeping and bath areas had clothes storage dividing them, and the back of the seat was a cabinet for more clothes. Above the bed and next to the desk were bookshelves, and the desk had cabinets for stationery supplies.

The kitchen walls were covered with cabinets and open shelves; dishes and glassware could be kept out to ornament the walls, whereas the pots, pans, and packaged food could be concealed in the cabinets. Firewood was kept in a basket that could be carried out to the woodpile to be replenished. Other miscellaneous things were kept in the back storage room.

The only furnishings not built into the house were the rugs. A woven rug in the living area and a sheepskin in front of the bed were added to give a soft texture and cover the hard concrete floor.

This house is not an architectural anthology of ideas and details all put together side by side under one roof. It is a single opus developed from one general idea in which detail is subordinate to the main idea.

This dwelling was planned for the comfort of one or two people, with the least possible upkeep. With nothing to paint and nothing to deteriorate with time, this house requires a minimum of cleaning, and almost no tacked-on "decoration." Every part is designed to serve not only a definite purpose, but in some cases several purposes. The three main materials—concrete, redwood, and glass—are used to the best advantage of the particular material and are not interchangeable. The concrete supports, the wood spans and trims, and the glass creates transparent planes. There are no tricks. Each material is doing what it should be doing. There is nothing done to be fashionable or "modern." Everything was worked out to combine most easily the needs of the owner with the limitations of the site, the space, and the amount of money to be spent.

Commentary

This low-cost weekend house designed by the author in 1951 is treated in greater detail than the other examples because it would be more difficult for the author to convey as clear an understanding of how someone else's work had developed.

Another reason it was used as an example is that this house was designed for one person and is therefore one that few people could use or want to copy. Since this book is not trying to offer *the* way of doing things, the house is to be looked at only as one result of a type of thinking. It is an example of one way in which ideas can take form in materials and space.

It might also be of interest to the reader to know that this tiny house took ten weeks to plan. This is mentioned because too often it is assumed that a plan can be drawn on the back of an envelope, handed to a carpenter, and out comes a house. It is possible to keep the rain off your head this way, but to efficiently organize space so that every convenience is incorporated into it takes a great deal of planning.

DESIGNER: LOIS GOTTLIEB; PHOTOGRAPHER: MORLEY BAER

136. The concrete provides support, the wood spans and trims, and the glass create transparent planes which protect but do not restrict space visually.

137. A rough stone wall built by primitive people, yet obviously highly trained and specialized in their field.

PHOTOGRAPHER: ROBERT GOTTLIEB

PROFESSIONAL ASSISTANCE

THE RAMIFICATIONS OF HOMEMAKING

Although many young people design attractive rooms for themselves while they are at school, or fix up their apartments afterwards, the serious business of making a home doesn't usually start until a couple gets married.

It is well understood that one of the major occupations of this couple is going to be involved with creating a family and an environment for them. Although they must take out a license in order to proceed, the license requires no qualifications or knowledge for homemaking. There is usually an unspoken assumption that they have absorbed the needed knowledge as they grew up, and if not they will learn by the trial-and-error method. Unfortunately, this is what often happens. Nevertheless it is not the best method to prepare for homemaking because it is not efficient and does not lead to peace of mind.

Another attitude toward the occupation of homemaking is that it is "nothing" or of little importance. An answer to the typical question "What does Jane Doe do?" is "Oh, nothing," or "She doesn't work, she is just a housewife." Yet this housewife is supposed to do most of the buying for the family, keep them all in good physical condition, keep them attractively housed and clothed, see to it that the children are educated, and so on and on.

In other situations any one of these tasks is considered a field of specialized knowledge. Any department store trains its buyers over long periods of time. Sheep and cattle raisers spend much more time studying how to keep their herds in top physical condition than most housewives spend concerning themselves with the nutritional needs of their families. The professions of architecture, interior decoration, medicine, and education are also considered highly specialized fields. But the homemaker is supposed to have absorbed and be all these things at once, a sort of twentieth-century version of the Renaissance man.

When one looks at the situation squarely it is obviously not possible for one person to be all these things. Businesses and governments have found that it pays in the long run to consult advisors for specialized or technical information. In making a home for a family, the situation must also be looked at in the same way if it is to be successful enough to be enjoyed. Particularly in areas where each person is without training or knowledge, he or she must turn to professional assistance without a feeling that everyone is supposed to be able to know how to manage the complex job of creating a comfortable home and environment.

With most people the major concern is the cost of such advice, but cost need not always become involved since with some careful shopping much advice can be had for nothing. Many free advisory services are paid for by taxes or included in the public services of large companies.

Some of the more easily accessible sources are included here to guide those who want to deal more effectively with the problems of creating a home.

GOVERNMENTAL AND OTHER SERVICES

The Classified Telephone Directory

The classified telephone directory can guide you to a world of knowledge and with the phone you can quickly bring that knowledge into the home. If you need a new floor covering or want to know about the various possibilities of mobile homes, it all can easily be looked up in the "yellow pages" of any city telephone directory. Several calls on any subject will usually furnish you with enough information to know more about exactly what is needed and what to do about it. Not only can you usually discuss your needs with someone on the phone, but most companies will also forward brochures with more detailed information. This modern method of preliminary investigation can save hours and days of shopping.

The Government Printing Office, Washington, D.C.

The Government Printing Office in Washington, D.C., prints thousands of pamphlets on practically every subject. It would be impossible to list all those pertaining to housing alone, and many new ones are being issued each month. Any person can write to this government office and request what they have on any particular subject. Most of these printed brochures cost little or nothing. (See list in Appendix A.)

University Extension Services

Land-grant educational institutions throughout the United States offer information and advice to the public as well as to their students. This is handled through university departments of agriculture and county agricultural offices which are scattered throughout the state. Most of the publications put out by these agencies are directed primarily toward farm needs, but many would also be useful to the urban dweller. (See list, Appendix B.) In some of the county offices of the agricultural extension there are home economists who are able to answer or aid in finding the answer to such questions as how to roast a turkey, or how to remove a stain on the carpet, or how well one's new kitchen plan will work. Other experts connected with the agricultural extension can be consulted as to why the lawn is not growing, or what will kill the bugs on the roses. For information concerning local extension services, one can contact the nearest university or county office.

Public Utility Companies

Public utility companies often have home economists who can be consulted about the installation or operation of household appliances. Many companies have heating engineers who will design a whole heating or cooling system for a new or remodeled house. All this is part of the company's service and costs nothing extra.

City Planning Department

All cities and most towns of any size have a city planning department. Here one can find out about zoning regulations, future street requirements, and the location of highways, freeways, shopping centers, industry, parks, and other land-use trends.

Zoning regulations control such things as building heights, minimum lot sizes, setbacks, and parking requirements. In turn this will control or limit the location of the building on the site and the size of the building. There is no reason to buy a piece of property and find out later that it cannot be used for the purpose planned for.

Property adjacent to your own is also important. One may want a particular house because it is in the country and has a pony corral, and yet the picture becomes quite changed if the city planning department finds on its maps that someone is about to put up a ten-story apartment house 6 feet from the pony corral. A city apartment which commands a high rental because of its view may suddenly be left without a view if a fifty-story apartment is built in front of it. Or a house you may be thinking of buying may not seem a good choice because there is no school, yet your mind can be easily changed if the city planners tell you that there will be one soon.

Here we are talking about total environment. It does not matter how beautiful the interior furnishings are if the local airport expands for jet planes and all conversation has to stop every time one takes off. All plans for the relatively near future are listed with the city planning department, and often one can uncover startling facts which will change many decisions about a dwelling.

The city planners can also direct one to other city offices that have information concerning sewers, water, electricity, gas, storm drains, and easements. A house may look like a bargain until one finds out that it lacks some of these necessities. Or, for instance, a house may have a septic tank that works perfectly well, but if the city is about to install a sewer, the owner is then obliged to use it and this small detail can add $1,000 to the cost of the house.

The building department should also be consulted if one is planning to build or change the existing structure extensively. This department controls regulations pertaining to construction, and may demand special preliminary building precautions costing a great deal. Usually most limitations can be overcome, but it is best to know of any before purchasing a site or starting to build.

Banks

Another important area of concern for homemakers is the financing of a home. This is going to affect how well one lives on available income. The point was made earlier in this book that $10,000 borrowed is not $10,000 when returned. Some understanding of finances is necessary because the monthly costs of a house can almost double due to different financial arrangements. Since each family's circumstances are somewhat different, arrangements for financing can be worked out to suit the particular circumstance. Almost every bank employs someone whose job it is to advise people on these financial matters. There is no charge for this information service.

Many banks can offer the potential home builder or remodeler a list of reliable contractors and some information as to the type and quality of the work they do.

Contractors

A good contractor is able to give much useful advice based on knowledge and experience. If one is planning to buy or remodel a dwelling, an experienced contractor can quickly give some idea of what the changes will cost, or whether the changes desired are possible. It is best to ask three contractors their opinion, since methods and prices vary. It is not unusual for one estimate to be double another. It may be that one man has better work methods, or the quality of craftsmanship may differ considerably. Contractors can best be judged by seeing their previous work.

Estimates

The contractor's educated guess as to costs is called an estimate. But it is only a guess. It in no way binds the contractor to do the work for that price. Estimating is, however, part of the service he offers with the hope that he will get the job.

Bids

A bid is a binding statement as to the price for which a contractor will do a particular job. Whereas he might estimate that he can probably install a new bathroom for $1,000, his *bid* may be $970 or $1,125. The exact figure will be based on the more specific details of what the owner expects of him. The bid is also a service that all contractors offer for nothing. One can get three bids and choose between them. However, it is important to distinguish between the various types of bids.

A *fixed bid* is a definite price for the entire job. Once the agreement has been made, the contractor will be paid that price no matter how much it actually costs him. He may earn more than planned, or he may lose money. He takes the chance so will raise his figure enough to take care of some contingencies.

A *cost-plus* contract indicates that the contractor will do the job for an agreed-upon percentage of the total costs. The owner in this case pays all the bills for materials and labor plus the agreed-upon percentage to the contractor. This may be cheaper because the contractor does not have to worry about taking a chance on losing money, but it also can be very expensive—particularly if the contractor is not totally honest. In this case it is no advantage to him to complete the work faster. The best type of bid arrangement will depend on the contractor himself.

Combinations and variations of these bids are also used. One can work out any arrangement that is most satisfactory to both parties. On small jobs a good arrangement is to get a definite figure on the labor costs and let the owner pay for all the materials. This way the contractor can't lose money because he is not spending any, and yet he has the incentive to do the work as quickly and efficiently as possible.

Through consulting several contractors, one can get enough advice for nothing to know approximately the total cost of a dwelling to be purchased or rented and then remodeled.

Termite Inspectors

The need for termite damage repair can increase the cost of a dwelling by hundreds or thousands of dollars. A house can be freshly painted and look in perfect condition to most people, but may have a rotten foundation. A termite control company has men trained to know exactly where to look for termites or dry rot. This service does cost a few dollars for an inspection, but it is certainly worth this expenditure rather than taking a chance on spending thousands on a house full of termites. Most banks and loan companies will require a termite report in order to secure a loan on a house. If repairs must be made, one may obtain several bids from either termite companies or general contractors to see who can do the work most reasonably.

The Decorator

The service of a decorator can often be procured as part of the price of interior furnishings. The decorator is a person usually trained in the field of design and is an experienced shopper. If one needs help in deciding what is needed to make a dwelling attractive and comfortable, the knowledge of the decorator can help; and even if one knows approximately what is needed, the shopping skill of a decorator can be very useful. Now, every city offers products for the home from all over the world, and the decorator knows what is available and where to find it.

Decorators are able to offer this service because they are issued a resale license by the state board of equalization. This permits them to buy any home furnishing directly from the wholesaler or importer and resell it at the standard retail price. His price is not more than the prices in other stores, but the profit he makes from the standard mark-up enables him to offer his designing knowledge with the products. Because decorators make their living from selling, it is understood, unless otherwise arranged, that the customers will buy from them whatever they need. The other type of agreement that can be made is to pay the decorator separately for his advice and not be obligated to buy from him.

Some decorators work from their homes. Others have small shops, and others are hired by large stores to help their customers. Most of them deal in the better-made, more expensive furnishings because they have found it to be most satisfactory and economical in the long run. Even if a couch costs twice as much as another to begin with, it will probably last five times as long, and it is a better buy and worth waiting for until one can afford it. It is usually the person who can least afford it who has tried to economize and who ends up making the most replacements in his home. A good decorator knows the lasting quality of the better products, so offers greater long-range economy.

The decorator is also willing to bring samples to one's dwelling. Since color and form are so related to the surroundings, to see something in one's home is a great help.

Some decorators are also interior designers. This means that they can design furniture, built-in cabinets, or other minor architectural changes, and can recommend craftsmen who can make them. Often to have something made especially to fit one's particular needs is no more costly than trying to find a mass-produced piece that may or may not fit. Since the designer is a good customer of the craftsmen who build such things, he will no doubt get better service and prices from cabinet makers, drapery makers, upholsterers, painters, and other craftsmen, than will the one-time customer. In these ways the decorator can offer the homemaker more for his money.

ARCHITECTS AND DESIGNERS

The Role of the Architect

Louis Sullivan defined the architect's role in the following way: "The true work of the architect is to organize, integrate, and glorify utility. Then and only then is he the true master-worker."

In order to pursue these aims effectively, an architect must possess knowledge in the fields of art and engineering as well as human relations. He must understand the use and structural potentials of materials, and he must also understand how to make these materials the most usable and beautiful for the kind of life his clients want. An architecturally designed house should reflect the character of the owners as well as provide them with the necessities of living.

Although any good architect is going to gradually develop an individual way of doing things or a style of his own, the subjects should be recognizable. A Frank Lloyd Wright house may obviously be a Frank Lloyd Wright house, but it is also the Smith or the Jones house and reflects the lives and interests of these people. So it is with a Rembrandt or Van Gogh portrait in which both the style of the painter and the particular subject are clearly recognizable.

"Architects" and "Designers"

There are two labels for architects. One group have passed certain examinations, belong to the AIA (American Institute of Architects), and are "licensed architects." The other group have not taken these examinations, do not belong to the AIA, and are called "designers." In general their training is the same, the work they do is the same, and they are often associated in the same offices. Although the license means that certain skills have been tested and approved, the unlicensed architect may have equal skills, but for various reasons prefers not to belong to the AIA. One can judge the merits of a particular architect or designer only by seeing his past work and talking to his former clients.

When an Architect Is Needed

Often people are under the impression that one does not hire an architect unless they are planning an elaborate and expensive house. Actually the opposite is true. It is like planning a budget. If one has unlimited amounts of money, there is less need to plan for spending it, whereas the less one has the more carefully it should be spent in order to make it go as far as possible. In the case of building a house, or even a small remodeling project, the lower the amount the less materials can be purchased, the less money there is for the labor to put them together, and the less space can be enclosed. This means that the most economical materials available must be used to their greatest advantage. Each piece of wood must be in the right place, and the structure must be efficiently designed so that it can be put together as easily as possible to keep labor costs to a minimum. In other words, every inch of available space must be useful. In general, the less money one has to spend the more time will have to be spent in wise planning.

It is also important that the planning be done as early as possible, preferably before the property is purchased. There is the woman who called an architect to design a little house for her on a lot she had already purchased for a goodly sum. The property turned out to be a 25-foot slot between two buildings. On either side were three stories of blank wall. To the rear was another building with a shabby stairway and laundry hanging on lines, and in front was the street covered with streetcar tracks and wires. The scene was ugly in every direction. The architect seeing this was so surprised that anyone would pay a high price for such ugliness that he finally said, "This is difficult to do something with." To which the owner replied, "That's what I hired you for!"

The owner was half right, she certainly needed an architect, but by this time she needed not only a first-rate architect but a wizard. To ask anyone to glorify this ugly site was expecting almost the impossible. Limitations were everywhere and there were no tangible assets. What this woman should have done was to seek the advice of the architect before she bought the lot. He would have then advised her to look further and start with another lot that had less limitations and more assets.

As things turned out, even this difficult site was made into something attractive; however, if the same amount of money had been invested in a better site, a more enjoyable and valuable environment would have been produced. The experience of the architect gives him a great deal of insight into the potentials of either a lot or an existing building that needs remodeling.

Costs and Payments

The standard architectural fee for designing a house is about 10 percent of the cost of the dwelling. There are a few architects who charge more, and there are some who charge less. One should be more dubious about the latter because for much less than 10 percent a livable structure can be produced, but it is impossible for the architect to do a very thorough job and at the same time realize some profit. For a small remodeling project most architects will probably charge at least 15 percent of the total cost. This higher rate is generally valid since, in many ways, to design something to fit in with what already exists involves more work than starting from scratch.

Small projects can also be handled on a consultant basis by the hour. Sometimes an hour or two of advice can save hundreds or thousands of dollars' worth of errors and can produce a much better idea for the same amount of money that would have been spent without the advice. A few sketches and a list of things to be done costs little and can help to make a much better house.

Not all architects want to be involved with small projects for the reason that the large ones make more money. There are, nevertheless, excellent architects who will do small projects.

The payment for architectural services can be handled in various ways and every architectural office has its own method of specifying payment. In general an architect will expect a retainer before starting in order to know that the client is serious. A second payment is expected when the preliminary drawings are approved and another payment when the working drawings are completed. A final payment is made when the project is completed to everyone's satisfaction.

Work Included

For a 10 percent fee the architect will make a set of preliminary drawings, a set of working drawings, and specifications, and will also supervise the construction. He will see to it that the contractor builds the structure as planned, and will make minor decisions and necessary changes as the building progresses.

Since all the major ideas of the plan are shown in the preliminary drawings (see Part IV), the owner should know about what to expect from the building. Any changes can be made when these drawings are completed, and most architects are willing to work on these until everyone is completely satisfied. However, once these drawings have been approved and the working drawings started, the architect is proceeding on the assumption that there will be no more major changes and only relatively few minor ones. Some changes are to be expected as the plan develops, but if the architect is constantly being asked to retrace his steps because the client cannot make up his mind, he will then be justified in asking to be paid extra.

Some people, after having the working drawings completed, feel that money can be saved by eliminating the supervision fee from the contract. Even though the drawings may be complete, the many working details and problems that come up during construction are best solved by the architect. If he is not on hand during construction to see to these details, the completed work may lack a totally finished look. One will get the most for the money spent on architecture by letting the architect take responsibility for the entire job.

Choosing the Architect

One sometimes first meets an architect at a social gathering such as a cocktail party or club. This may be a fine way to meet an architect, but it is no way to judge his work. There is little correlation between charming company enjoyed at a social gathering and an architect's abilities to design a good house. Knowing a pleasant architect is a good beginning, but an architect should be shopped for as carefully as any other expensive item or service. One should look not only at the salesman but at the product.

A more practical way of finding an architect is to look at architecture that appeals to you. If you have a friend with a fine house, ask who designed it. If there is a beautiful house in the vicinity, stop and ask who designed it. There are very few people who will not be pleased and proud to show even a stranger their home if one is truly interested.

One can also call the local chapter of the AIA and ask for a list of local architects. The nearest university department of art or architecture may know who does work locally.

The classified section of the phone book lists both architects and designers.

If you like the work of an architect shown in a publication, it is worth talking to him even if his office is quite far away. For a project of any size, most architects are willing to travel a long way if necessary, or they may know of someone who does similar work in the area in which you intend to build.

Most architects have pictures of their work in their offices. If these seem interesting to you, ask to see several of the houses. It is important to see work which is in your price category. Talk to the owners of the houses, not only about the design of the house but how the whole project went both as to organization and cost. Some architects may produce wonderful results, but not within a proposed budget. One can deal with this problem if it exists by proposing a lower budget than is necessary. Other architects may do good work but in a disorganized fashion. This problem can also be dealt with if you find an experienced contractor who is very organized. Only by finding out as much as you can about the architect or designer will it be possible to make the right choice.

Cooperation of Client and Architect

Most architects have designed some houses or projects which are better than others. Even the best architects usually have some ill-fated projects that turn out poorly. Since there are at least two parties involved in each building project—the architect and the client—it therefore takes a cooperative effort from both sides to produce a good result. Many of the poor architectural results can be attributed to the client's lack of understanding. In these cases the clients do not understand which decisions are theirs and which decisions must necessarily be left to the architect.

There is the "I know just what I want" variety of client. They usually come prepared with a mass of pictures and plans cut out of magazines. This type of client wants the architect to stick these ideas together under one roof and also see to it that a beautiful result is produced. Such clients need not spend money on an architect—a good draftsman can make a working drawing which will combine these varied ideas. However, trying to solve your architecural needs in this manner is like the person who has heard that a certain pill will cure his pain. All he needs to do is to go to the druggist and ask for it. There is no need to discuss other possible remedies with the doctor. His mind is made up and no longer open to suggestion or discussion.

Another type of client says, "I don't know anything about art, but I know what I like." The problem with this approach is that most likes or dislikes are based on knowledge and understanding as well as lack of it. Just as one may change his or her opinion of other people by knowing more about them, so one may change their ideas about a certain style of architectural form with greater understanding of it. Most architects will take the time to explain to a client what he has done and why. The client must, however, be willing to listen and learn if he has faith in the architect.

There are also unrealistic and uncompromising clients who ask the impossible in terms of space or some other luxury for the amount of money that there is to spend. The client in this case is unwilling to compromise in any way when the architect says that his requirements are impossible within the budget and that other alternatives must be substituted. This type of client will usually end up with no house at all, or with a house that they cannot afford. It is better to have part of a dream or a modified dream than to give it up entirely.

Dreams can also get lost in less important details. A typical example of this situation is the couple who start out with a small budget: For their needs this may at first be adequate because what they say they want is one beautiful room with a kitchen, bath, and small sleeping area. The idea is fine and the preliminary drawings are made. They are thrilled with what is there, but they have been thinking about it and decide that a little dressing room would hardly cost anything and this would give them real comfort. So this is squeezed in and the drawings proceed. Soon they call to say that it is all so lovely that they might as well have it perfect and have a guest room too—just a tiny one. Since the money to be spent remains the same, the extra rooms must necessarily keep coming out of that one beautiful room that they started with. This can go on and on until finally there is no beautiful room left. They may have many little luxuries of minor importance, but the big thing that they originally felt was most important has dissipated into the details.

Then there is the client who simply cannot make up his or her mind. For the architect it is like trying to paint a portrait of someone who keeps wiggling around. Finally everyone is unhappy and the project either disintegrates or turns out as confused as a photograph of a wiggling person. Everyone will no doubt have some changes of mind, but if this turns into an indoor sport to keep the architect drawing in ten different directions at once, he will not be able to do a good job.

Sometimes such problems stem from disagreements between a husband and wife, and the architect is put into a role of mediator. He is really being asked to satisfy two diverse ideas at once. Once in a while it can be done, but not usually, so again these clients will probably not end up with a house.

Another less difficult but still confusing situation to the architect is the client who has no idea of how he wants to live or what he wants to spend. It sounds fine to have such a free rein as to what to do and spend, but trying to design a house with no limits at all is difficult. One is left mentally wandering around in a large desert with no roads leading anywhere. It is necessary for the clients to supply the architect with some ideas of what is wanted and how much is to be spent. These will guide him to a surer conclusion.

The best way one can help an architect is to let him have the clearest picture he can of you and how you want to live. The following information and attitudes will surely help any architect to do a better job.

1. Make a list of your family, their activities, and possessions.
2. Invite the architect to your home so that he can see how you are now living and the things you own. Even if it is not what you want, it will give him some idea of you and you can tell him which things you particularly like about your present dwelling and what you want to be different.
3. Collect some pictures of houses you like best, but use them only with the idea of giving him a better understanding of your tastes, rather than asking him to reproduce these pictures.
4. Establish a happy medium of limitations for him to work in.
5. See to it that the big and important needs are fulfilled and, if necessary, let other minor ones go. Sometimes it is impossible to have everything all at once.
6. Since most architects tend to be somewhat optimistic about costs, and most clients do think of some extra things that are needed as the drawings progress, start with a budget several thousand dollars less than one actually has to spend.
7. Think of your architect as a doctor. Explain your problems and needs to him and let him prescribe a solution. He is not a druggist handing out pills at your request, or a draftsman drawing up your ideas. You have come to him because you like his work and believe in his ideas.

   Don't hire an architect or designer until you find one in whom you have total faith. Then put yourself in his hands and trust him to organize, integrate, and glorify your environment.
8. Think of the architectural results he creates for you as a portrait which should be treated with the same respect you would treat any expensive

portrait. You may choose a frame for it or decide where to hang it, but don't rush up and put a mustache on it. You may own the house he creates for you and live in it, but if it is a truly fine house, it is someone else's work of art and should be treated with the same respect any other work of art would be treated.

LANDSCAPE ARCHITECTS

The Role of the Landscape Architect

A landscape architect is an architect or designer of outdoor space. This thoroughly trained person is not a sort of high-class gardener or a ground decorator, but a professional planner of space just as the architect is.

And just as the good architect leaves one with a comfortable home ready to be lived in, so the landscape architect can produce a comfortable outdoor environment that can be enjoyed for living. A dwelling need not be a floor, four walls, and a roof; and a garden need not be a lawn, a hedge, and a tree. A garden can become an outdoor living room in which there can be a place or several places for eating, a place for outdoor cooking and a kitchen garden, game areas, children's play areas, service areas, and numerous other possibilities based on one's individual interests. If properly planned, outdoor living areas will cost much less per square foot than areas inside the house, and be just as usable a good portion of the year. It is the landscape architect that can design such space.

The training for this profession requires not only a knowledge of art and design, but knowledge of ground formations, plants, outdoor building materials, and outdoor engineering problems such as drainage, retaining walls, etc.

When a Landscape Architect Is Needed

The services of a landscape architect should be had before one buys the site, if possible, and certainly before one builds. This does not apply only in cases where one is contemplating acres of garden, or thousands of dollars worth of outdoor planting, but applies even more so to cases where less space and money is available, Just as with hiring an architect, the less one has to deal with the more necessary it is to have clever planning. Anytime one is going to do something with some outdoor space, be it a 10 × 10-foot patio, the simplest backyard, or an elaborate garden, the landscape architect will know what to do to best use what is available.

If money is going to be spent on plants, they might as well be the right plants and might as well be in the right places. If the area needs some paving, it might as well be attractively paved, and so on. Whatever is going to be done can be done better and planned for greater long-range economy of maintenance if planned by someone with knowledge and experience. Even if the owner plans to gradually build the garden himself, the end result will be better and it will be more rewarding along the way if there is an over-all aim in mind.

Advantages of Early Planning

Outdoor areas should be planned at the same time the house is planned. This way the landscape architect is actually helping to plan the space rather than simply trying to rescue from ugliness or decorate space left over after the building has been completed.

Not only are there aesthetic reasons for planning ahead, but if an over-all plan for the outdoors as well as the indoors is made to begin with, both money and effort will be saved. For instance, most sites will require some bulldozing in order to level an area for the house. It is costly to bring in this large equipment; but once there, it can be used for terracing any outdoor areas as well for very little additional cost. Flat terraces, new ground levels, drives, or walks can easily be made at the same time the place for the house is bulldozed.

Another important consideration is the preservation of the topsoil. If a bulldozer operator is simply told to make a flat spot in a certain place, he will do just that. However, as is usually the case with bulldozing, the topsoil will be pushed off to one side and covered with whatever earth or rock is underneath. The owner will then find himself in the impossible situation of trying to grow a garden in this rock or clay or whatever it is, and as a result many owners either continually struggle with it for years or spend money to bring in new topsoil. Early planning of outdoor space can prevent such waste. With proper planning this soil can first be pushed aside and then redistributed where it will be needed.

Any available rocks can also be covered over and lost. Rocks make beautiful ornaments for a garden, so if they are left in place when possible, or moved by the bulldozer to where they can be used to advantage, something valuable has been preserved rather than thoughtlessly pushed aside or buried.

Existing trees can also be planned around and protected if there is someone there to do so. Otherwise they can be permanently damaged or even buried by the bulldozer. It is not only costly to replace a large tree, but it will take many years for a small one to replace it.

The proper grading of a site can save thousands of dollars in the long run. Early planning for the distribution of topsoil, piping for water for the plants, and terracing will all effect a saving. While the garden area is easily accessible from the street before being obstructed by the building, it is convenient to dump a load of topsoil out of a truck where needed, but it is either costly or backbreaking to wheel a few tons of it around a house, through a path, and maybe up or down steps.

If one knows beforehand approximately where there will be plants, a watering system can be installed at the same time the plumbing for the house is installed. Again the total costs are reduced, since the workman is there anyway. Nothing is more discouraging in gardening than not being able to water conveniently. Some home owners ultimately conclude that they don't have a "green thumb" and give up gardening. It does not matter what the color of one's thumb—if the plants are not in adequate soil and do not get enough water, they will not grow.

Another advantage of early planning makes it possible to start the major planting before building the house. Since it is usually at least a year from the beginning of the planning to the time one moves, if some of the trees are planted as soon as the preliminary drawings are completed they can have a good head start and will offer shade and comfort by the time the house is complete.

Costs

The landscape architect works in a manner similiar to the architect. If he is planning and supervising the construction of a whole garden, he will charge a percentage of the cost of the garden. Because many people prefer to do the outdoor work themselves, or are redoing or adding to older gardens, landscape architects are willing to work on an hourly basis. An hour of professional advice can save much wasted time, money, and effort. A homeowner can struggle with a garden for years, and pour money into it, for plants and fertilizers, and yet nothing seems to happen. With an hour or two of good advice and a basic plan, the right efforts and materials can be used to make something more beautiful and usable. If one has the landscape architect come back for another hour or so each year, enough planning can be discussed to keep most homeowners as busy with gardening as they wish all the rest of the year. Here we are talking about investing a few dollars in order to save countless hours of effort misspent on getting only minimum rather than maximum results.

Work Included

If the landscape architect is planning and supervising the construction of the entire garden, it will be handled in much the same manner as the architect plans and supervises the construction of a house. The landscape architect will furnish a preliminary plan to show the basic ideas, and then a detailed drawing showing all grades, roads or drives, paths, drainage facilities, terraces, and structures or pools. All the materials for building, as well as plant specifications, will be indicated.

If the work involved is not too extensive, a sketch and a list of things to be done will be just as sufficient and less costly.

How to Find a Landscape Architect

If one has already chosen an architect, he would be the first one to ask. If there is someone he likes to work with whose work you also like, this would probably be the best combination. Otherwise you can look in the same places one looks for an architect and with the same approach in mind. Look at his work. It does not matter how charming the person. It does matter if the gardens he has produced feel comfortable and beautiful to you. A landscape architect may even be very well known and considered very fashionable. This is good, but the real question is, "Do you enjoy being in his gardens?"

The Long-Range Garden

An important difference which affects the planning of a garden and a house is that the garden is a growing and changing thing. One may suffer with mistakes in the house, but they don't get much worse as time goes by. However, the mistakes in the garden do get worse. The poorly graded earth either fills with puddles or washes away, and the mistakes in planting either die, take more upkeep than they are worth, or grow out of control. Only the well-planned garden becomes more beautiful as it grows and matures.

CONCLUSIONS

The study of environment becomes increasingly important with man's greater ability to change his environment to fit his needs. Therefore it concerns everyone, since today every man and woman has more control over some corner of the world than ever before. It is each person's responsibility to try to make both his immediate and his total environment more useful and beautiful, whether it be a single room or a vast building project.

Each age or civilization has created an architecture to fit its needs and satisfy its most important values. The great architecture of the past or present is not something to be mimicked, but something to be understood. How did the forms develop? Why is the result as it is? What is the idea behind this building or object?

Each person's style develops as his or her needs are satisfied, interests are provided for, and values are expressed in every facet of his or her dwelling. As a result of these things the dwelling becomes delightful because it has meaning and significance. Within almost any limitations the principles of good design can be applied to make a better environment. The following illustrations show that beauty can be within the reach of everyone.

ARCHITECT: GORDON DRAKE; PHOTOGRAPHER: JULIUS SHULMAN

The amount of space is not as important as how it is *arranged* and *limited*. This tiny entry to a house built in 1946 for $4,700 has beauty and grace comparable to an expensive dwelling.

ARCHITECT: FRANK LLOYD WRIGHT; PHOTOGRAPHER: JULIUS SHULMAN

The materials used are not as important as *how* they are used. Here ornament is created by the shadow patterns of the rough redwood boards of the door.

ARCHITECT: LESTER WERTHEIMER; PHOTOGRAPHER: JULIUS SHULMAN

The efficiency of a dwelling is not as important as how one *feels* while there. The straight line may be the shortest distance between two points, but it is not necessarily the only or best way to get from one to the other.

The beauty of comprehensible form is timeless and should be strived for rather than the fads or "good taste" of the moment. This apartment fireplace is as beautiful now as when it was built in 1947.

ARCHITECT: R. M. SCHINDLER; PHOTOGRAPHER: JULIUS SHULMAN

ARCHITECTS: BUFF, STRAUB, AND HENSMAN; PHOTOGRAPHER: JULIUS SHULMAN

The amount of money spent is not as important as the arrangement and *meaningfulness* of the things bought with it. These Japanese lanterns can be purchased for a few cents in most variety stores.

ARCHITECT: RICHARD NEUTRA; PHOTOGRAPHER: JULIUS SHULMAN

Immediate economy is not as important, or as economical, as *lasting quality*. This house built of fine woods, masonry, and handsome forms will not deteriorate, but will increase in value as the years go by.

The cost of professional advice for any project is small in comparison to the savings it can provide by making it possible to get more for one's money, avoid costly mistakes, and create great beauty. It was one of the world's most experienced architects who created this elegant lath house from the most common and cheapest of materials.

ARCHITECT: RICHARD NEUTRA; PHOTOGRAPHER: JULIUS SHULMAN

ARCHITECTURE AND DRAWING: PAOLO SOLERI

Such incidentals as the color of the draperies or the texture of the bedspread are of relatively little importance in comparison to the conditions of one's total environment. Although most people can completely control only their own dwelling, it is becoming more essential for all people to be aware of the total community and guide its direction and type of growth whenever possible. This is a fragment of a schematic concept for a community presently feasible. From such concepts that may seem like far flights of fancy today come the realities of the future.

BIBLIOGRAPHY

A. THE PHILOSOPHY OF ARCHITECTURE AND DESIGN

LEWIS MUMFORD, *Roots of Contemporary American Architecture*. New York: Reinhold, 1952 (also Grove Press, 1959). One of America's finest architectural critics has compiled thirty-seven essays dealing with every aspect of environment and design. These collected essays give the reader an introduction to the best writers in the field.

FRANK LLOYD WRIGHT, *An Autobiography*. New York: Duell, Sloan & Pearce, 1943. Mr. Wright expresses his philosophy along with the story of his eventful life.

JOSEPH HUDNUT, *Architecture and the Spirit of Man*. Cambridge: Harvard U.P., 1949. A delightful study of how man has expressed himself in his buildings and cities.

J. P. GRILLO, *What Is Design?* Chicago: Theobald, 1960. A discussion of the elements of good design with remarkable examples from both natural and man-made design.

B. THE HISTORY OF ARCHITECTURE

C. W. CERAM, *Gods, Graves, and Scholars.* New York: Knopf, 1952. A fascinating story of how archaeologists pieced together the stories of ancient civilizations by studying their architectural remains in Italy, Greece, the Middle East, and Central America.

BANISTER FLETCHER, *A History of Architecture on the Comparative Method.* New York: Scribner's, 1961. An encyclopedia of architectural knowledge which minutely describes all periods and styles.

SIGFRIED GIEDION, *Space, Time, and Architecture.* Cambridge: Harvard U.P., 1946. The development of modern architecture as seen by Mr. Giedion. He says, "History is not a compilation of facts, but an insight into a moving process of life." It is this insight he offers.

NIKOLAUS PEVSNER, *Pioneers of Modern Design from William Morris to Walter Gropius.* New York: Museum of Modern Art, 1949. Well-illustrated studies of the work of the men who have made our environment what it is today.

C. THE CITY

LEWIS MUMFORD, *The City in History.* New York: Harcourt, 1961. The most brilliantly written and complete book dealing with the city, its development, and its future possibilities.

F. STUART CHAPIN, *Urban Land Use Planning.* New York: Harper, 1957. A good over-all presentation of today's ideas and methods of city planning.

MARY MCLEAN (ed.), *Local Planning Administration.* Chicago: International City Manager's Association, 1950. A reference on the structure of the city-planning functions. An aid to the voter who wants to know what he is voting for and why. (Available in reference libraries or city-planning offices.)

D. THE DWELLING

FRANK LLOYD WRIGHT, *The Natural House.* New York: Horizon Press, 1954. Mr. Wright states, "I believe a house is more a home by being a work of art." In this book, well illustrated with pictures and drawings of many of his best houses, Mr. Wright discusses what makes such a home.

W. A. KIRKPATRICK, *The House of Your Dreams.* New York: McGraw-Hill, 1958. One may feel as if in a dream with the comforts Mr. Kirkpatrick describes, but the book is actually very down to earth. It is full of data on building materials, utilities, costs, and planning.

ELIZABETH MOCK, *If You Want to Build a House.* New York: Museum of Modern Art, 1946.

Henry Wright and George Nelson, *Tomorrow's House.* New York: Simon & Schuster, 1945.
Ray and Sarah Faulkner, *Inside Today's Home.* New York: Holt, 1960.
Russell and Mary Wright, *A Guide to Easier Living.* New York: Simon & Schuster, 1951. All four of the above books are thoughtful discussions of the most important aspects of the dwelling. All are well illustrated and easy as well as good reading.

E. THE GARDEN

Thomas D. Church, *Gardens Are for People.* New York: Reinhold, 1955.
Garret Eckbo, *Landscaping for Living.* New York: Duell, Sloan & Pearce, 1950. As their titles imply, both of these books describe outdoor space in relation to the house, people, and living. Both are beautiful and informative books for anyone interested in gardens.

F. TECHNICAL DATA

Charles Ramsey and Harold Sleeper, *Architectural Graphic Standards.* New York: Wiley, 1949. Although this reference work was compiled especially for architectural offices (and is used in all of them), the drawings are clear and should be understandable to anyone. It contains almost all of the technical data needed to build a house—for example, basic dimensions needed for planning and furnishing, stairway planning guides, bath and kitchen planning, parts of the wall, floor, roof; framing, foundations, plumbing, electrical data, etc.

G. PUBLICATIONS FROM THE GOVERNMENT PRINTING OFFICE, WASHINGTON, D.C.

The following sample titles from the vast list of material published by the Government Printing Office were selected merely to give the reader some idea of the wide scope the material covers. Complete catalogues can be found in most libraries, and the publications can be ordered from Washington, D.C., at little or no cost.

1. Before You Buy a House
2. Low-Rent Housing in Alaska
3. Housing and Urban Redevelopment
4. Loans for Building Small Homes
5. Bamboo Houses for Low-Cost Tropical Conditions
6. Insulation of Concrete Floors

7. Floor Heating of Small Homes
8. Behavior of Paint on Different Woods
9. Care and Use of Hand Tools
10. Slipcovers for Furniture

H. PUBLICATIONS OF THE OFFICE OF INFORMATION, THE U.S. DEPARTMENT OF AGRICULTURE, WASHINGTON, D.C.

A complete list of pamphlets published by this department can be sent for. The following are a few of their titles:

1. Better Lawns
2. Pruning Shade Trees
3. Home Propagation of Ornamental Trees and Shrubs
4. Subterranean Termites—Their Prevention and Control
5. A Step-Saving U Kitchen
6. The Beltsville Kitchen Workroom with Energy-Saving Features
7. Easy-to-Build Kitchen Cabinets
8. Washing Machines—Selection and Use
9. Home Freezers—Their Selection and Use

I. PUBLICATIONS OF THE UNIVERSITY OF CALIFORNIA AGRICULTURAL EXTENSION

These titles are representative of the type of publications put out by land-grant colleges. Anyone can send to his own state institution for a list of its publications. Some universities also have special departments concerned with housing, and these also publish pamphlets. (For instance, the University of Illinois publishes "The Small Homes Council.")

1. Planning the Garden
2. Landscape for Summer Shade
3. Care of House Plants
4. Adobe Construction Methods
5. Smooth-Surface Floors
6. Build Your Own Shop Bench
7. Plan Your Kitchen Storage
8. Selecting a Window-Type Room Air Conditioner
9. How to Finish Furniture
10. Draperies Made to Order